For Maurice—my dance partner for life

Salsa World

In the series *Studies in Latin American and Caribbean Music,*
edited by Peter Manuel

Also in this series:

Ketty Wong, *Whose National Music? Identity, Mestizaje, and Migration in Ecuador*
Peter Manuel, ed., *Creolizing Contradance in the Caribbean*
Cathy Ragland, *Música Norteña: Mexican Migrants Creating a Nation between Nations*
Alejandro L. Madrid, *Sounds of the Modern Nation: Music, Culture, and Ideas
    in Post-Revolutionary Mexico*
Christopher Washburne, *Sounding Salsa: Performing Popular Latin Dance Music
    in New York City*
David F. Garcia, *Arsenio Rodríguez and the Transnational Flows of Latin Popular Music*
Sergio Navarrete Pellicer, *Maya Achi Marimba Music in Guatemala*
Peter Manuel, *East Indian Music in the West Indies: Tân-Singing, Chutney,
    and the Making of Indo-Caribbean Culture*
María Teresa Vélez, *Drumming for the Gods: The Life and Times of Felipe García
    Villamil, santero, palero, and abakuá*

Salsa World

*A Global Dance in
Local Contexts*

Edited by Sydney Hutchinson

TEMPLE UNIVERSITY PRESS
PHILADELPHIA

TEMPLE UNIVERSITY PRESS
Philadelphia, Pennsylvania 19122
www.temple.edu/tempress

Library of Congress Cataloging-in-Publication Data

Salsa world : a global dance in local contexts / edited by
Sydney Hutchinson Mengel.
    pages cm. — (Studies in Latin American and Caribbean music)
    Includes bibliographical references and index.
    ISBN 978-1-4399-1006-1 (cloth : alk. paper) —
ISBN 978-1-4399-1008-5 (e-book)   1. Salsa (Dance)   I. Mengel,
Sydney Hutchinson, 1975–
    GV1796.S245S27 2013
    793.3′3—dc23

                                                        2013013288

Printed in the United States of America

2 4 6 8 9 7 5 3 1

Contents

Acknowledgments

During the preparation of this book, I received support from the Alexander von Humboldt Foundation in Germany, and I was hosted by the Department for Ethnomusicology (also known as the Berlin Phonogram Archive) of the Ethnological Museum in Berlin. I am grateful to the foundation and to my colleagues at the museum for their support; to my husband, Maurice Mengel, for his; and to my dance teachers and partners, past, present, and future. In this capacity, particular thanks go to Angel Rodríguez, Addie Rodríguez, Ivan Rivera, Miguel Rosado, Jill Redondo, and Amanda Cardona.

—Sydney Hutchinson

1

Dancing in Place

An Introduction

Sydney Hutchinson

began dancing salsa as a teenager in Tucson, Arizona. My formal training consisted of a single dance lesson in a nightclub, which was soon shut down (perhaps my age—only sixteen at the time—had something to do with the closure). More important for my early salsa learning was the simple practice of spending many, many nights dancing with partners from all over the globe, not only in Tucson but also wherever I traveled, and sometimes taking opportunities to learn in a more structured way from especially skilled friends or from visiting professionals brought in by local aficionados of Cuban *rueda* dancing, a kind of salsa in the round (see Chapter 6). Eventually, after years of practice, I was regarded as a skilled dancer myself, and I taught classes in salsa and rueda while studying at Indiana University, also leading a salsa band on piano.

At age twenty-five I moved to New York and had to learn to dance salsa all over again. Nothing was the same there: not the steps, not the turns, not the timing or count, and not the relation of dance to music. It did not even have the same social qualities: in Tucson the diversity afforded by salsa clubs was one of the dance's principal attractions,[1] but in New York the salsa scene, very much dominated by New York–born Puerto Ricans, had a strong element of ethnic pride.

Most surprising to me, however, was that my Puerto Rican housemates told me I danced "Colombian." It seemed that this evaluation rested on my frequent use of a basic step in which I crossed behind with my foot on the first count, rather than stepping straight backward or forward, and my tendency to slightly kick on the rest count in preparation for that crossed step. Intriguingly, I had never been to Colombia or had much—if any—contact with Colombian dancers. These were movements I had picked up through social dancing in Tucson—they were taught neither in my one nightclub dance class nor as part of Cuban rueda.[2] Thus, it seemed the explanation was the geography of my learning experience: in Tucson as elsewhere in the Southwest, salsa is strongly flavored by the long-standing popularity of *cumbia* music and dance, one of many links between Mexican and Colombian popular cultures.[3]

Over the next year, I worked hard to retrain my body to dance New York style. In exchange for teaching his beginner classes, I received private lessons from lifelong New York *salsero* Ivan Rivera, during which I learned how to style my arms, execute lifts and aerials, perform an entire syllabus of "shines," or solo footwork—something that did not yet exist in Arizona—and most importantly, count and step to the more syncopated "on-2" timing. Eventually I joined and performed with Razz M'Tazz, one of the foundational New York salsa-mambo companies, and taught others how to dance New York style in classes and workshops. Even though I lost that Colombian touch through retraining, my former style would continue to resurface on visits home, underscoring the intimate ties between body and place as constructed through dance.

Studying Salsa Dance

I begin this chapter with a personal anecdote for two reasons. First, I wish to illustrate how dance creates a sense of place that is felt in the dancer's body, learned and experienced through interactions with other dancers on and off the dance floor. That Puerto Ricans in New York City could read the bodily movements of a southwestern U.S. dancer as "Colombian," a connection made possible through long-term affinities between that South American country and the northern Mexican border area, affinities so deep-seated that they affected the bodily style, or habitus, of even an urban Anglo, is just one indication of the complexity of those interactions. That those same dancers could recognize perhaps a half dozen such geographically denominated salsa styles, often by minute bodily cues, demonstrates how popular social dances like salsa become deeply localized. The anecdote also shows how my interest in the interplay between dance and place developed, an interest that led first to my work on *quebradita* and other border dances[4] and eventually to this book. *Salsa World* is about a particular dance genre, but it is also a study of how and why some forms of global popular culture become localized and, in particular, how dance and place relate to one another through the body.

Salsa has a particular history and a particular discourse about that history, one bound up with competing claims of ownership and ties to a different sort of place, that of the nation-state. Although dance has played a central role in Latin American nationalisms for over a century—who can imagine Argentina without tango or Brazil without samba?—in recent years it has also come to play a role in establishing pan-Latino identifications and in bringing Latino popular culture to even broader audiences. Salsa, for instance, began as a symbol of Nuyorican (New York Puerto Rican) pride, later became an emblem of pan-Latinism, and is today a globalized form of popular culture. At the same time, because dance is a participatory activity that relies on face-to-face interactions, or more precisely body-to-body ones, salsa (like other forms of popular dance) has not become a homogenized, mass-mediated product but has instead assumed intensely local forms in many communities. New Yorkers, Angelenos, Puerto Ricans, Cubans, Colombians, Dominicans, and others all have their own, unique ways of dancing salsa that distinguish them as much as their spoken accents do. In fact, I suggest that those minute cues of bodily movement, posture, and musical timing that allow dancers to identify those who come from elsewhere be termed "dance accents."[5] As with speech, losing one's accent—in other words, adapting to the habitus of a location that is not one's home—is difficult.

In this book, I and the other authors examine how salsa dance is localized—or how the body acquires an accent—and how concepts of geography, ethnicity, and local and national identities interact with the globalized salsa industry. While some of these topics have been treated in earlier works on salsa music (e.g., Waxer 2002a; Quintero Rivera 1999), to date no book in English has dealt specifically with salsa as a dance practice, despite the centrality of the body and movement to the genre. This book collaboratively constructs a multisited ethnography of salsa dance, by including multiple authors who write about the places they know best, while attempting to answer a common body of questions: How and why do salsa dance practices vary? At what points does this salsa scene connect with others? What disconnects still exist, and why? What role does salsa play in local cultures, contexts, and identity constructions? What do people in a location get out of dancing salsa? Our observations have wider implications for understanding the localization of popular culture in general.

Elsewhere (Hutchinson 2009), I have discussed the sidelining of dance in the social sciences, a situation that often continues in the present despite the early importance of the topic to foundational figures such as Franz Boas. Thus, another task of this book is to implicitly address the issue of reintegrating dance into the ethnographic fields by presenting studies of dance coming out of a variety of disciplines. I argue that although recent currents of theory have been successful at dismantling, or at least seriously questioning, many of the long-standing dualisms of Western thinking, such as nature/culture and mind/body, the division between music and dance has remained and even been reinforced by entrenchment in the respective scholarly disciplines. However, for many—perhaps even most—people, communities, and cultures, music and dance are inseparable as cultural forms, so that drawing lines around them distorts people's actual experiences.[6] It is therefore important to acknowledge the interdependence of the two fields, to recognize the contributions that different academic disciplines can make to their study, and to attend to the interactions of dance practice and music.

Salsa World challenges traditional disciplinary boundaries not only by combining these two areas but also by including Latin American scholars from very different traditions, ones less familiar to those of us in the northern academy. Because this book emerges primarily from the ethnographic disciplines, particularly ethnomusicology and anthropology, it will perhaps be of most interest to scholars in these fields. It may show them that focusing on dance can reveal previously untold stories about issues of concern across the social sciences such as nationalism, identity, ethnicity, and globalization and that it can do so precisely because of the intensity with which place and community are produced through bodily practices.

Anyone who has trained as both musician and dancer can attest to the very different points of view each side holds over the other's subject matter—for instance, when reconciling musicians' and dancers' counts: each side has a unique point of view that can lead to revealing observations about the other. I therefore believe this book has something to say to dance scholars as well. In the 1990s Jane Desmond noted that gaps within the dance literature included the "commodification of movement styles, their migration, modification, quotation, adoption, or rejection as part of the larger production of social identities through physical enactment" (1997: 30). This book adds to the work done on such issues in the intervening years through its focus on the migration and modification of a particular popular social dance and its inclusion of perspectives from outside the northern English-speaking academy. It shows dance to be a significant part of the migration and flow of ideas, capital, and even people around the world.

Salsa Music: History and Literature

The history of salsa music is well known and extensively documented in widely available books; thus I present here only a brief outline, which contextualizes the discussion of dance, our main topic, in the existing salsa literature. The music we today know as salsa emerged in New York City in the 1960s. It was a combination of Cuban musics like *son*, *guaracha*, and *guajira* with a little bit of flavor from Puerto Rican *plena* and *música jíbara* and a touch of Latin jazz. It also depended on the networks and tastes already set up by previous Latin music crazes in the city, particularly the 1950s mambo. Fania Records was the driving commercial force behind the music, popularizing the term "salsa" and making sure virtually all the artists playing the style were a part of their Fania All Stars ensemble.[7]

Early salsa artists came from a variety of backgrounds, but New York–born Puerto Ricans were the most numerous and among the most influential of this new crop of Latin musicians. Stylistic innovations such as Eddie Palmieri's addition of trombones to the Cuban *charanga* ensemble, Rafael Cortijo's experiments with *bomba* and plena, and Willie Colón's use of jíbaro music produced a distinct musical sound. Jorge Duany explains that salsa differs from its close relative, the Cuban son, in its emphasis on brass instruments, the addition of the timbales, more "violent" arrangements, and the influence of jazz harmonies (Duany 1984: 198).

Debates over salsa's Cuban or Puerto Rican origin are ongoing. Salsa's indebtedness to Cuban styles is indubitable: even Tito Puente, considered a salsa progenitor, frequently stated, "I play Cuban music, not salsa." But as Johnny Pacheco explained the Fania artistic process, "What we were doing was taking Cuban music and adding more progressive chords, emphasizing rhythms, and highlighting certain aspects" (quoted in Washburne 2008: 20). The music produced in this way sounds far different from both its Cuban predecessors and current Cuban styles such as *songo* and *timba*. It thus became an important symbol of Nuyorican identity and culture (see Berríos-Miranda 2002), although Chris Washburne argues that it should more properly be viewed as "inter-Latino" or "trans-Caribbean," because it is consumed, performed, and produced by many groups and has roots in other Caribbean musics as well (2008: 11).[8] As we will see, the debate over origins is also very much a part of the dance scene.

Fania's phenomenal success led to the creation of numerous local salsa scenes and labels in various parts of Latin America, decentralizing production and, ironically, leading to Fania's own demise (Washburne 2008: 22). The label was eventually embroiled in lawsuits related to its brutal treatment of artists and neglect of royalty payment, and it was sold off in 1997. Nonetheless, the hard-driving, rootsy style and gritty lyrics of the early Fania artists endure; this style, termed "*salsa dura*," is the one preferred by most New York salsa dancers today, many of whom vehemently reject newer styles.

The decline of Fania opened the door for other labels, promoters, and styles. In New York, Ralph Mercado Management began promoting a new, softer style with romantic or erotic lyrics, a focus on star singers, and a de-emphasis on improvisation; this style is known as *salsa romántica*. While music critics and scholars lambaste it for its depoliticized content, blatant commercialism, and less adventurous, pop-driven sound, Washburne rightly notes that salsa romántica succeeded in attracting listeners not previously involved in the music—particularly women, who had been largely excluded from salsa dura's masculine ethos. This style dominated the market in the 1980s–1990s, gaining extensive airplay just when some observers had been lamenting merengue's gain on salsa's territory in New York (see Washburne 2008: 183).

Meanwhile, other histories of salsa were developing elsewhere. The ones Alejandro Ulloa Sanmiguel (Chapter 8) and Rossy Díaz (Chapter 9) contribute to this volume give alternative perspectives on the typical salsa narratives, which tend to position the music as a "new" style emerging in New York and later spreading throughout Latin America. In fact, salsa was frequently experienced not as a break with but as a continuation of earlier dance practices in these countries, as salsa culture grew out of son culture in Santo Domingo, Dominican Republic, and out of the *champú* dances in Cali, Colombia.

Perhaps the most influential alternative was being developed in that distant neighbor Cuba. A distinctive circle dance called *casino*, *rueda*, or *rueda de casino* developed in social clubs there in the 1950s and resurged in the 1980s, partly a result of the influence of U.S. salsa, alongside a new musical form called *timba* (see Perna 2008: 12). With its technically demanding, ultrasyncopated jazz- and funk-influenced arrangements and the combination of the violins and flutes of the charanga ensemble with drum sets and multiple synthesizers, timba sounded unlike any U.S., Caribbean, or South American salsa; it also developed outside the world capitalist system, although today it participates in that system.

On a musical level, salsa is fairly simple to define because of its rhythmic structure; in New York, at least, both this structure and salsa performance practice have been relatively stable since the 1970s (Washburne 2008: 166–167). The basic steps, counts, and bodily movements of salsa are also clearly recognizable, despite their innumerable variations and permutations. Nonetheless, in the discourse surrounding the music, salsa appears undefinable and unlocatable: it is Nuyorican and pan-American; it is revolution and resistance, and it is conformity and commercialism; it is an exotic encounter with the Other, or it is our own. This ambiguity has a purpose, because salsa must serve many different affiliations, as Washburne argues, so that regional, national, and international levels are mixed and constantly interact in salsa. Therefore, salsa continues to be marked today, as it has always been, by the tension between commercial interests and lived experience, between Anglo-American and Latin American cultures, between U.S. imperialism and Latin American resistance.

Salsa Dance Panorama

Just as salsa music functions on many different levels to serve different affiliations, so does salsa dance. Throughout the developments just described, salsa dancing continued to grow and change in New York (see Chapter 2). The result was a split between those who danced for fun and to socialize, often termed "social dancers" or "street dancers," and those who also had the goals of performing and competing, often termed "studio dancers." (In Spanish, the respective terms are *"bailador"* and *"bailarín"*; see Chapter 8.) Street dancers may or may not feel connected to a global community of salsa dancers, but studio dancers certainly do. They are connected to one another virtually, through dance websites, discussion groups, and online social networking, and also in person at various times throughout the year. The discursive separation of the two groups parallels the debates over politicized and commercialized salsas, like salsa dura and salsa romántica. Studio dancers are the primary focus of this book: their practices most clearly reveal the tensions, arising through bodily movement, between the global and the local.

Washburne sees a decline in interest in salsa music in the twenty-first century that has resulted in the closing of many clubs and declining opportunities of gigs for musicians. It might, then, seem paradoxical to note salsa dancing's growth in the same period, except that competitive salsa dancers generally prefer to dance to recorded music. In New York, at least, the venues such dancers gather at are "socials," informal parties for serious dancers inspired by ballroom studio practices, and "congresses," large conventions often featuring both the-atrical performances and competitive events. The first are local in scope, the second transnational.

The number of congresses has increased drastically in the past decade. In 2003 I noted events occurring on the West and East Coasts of the United States, in Canada, in Puerto Rico, and in Italy, among other locations. At the Ber-lin Salsa Congress in 2008, the information table had flyers for congresses in Stuttgart, Frankfurt, Hamburg, and Munich, as well as Athens, Amsterdam, Istanbul, Marrakech, Slovenia, Monaco, Estonia, Switzerland, and Poland, each brought by dancers representing those locations. The instructors at the same event had African American, Latino, East Indian, Polish, Moroccan, and even Iraqi British backgrounds. Meanwhile, the 2009 World Salsa Championships in Fort Lauderdale advertised participation by dancers of thirty nationalities. Congress advertising tends to announce dancers' country of origin as a nod to diversity but eliminates any discussion of politics or difference. Yet even as this kind of salsa was increasing its globalizing tendencies, other, more local kinds of salsa were emerging. Just as local salsa music industries have sprung up in diverse locations, so have local varieties of salsa dance, even more varied than the musical styles available.

Salsa dance today is clearly a commodity, being sold though dance lessons, videos, recordings, and attire. But movement is a slippery sort of commodity, not easy to pin down or package. As Juliet McMains writes of ballroom dance, it is limited in its reproducibility because of its dependence on one-to-one in-teraction (2006: 56). One might add that touch, a necessary component of that interaction, still cannot be transmitted through any standard mass communi-cation technologies, limiting the ability of marketers to commodify dance. So while music is easily transportable through recordings, meaning that people anywhere can reproduce it with exactitude and hear exactly the same song in any place and time, the dance experience is less replicable. Even though one can learn dance steps from videos, a practice made even easier now by the advent of YouTube and similar sites, most people still learn to dance through face-to-face, body-to-body transmission, and in a partner dance like salsa, direct contact with others is a prerequisite for dancing. In addition, while today music listening is often conducted in private, dance is a social activity.

For these reasons, dance, unless subjected to standardizing regimens (as in competitive ballroom dance), is supremely susceptible to localizing processes. When one learns any dance, prior bodily dispositions enter into a performance of that dance, intentionally or not. This reliance on muscle memory means that when a new community adopts a dance, the prior movement experiences of the members of that community may enter and become part of that dance. As Ángel Quintero Rivera explains, dance is not just virtuosity; it is "corporeal intercommunication of emotions and knowledges" (2009: 29).

What all this means for salsa is that, although a commercialized, mass-mediated, and transnational product, it is also something that many people in disparate locations experience as their own (cases in which dancers take up salsa as an exotic Other are discussed below). This is the case for street as well as studio dancers. Some believe this ownership to be natural: for instance, some Puerto Ricans and Cubans feel the dance originated with them. Others, like Colombians, acknowledge that it came from elsewhere but still internalize it. They turn it into part of their local culture, transforming the dance and their relationship to it through repeated social interactions (at parties, nightclubs, concerts, or classes) and the effects their bodily experience (dance training, social dancing, or socially acceptable postures and ways of walking) bring to bear on it. These prior movement experiences may vary widely (I may have training in ballet, while my partner is into hip-hop), but some shared experiences may also predominate (cumbia is popular in Colombia and the United States–Mexico border area; U.S. dancers are likely to be familiar with movie musical conventions; most Dominicans can dance some merengue). Dancers' attitudes and understandings of these experiences may likewise vary from place to place, causing them to accept or reject practices.

Concurrent with the commercialization and spread of salsa music, as I have mentioned, salsa dance became commercialized and professionalized, processes detailed in several chapters in this book. The dance was also standardized, so that a few basic steps are taught in a couple of different but easily recognizable forms around the world. Beyond the basics, teachers may develop a syllabus of steps particular to their school. This practice is not unique to salsa and indeed was adapted from ballroom dance, but it is particularly extensive in this genre. So while Karen Backstein found that New York teachers of Brazilian and Afro-Caribbean dance were just beginning to develop teaching methodologies around 2000 and they were not yet standardized (2001: 469), among New York salseros this process has been under way since the 1980s.

While New York (on-2) and L.A. (on-1) styles have dominated the transnational salsa scene for some years, particularly at congresses, the so-called Cuban style is also danced in many locations and presents an important alternative. This style, with more focus on bodily movements and isolations and with rounded turn patterns in place of the slot form that characterizes North American salsa,[9] derives from Cuban casino or rueda, a round dance in which multiple couples exchange partners and perform coordinated moves according to a leader's calls. It is appearing increasingly often alongside the other two styles at congresses, and it even seems poised to overtake the aforementioned styles in some areas. Meanwhile, in Cuba itself *despelote*, a kind of autoerotic display by women dancing solo, may be more common, sometimes interspersed with newly created rueda moves (see Chapter 6). Rueda has become known internationally as Cuban salsa, and while this is clearly a misnomer, since it existed before New York salsa and came from an entirely different socioeconomic system, the term is now used to lend weight to the Cuban-origin argument.[10]

Looking at the styles named in salsa congresses shows that studio salsa dancers around the world categorize salsa styles in two principal ways: by nationality or region (e.g., Cuban, U.S. West Coast, or Colombian style) or by musical relationships (generally, on-1 or on-2, referring to the count on which the dancers break, or change direction). As with many classifications, this one simplifies, obscuring (a) historical connections between locations, (b) the very recent emergence of emic theories of dance counts, and (c) local meanings of music and dance styles. This book provides important correctives to all three errors.

First, Ulloa and Jonathan Marion concur that United States–based on-1 dancing depended on Colombian-style salsa, which emphasizes the downbeat and provides a counternarrative to the Puerto Rican focus on Cuban clave and its off beats. Ulloa adds to this his own hypothesis, which is that Colombian dancers gained their predilection for dancing on-1 from Mexican films of the 1940s–1950s and the *guaracha* and mambo dance styles they featured. In this description, we see a dialectical relationship between Colombian and Mexican dance practices, often via outposts like Los Angeles and including input from Cuban and other Caribbean sources. Such a hypothesis surely complicates any simple view of salsa as evolving in linear fashion through the unidirectional movement of Caribbean Latinos to New York, for example. As Cindy Garcia (2008) and Joanna Bosse (Chapter 5) point out, however, these transnational interactions occur within a framework of power relations in which Mexican dance styles may not be as highly valued as Caribbean ones.

Second, Sydney Hutchinson and Ulloa demonstrate that on-2 and on-1 counting systems are recent phenomena dating back no further than the 1980s, much as Washburne's recent (2008) work has shown that salsa musicians' dogmatic adherence to the clave rhythm is a 1960s Nuyorican preoccupation possessing few Cuban precedents. Meanwhile, Díaz and Priscilla Renta show how little the count matters to the many Caribbean dancers who value freedom and spontaneity over a close fit with clave.[11] Codification of steps and standardization of counts is thus a matter for professionals hoping to sell dance to students and audiences. That such an elaborate theorization of music and dance interrelationships has arisen in this community before scholarly intervention (the first scholarly publications to discuss on-2 dancing were Hutchinson 2004 and Renta 2004) is striking and demands attention.

Third, although all the chapters in this volume describe dance scenes that participate to some degree in a transnational dance community, they also demonstrate the vastly different meanings dance practices acquire locally. Salsa can mean upward mobility for working-class Latinos in New Jersey (Chapter 3), a cosmopolitan connection to others for middle-class midwesterners (Chapter 5), Puerto Rican pride to New Yorkers (Chapter 2), a competitive challenge for Angelenos (Chapter 4), an alternative, nonviolent imaginary to Caleños (Chapter 8), a tropical vacation for Parisians (Chapter 10), national differentiation in Barcelona (Chapter 11), or even socialist resistance to capitalism in Cuba (Chapter 6).

Globalized Salsa

The choice of the cities we examine in this volume—Tokyo, Paris, Barcelona, Havana, Santo Domingo, San Juan, Los Angeles, and New York—by and large reflects the fact that salsa culture is an urban culture that has been transnational since its inception.[12] While drawing its style and its means of legitimization from earlier, rural styles like Cuban son, guajira, and guaracha and Puerto Rican música jíbara, salsa's typical origin stories, when unraveled, reveal connections not only between Cubans and Puerto Ricans but also among African Americans, Italian Americans, Anglo-Americans, Mexicans, Colombians, Dominicans, West Africans, and many others. Just before the emergence of salsa, Latin American popular music was being disseminated throughout the Americas through Cuban recordings and Mexican films, often making its way from there to West Africa, where it contributed to or directly spawned a vast array of local popular musics, including Congolese rumba, Nigerian highlife, Angolan *kizomba*, and Guinean *maringa* (see, e.g., Charry 2000: 263). These styles themselves rest on an earlier layer of African-Caribbean genres like *gumbe* (or *goombay*), once found in Jamaica, Louisiana, Cuba, Guinea, Sierra Leone, and beyond (see Bilby 2011).

Transnational connections and interchange are thus nothing new in Caribbean music and dance. Such processes have been described variously as creolization, *créolité*, *mestizaje*, hybridity, and transculturation by analysts. Each term has a different history and connotation. For instance, numerous scholars have rejected "hybrid," "mestizo," and "creolized" for their racial implications, but others have recently found emancipatory potential in reclaiming such terms. For instance, Quintero Rivera suggests that "mulatto" music and dance styles like salsa demonstrate the value of hybridity to a "world obsessed with the idea of only one governing, centralizing principle" (2009: 65), and his analysis of such styles is thus a kind of decolonization project. Yet among the several options, the term "transculturation" may be particularly apt for the case of salsa. It is proposed by Cuban scholar Fernando Ortiz to describe the uneven "process of transition from one culture to another" that involves both loss and new creation (Ortiz [1947] 1995: 102–103). He sees transculturation as being particularly typical of the Caribbean because of the diversity of cultures involved, the prolonged intensity of their interactions, and the speed and thoroughness with which it occurred, all of which made the region distinct from Europe (99). Today, however, such intensive interactions of multiple cultures have spread to many—if not most—urban areas around the world. Transculturation, like salsa, is thus a part of globalization, but it is a part that is rooted, theoretically at least, in a Caribbean past.

Mixture is thus old news in the Caribbean, which means that our use of the term "globalized salsa" requires further explanation. Terms like "globalization" and "transnationalism" express the common feeling that life today is qualitatively different from life in centuries past, despite prior mixtures, fusions, and travels. What is new, John Tomlinson tells us, is not movement and dialogue but rather the degree of complexity in the social connectivity many take for granted today (1999: 1–3), the transformation of our experience of space and time through mass mediation and the ease of travel (3–10), the widespread use of communication technologies in all aspects of daily life, and the changing relationship between place and culture resulting from deterritorialization (106–149).

"Globalized salsa" thus means complex connections between different and distant groups of dancers facilitated by technologies like the Internet; a sense of proximity to dancers half a world away, perhaps one that is greater than what the dancer feels toward his or her own, non-salsa-dancing neighbors; and a clear sense of locality through local dance styles that are nonetheless infused with "the ghostly presence of distant influences" (Tomlinson 1999: 58). Salseros themselves actively imagine the global in their discourse, promoting the dance as "a new common element of communication around the world" and as a global unifier (Delgado 2003; my translation).

It also means increasing links to global institutions through the global capitalist system, or rather the music and dance industries that form a part of it. It is no secret that salsa music has been a commercial enterprise from the beginning, as described above. Salsa dance classes spread as a commodity on a similar trajectory. In places without a prior tradition of son or mambo dancing, introductory classes given at nightclubs before salsa band performances and included in the admission price played an important role in spreading the style. Student interest in acquiring dance competence allowed specialists to emerge and impelled them to complicate the style with a plethora of new steps and turn patterns. The more complicated style in turn helped establish a dedicated community of salsa dancers willing to invest time and money in lessons, videos, shoes, and clothing. Promoters created congresses, which made money while also enlarging and intensifying dancers' networks. Commodified salsa dancing, reified as a set of specific steps ("a dance") rather than a social practice ("dancing"), then spread even to those locations where a strong tradition of social salsa dancing already existed.

Globalizing processes in salsa today can perhaps be found even more often in dancers' outlooks and complex practices of connectivity than in the salsa music recording industry—especially since studio dancers tend to use older music rather than supporting new artists. But mass media continue to play important roles in the development, spread, and popularization of salsa music and dance by establishing connectivity between dancers and disseminating dance practices. All the chapters mention these issues, but they are particularly highlighted in the Colombian (Chapter 8) and Japanese (Chapter 12) contributions. While these two places are culturally and geographically far different, they share the practice of relating to salsa primarily through media, recordings and films being decisive in the Colombian case, Internet and print media in the Japanese one. In Spain, radio is the principal means through which a salsa community is built. In the Dominican Republic, salsa's role in tourism and local cultural industries is another way the dance establishes connections between people and places.

Salsa is different, then, from earlier transcultural Caribbean dances in the degree of its commercialization—as long as the genre label has existed, it was always made to be marketed—and in that it was never a rural music or a purely oral tradition. In addition, it inhabits a special position as a dance that exists in both a professional, globally marketed, performance-oriented form, that of studio salsa, and an amateur, local, social form, that of street salsa. In certain places, the two forms are in constant and intense contact, even though they may serve different social groups, demonstrating that this is not a simple dichotomy but rather a scale in shades of gray. The linkages between salsa and mass communication technologies are also an important factor in establishing salsa as a globalized form of popular culture. The Internet, in particular, facilitates not only the spread of steps and styles but also dialogue between distant dancers, and it has even contributed to spreading the ways of classifying and debating salsa styles I have already mentioned.

Finally, and related to this last point, salsa is also different because of the wide audiences it reaches, which now include all classes; because of its deterritorialization and hence relatively greater distance from national discourses (even in Puerto Rico, salsa is not the national music); and because of the geographic spread of its influence, affecting every inhabited continent. Thus, in this book we look at salsa as a "globalized dance," even though it is obvious that not everyone around the globe participates in salsa dancing.

When we look particularly at studio salsa, we find that in most countries it is the practice of that select group that might be termed "cosmopolitan" (for useful discussions of the term, see Turino 2000: 7–9; Tomlinson 1999: 198–199). Salsa scenes are frequently cosmopolitan ones in several senses. In most places salsa dancing is not firmly tied to a concept of nation, with the possible exception of Puerto Rico (see Chapter 7), so that most salseros do not choose the dance for nationalist reasons. In general, salsa cosmopolitanism instead relates to a generalized concept of *latinidad*, or a sense of Latino identity (tropicalized into a stereotypical "Latin heat" for some non-Latinos) and to specific notions of locality, local pride, and localized conceptions of Latino identities. In most cases, again with the possible exceptions of Puerto Rico and New York, salsa is also not tied directly to colonial experiences, since it is not primarily spread by a colonizing power but rather by dance aficionados in conjunction with the transnational music industry. Most importantly, many salsa dancers feel connected to other salseros in disparate locations throughout the world through their dance practice. Particularly in places far from cultural centers, people may get involved in salsa precisely because it offers them a way of making a connection with cultural Others (see Bosse 2008 and Chapter 5). Yet the possibility of making those connections is limited to those with the means of doing so, for instance, by accessing the Internet or traveling to congresses. This means that while congresses may create an ethnically inclusive community, it is one with little class diversity—and in fact, critics of cosmopolitanism often note the tendencies of cosmopolitans to gloss over class divisions and inequalities in their imagining of the idealized coexistence of cultures.

Salsa dancers are not always cosmopolitans, however. In fact, social, or street, dancers may not necessarily feel themselves to be participating in a global popular culture, and so local salsas are still not particularly globalized or even known outside their home places, as Díaz (Chapter 9) and Bárbara Balbuena Gutiérrez (Chapter 6) show in this volume. This became especially clear to me when I was dancing with Santo Domingo salseros: although stepping forward on the left foot and back on the right is a basic tenet of international studio salsa, one that enables even those with divergent movement styles to dance together without colliding, these dancers all did the reverse—that is, they stepped forward on the right (and were surprised at my surprise). Many toes were stepped on as a result of this intensely local practice.

The division present in salsa between local social dancers and cosmopolitan, semiprofessional studio dancers is often one of class and access to cultural, economic, and kinetic capital. Nonetheless, frequent border crossings between the two realms blur the dividing line. As Katherine Borland, Díaz, and Ulloa note, becoming a studio dancer can be a strategy of upward mobility; similarly, the adoption of movements coded as "street" can be a legitimization strategy for studio dancers. Nonetheless, mobility through dance practice is often impossible for those with insurmountably low social status, like the Mexican migrant dancers Bosse describes. In addition, dance movements and bodily habits themselves change by moving across categories, as Ulloa suggests.

Thomas Turino finds that cosmopolitans are considered elite and sophisticated because they themselves define these terms (2000: 10–11). Similarly, studio salsa now functions as cultural capital because its originators had already transformed social salsa practices to fit middle-class, cosmopolitan aesthetic principles (see Bosse 2008). Its degree of complexity has been raised through the creation of numerous complicated steps and turn patterns, improvisation has been de-emphasized in favor of learned sequences (see Chapter 7), and every aspect has been codified and standardized. Now too difficult to learn at home or on the street, studio salsa is a commodity to be bought and sold. And its professionalization may be accompanied by an unwarranted devaluation of local social dancing that can reduce the dance's power to create community cohesion (see Chapters 2 and 7). Like the move from salsa dura to salsa romántica, the increasing predominance of global (studio) over local (street) salsa carries the risk of depoliticization and exclusion, even as it brings new populations into the dance.

In sum, if salsa was once thought of as a local music, this situation changed long ago. It would indeed be difficult to conceive of the "Salsa Bollywood" style created by Bangalore, India, dancers Ree and Prithvi and taught at the 2008 Berlin Salsa Congress as a local one. And the commonly told history of salsa's origins, which focuses on the genre's emergence in New York, itself leaves out the dance's shifting and multiple prehistories. Salsa dance epitomizes many of the features that have been associated with globalization: hybridity, deterritorialization, commodification, and cosmopolitanism. It has been spread through migration, mass media, new technologies, and tourism. But the spread of salsa is not a top-down affair in which mass-mediated popular culture is imposed on hapless locals; it is a dialogue in which the locals also impose their own tastes and priorities, changing the nature of the very commodity they are meant to consume.

Localized Salsa

While deterritorialization is key for understanding global, mass-marketed studio salsa dance, reterritorialization is a process at least as important. This book therefore focuses less on how salsa has become separated from its origins, which, as we have seen, are themselves contested, and more on how it is continually relinked with place and community through dance practices. By calling salsa "globalized," we point out that salsa has spread to many continents, countries, localities, and communities, many of which have little in common *except* for their interest in salsa. By emphasizing that the dance is simultaneously "localized," we distance what is global from what is normative and underscore the roles of local actors in producing the global. Globalization occurs differently in different places, so that Japanese, Spanish, and Colombian experiences of salsa are very different, even though they deal with the same product. Even codification, stylization, and professionalization take place at the local level. Far from producing a single, homogenous movement style, then, salsa has developed differently in different locations; it has also taken on different gendered and racialized meanings as it has become embedded in local racial hierarchies, ethnic identities, and histories of gender relations.[13]

Just as non-Western modernities arise pluralistically from different histories (Featherstone 1990: 8; Tomlinson 1999: 65–66), so does globalization occur multidirectionally and in plural, as much for "the rest" as for "the West" (Hall 1996). Ana Maria Ochoa explains that major transnational labels dominate an increasing share of the music market at the same time that they spawn local branches that function as independents within the larger conglomerate. The "world music" some of these labels sell constructs authenticity based on ideas about nature, "true emotions and genuine sentiments," and time without history, thereby erasing differences (Ochoa 1999: 257–258). Salsa dancers do the same when they consider "authentic" dancers, those with a Latin American background, to be "naturals," while everyone else has to learn it. In both salsa and world music, authenticity as a commodity is tied to race and ethnicity, located in the bodies of performers and then marketed in tropicalized form as "hot" and "fiery" (see Backstein 2001: 458; Ochoa 1999; Aparicio and Chavez-Silverman 1997: 8).[14] Salsa becomes a "hot commodity" because the passion it is thought to encapsulate has itself long been mined from Latin America and sold in Europe and North America (see Savigliano 1995).

Localized salsas have complex and highly variable relations to notions of authenticity. Borland in Chapter 3 shows how outsiders with their exoticizing gaze are not the only ones engaged in tropicalization; New Jersey Latinos also tropicalize themselves. Marion in Chapter 4 explains that Mexican dancers in Los Angeles are sometimes grouped with other Latinos as authentic and at other times deemed inauthentic because they are not Caribbean. A similar dynamic occurs in Illinois, Bosse demonstrates in Chapter 5, where salsa is tied to often racist evaluations of kinetic capital; there, Cuban and New York styles are viewed as the most authentic ones. Kengo Iwanaga in Chapter 12 shows how Japanese dancers make very selective and strategic transnational connections: those who dance Cuban style are interested in authenticating their dance by acquiring and expressing knowledge about the music and dance's history, but they are in a minority; a majority dance L.A. style and have little interest in such matters. This tendency seems to be reproduced in many other local salsa scenes. But because local interpretations are, I argue, just as important as local performances, it is imperative to examine not only the product but also the processes that produce it and the discourse that surrounds it. The version of salsa taught in ballroom studios and tied to dancesport, formally regulated competitive ballroom dance, seems to be divorced from race- and place-based notions of authenticity; instead, it focuses on a technical competency completely separate from cultural knowledge. This new type of globalized salsa requires further research.[15]

Borland suggests that "while all scenes are local, not all locales produce the conditions for the development of a place-specific style," a statement that merits further analysis. How do place-specific styles like those described in this book actually arise? Elsewhere (Hutchinson 2012), I have proposed the term "kinetopia" as a way of examining the interactions of dance with place. Its literal meaning is "place of movement," and the relationship functions in two ways: some dances are kinetopias,[16] in that their relationship to place defines them, and some places are kinetopic, in that they are in part defined by their particular patterns of movement. A kinetopia is often constructed through dance, although styles of walking, driving, gesturing, and other motion-based behaviors can also play important roles, as do more large-scale types of movement, from crowds moving through streets during carnival to travel patterns or the displacements of labor migration. In other words, kinetopias are both places and dances: I am speaking of a dialectical relationship between localities and movement practices that is mediated through the body.[17] The kinetopia concept can help us understand how people dance in place and why place-specific styles develop.

Foucault's ([1967] 2002) "heterotopias"—sites of juxtaposition, difference, conflict, and conversation—construct our understanding of the world through inversion: mental hospitals, for instance, tell us what normal behavior is;

cemeteries tell us what it is to be alive; and through their separation, festivals tell us about ordinary time and museums tell us about ordinary space. Likewise, kinetopias produce local understandings of the world through bodily movement. Unlike utopias, they actually exist, but like them, kinetopias may also be aimed at producing a more perfected version of the outside society, as salseros speak of achieving global unity through dance. Kinetopias are both conceptual and physical spaces. They may be a region, a city, or a more specific location like a disco, a street festival, or a high school dance. People define kinetopias through contact and comparison—we move in this way, and they do not—and thus they are also sites for identity building. "Dance accents" are kinetopic in that they define social groups as related to place through their members' movement practices. Place-specific, kinetopic salsa styles tend to emerge in locations that already have a distinctive local or regional culture with a strong heritage of partner dance, a cultural connection to the dance either through geography or migration, a network of sites for dancing, media outlets that support the genre, and a large number of local salsa aficionados. Only such places seem to have the numbers, momentum, and dance vocabulary needed to create and sustain a kinetopia of salsa.

Salsa dancing might seem a curious kind of kinetopia. While the music was once strongly associated with a particular place—New York's Latino barrios—that connection has been gradually dissolved as the dance and music have become globalized. But salsa is a product of cultural mixture, and as Tomlinson notes, there is a "tendency of culture mixtures to re-embed themselves, however briefly, into 'stable' identity positions" (1999: 148). The chapters in this book evidence the process in which salsa dancing is reterritorialized in a wide variety of locations, giving rise to numerous kinetopias. As Josh Kun writes of "audiotopias," the local salsas we describe bring together "sites normally deemed incompatible"—like developing and developed nations, or First and Third Worlds—and may also be "spaces of effective utopian longings," as in the hope, frequently articulated at salsa congresses, that salsa dancing can bring the world together (2005: 23).

We might think of kinetopias as being the (re)territorialized aspects of the global "choreoscape." Arjun Appadurai (1990) describes the deterritorialized, or globalized, world as being constituted by the interaction of a variety of "scapes," or fields of action, from the "financescape" of global capitalism to the "ethnoscape" of human relations. The choreoscape, the vast array of dances circulating around the globe, is another part of these interactions and a part that frequently becomes re-embedded in localities. As commodified popular culture, and as a part of the migration and flow of ideas, capital, and even people around the world, salsa dance forms part of the choreoscape that produces embodied concepts of community, ethnicity, and gender, among others.

In attending to the role of the choreoscape in globalizing and localizing processes, this book argues for the restoration of dance to the central place it occupied in the early histories of the fields of folklore, anthropology, and ethnomusicology. But because salsa dancing has simply not been researched everywhere and every way it is performed, numerous places and topics are left out. For instance, salsa enjoys great popularity in many West African nations with a long history of not only consuming but also producing Latin American music. The continuing popularity of the mostly Senegalese salsa group Africando among New York salseros—their song "Yay Boy" has entered the on-2 canon, and dancers sing along to it even though its Wolof-language lyrics are unintelligible to them—is just one example of the transnational, transcultural connections occurring in African salsa (see Montes Pizarro 2008). And in India, the style seems to be growing concurrently with the new middle class (see "Salsa Mubarak," n.d.; I thank Naresh Fernandes for the tip). Yet I was unable to find any researcher working on salsa dancing in either Africa or India. Future researchers, I hope, will continue where we have left off, thus helping create a fuller picture of how popular culture in general, and salsa in particular, is localized through embodied practices.

Common Threads

This book brings together contributors from seven countries (United States, Japan, France, Spain, Colombia, Cuba, and Dominican Republic) and at least as many fields and disciplines (ethnomusicology, anthropology, communication studies, sociology, dance, humanities, Latin American studies, and performance studies). The contributions therefore reflect a wide variety of perspectives born from not only individual interests but also differences in the discourses of the authors' respective national traditions and academic fields. I believe the diversity of the authors and their styles to be a strength of this book, since it reflects the current state of salsa as a multisited practice. In addition, nearly all of these authors are or have been deeply involved in the local salsa scene in which they write, and two of them, Bárbara Balbuena Gutiérrez and Alejandro Ulloa Sanmiguel, are likely the best-known authorities on salsa in their own countries. Including these chapters is as important for the decolonization of our disciplines as it is for reminding those of us working in First World academies that not everyone has accepted our intellectual proposals. That some of these essays do not fit comfortably into current discourses in English-language social sciences reminds us that we need to hear other voices from other academies, as well as from outside the academy entirely, and that we need to work harder to forge international dialogues.

The book is organized into geographic sections, each of which shows a different facet of salsa today. All of them, however, have certain themes in common, so that issues of class, race, and ethnicity continually resurface. Its structure follows the trajectory of commercialized salsa's spread from New York to Latin America to points beyond. The first section thus consists of works on salsa in the United States, which illustrate salsa's social ascent and the changes it has experienced by transforming from a working-class, local, and strongly Latino genre into a middle-class, globalized, and multiethnic one. In the process, tensions have arisen between those identified as street and studio dancers, between Latinos and non-Latinos, and between the drive to commercialize and the need to socialize.

In New York, on-2 dancing arose as a unique local style tied to a sense of pride in Puerto Rican or Nuyorican heritage and in the local tradition of mambo dance. Today, it has evolved into a globally salable commodity, necessitating a de-emphasis of ethnicity as a factor in its performance. Instead, nostalgia, a clave-centered mythos, and a utopian idea of bridging differences through dance are factors in many modern-day aficionados' understanding of salsa. In Chapter 2, I detail the history of on-2 dancing, with special attention to its class and ethnic dimensions and street-studio tensions.

Katherine Borland writes of another salsa periphery, one located right next to the dance's perceived center. In New Jersey, salseros see themselves as outward-reaching cosmopolitans, but here salsa is both part of an inclusive latinidad and a way out of limiting socioeconomic spheres. Perhaps in reaction to nearby New York's emphasis on Puerto Rican roots, New Jerseyites celebrate diverse backgrounds while avoiding any talk that might increase divisions within the scene, particularly talk about class.

Jonathan Marion looks at the other big U.S. salsa center, showing how the L.A. salsa scene developed primarily through competition, reflecting the city's reputation for hustling. Savvy marketing has succeeded in gaining L.A.-style salsa recognition as *the* alternative to New York salsa, even though the dance marketed is not representative of diverse local dance practices. In contrast to the theatrical style of globalized L.A. salsa, local social dance often drew instead from the cumbia dancing popular in the border area. Marion's chapter therefore serves as an example of the transformations dance may undergo in passing from global to local levels, and vice versa.

In looking at a salsa scene in an area far removed from those usually associated with the dance, Joanna Bosse gives a valuable new perspective on racialization in salsa. In the historically homogenous but currently diversifying small-town Midwest, those considered to be salsa insiders and outsiders may differ markedly from the emics and etics of other places: here, Mexicans are considered natives to salsa because of their Latin American origins, even though they are also viewed with suspicion. While salsa provides midwestern "small-town cosmopolitans" with a way to connect to global popular culture and to meet others of different backgrounds, it also camouflages a particular form of racism, manifested in their scorn for Mexican dance styles. In this case, everyone is not equally cosmopolitan, and one's degree of cultural capital may be evaluated through bodily practices or dance accents. Perhaps we might introduce the term "kinetic capital" to describe the phenomenon.

Globalized salsa is now often considered a middle-class activity, since, as noted, it caters to those who can afford lessons, costumes, and visits to clubs and congresses. Yet the Latin American chapters in the second part of this volume demonstrate that salsa is not exclusive to that class. While Latin Americans are clearly aware of and engaged in the globalized salsa industry, in many countries salsa is still danced also or even primarily by lower and working classes. And salsa's ascent in foreign lands is no guarantee of a similar rise in status in those countries with which it has historically been associated.

Bárbara Balbuena provides an insider's look at salsa in Cuba, the island many outside observers associate most closely with the dance but a place that in reality has a conflicted relationship with the genre. In showing how unique local forms like *rueda de casino* have developed in this socialist country, she provides an important counterpoint to the other chapters in this book, which look at local salsas in the global capitalist system.

Next, Priscilla Renta analyzes the concept of *sabor* (flavor) from a personal, native-ethnographic perspective, placing her own experience in dialogue with developments in the Puerto Rico Salsa Congress since its beginnings as the World Salsa Congress in 1997. She demonstrates how the congress has contributed to the professionalization of salsa as well as to the Latinization of transnational popular culture. This example of transculturation shows the interplay of various commercial interests in globalized salsa as well as salsa's potential as a decolonization maneuver.

In Cali, Colombia, Alejandro Ulloa Sanmiguel similarly demonstrates how salsa helps create an alternative imaginary for the inhabitants of this city, long torn by violence and the drug trade. Dance can be a positive, creative outlet for Caleños, and when they bring their local style to international congresses, it can also improve outsiders' impressions of the city and of Colombia as a whole. Discourse on race in Colombia, as elsewhere in Latin America, can be quite different from that in North American and European scholarship; this difference is seen in Ulloa's chapter, which nonetheless seeks to explain how Caleño dance fits into the city's history of racial discrimination. Finally, he demonstrates how salsa and other Caribbean dances in Cali grew as a result of interactions with mass products like recordings, often mediated by local businesswomen.

In her chapter on the city of Santo Domingo, Rossy Díaz explains salsa dance as a class-delimited activity particularly associated with Dominican return migrants. It is also a practice through which some barrio dwellers construct an identity alternative to the official Dominican one, which is closely tied to merengue. In this Caribbean city, salsa is a local cultural industry characterized by ties to the growing tourist industry and, simultaneously, to the older, traditional son-dancing culture. Its economic growth is all the more noteworthy considering how it has occurred almost exclusively through dancers' own initiative in the vacuum left by the absence of any official cultural policy that might encourage the development of small-scale industries.

The third and final section of this book encompasses salsa scenes far removed from locations typically associated with the dance. While the general movement vocabulary was imported to these scenes from afar, it was incorporated in particular ways that depended on local social and cultural dynamics.

Dance practices and their ascribed meanings vary widely between locations with large and long-standing Latino communities, such as Barcelona, and those with no sizable Latin American immigrant communities to speak of, like Tokyo. In all these places, the media and transmitted stereotypes about Latinos play central roles in the localization of salsa.

Echoing Paul Gilroy's (1993) and James Clifford's (1997) concept of the intertwining of roots and routes, Saúl Escalona conceives of salsa in Paris as a "route" embodied in the dance's movements. Although Parisian Latinos do dance salsa, Escalona focuses instead on the reception and reproduction of salsa among non-Latino Parisians, for whom the dance is a set of movements devoid of any cultural meaning except that of a stereotypical "tropical heat." French dancers classify salsa styles geographically, codify movements as a list of steps to be performed, and seek to acquire kinetic capital by mastering the steps. In Escalona's analysis, these practices are more related to French ideas about individuality and competence than to Latin American ones about community and enjoyment.

Isabel Llano shows how the growth of salsa in Barcelona has been intimately tied to the growth of Latin American mass media in that city. Like Bosse, Llano shows that insiderness and outsiderness are judged differently in different locations: in Barcelona some of the earliest salsa teachers were from South America's Southern Cone, a region distant from salsa's usual centers. (The same teachers would likely be deemed inauthentic in places with large Caribbean populations, like New York.) The heightened popularity of Latino music in Barcelona has not produced an integrated dance scene: instead, each nationality has its own dance spaces, while Spaniards attend still others, and each group manifests distinct consumption practices. Nonetheless, Llano believes that the embodied nature of dance practice may be helping change Spanish cultural identities and attitudes toward immigrants.

In Japan, salsa is not connected to any large Latino immigrant community. Kengo Iwanaga shows how salsa has been assimilated into a culture where partner dance was historically not accepted, but where a progression of Latin dances from tango to salsa has nevertheless helped change attitudes. There, two types of dancers practice two different styles of salsa, with the minority Cuban-style dancers exhibiting an interest in learning about culture and the majority L.A.-style dancers interested in only performance. This focus is related to the business orientation of the salsa scene in Japan, which has grown through the efforts of businessmen promoters and the appearance of magazines and websites devoted to the style. The Japanese example underscores the importance of mass media, particularly the Internet, in the globalization of the dance.

In all, these chapters provide different takes on how dance produces place and vice versa. In cases like the Puerto Rican, Colombian, Cuban, Dominican, New York, and Angeleno ones, local salsa practices create a kinetopia in which the dance can come to stand for the place. Local dancers acquire obvious dance accents, detected either visually by an observer or tactilely by a dance partner.

In other cases, like the Japanese or French ones, there is a conscious attempt to re-create a dance from elsewhere rather than produce a unique kinetopia, and there is no definable localized dance accent. Even so, dance practices must change through their interactions with local beliefs, values, and bodily habits. The reverse is also true, as Iwanaga shows: the practice of partner dancing in Japan has itself given rise to a new habitus that represents a notable departure from prior ones, in which casual body-to-body contact had been avoided.

Conclusion

Eighty years after Curt Sachs (1933) attempted to create a generalized global geography of dance practices, one can today construct a quite specific, global geography of salsa by examining the distribution or diffusion of on-1, on-2, Cuban, or other styles. Dancers distinguish between styles defined by but divorced from locality, while the dance styles and their meanings are changed when they are recontextualized. To cite one example, as New York salsa becomes global salsa, dancing on-2 has gained prestige but, some might find, lost meaning. At the same time, the creation of a global salsa community may be seen as a positive development, since it creates common ground for people of diverse backgrounds who might never otherwise have the opportunity to interact. In itself, globalization is neither positive nor negative. As salseros themselves might acknowledge, it is not what you do but how you do it: dance can be performed differently in different places and times. The same is true of cultural globalization: however it takes place, it varies from place to place.

The related concepts of dance accents and kinetopias can help us understand this phenomenon. Our bodily habits are profoundly influenced by the contexts in which we live, their histories and politics, and these traces are manifested most clearly when we engage in aestheticized movement practices like dance. Even talk about dance—how we judge it, what we value in it—reveals the meanings dance acquires in local communities, the ways dance and place interact, and the many differences that exist between local dance scenes, even when they all participate in a form of globalized popular culture. This book demonstrates how very differently salsa is understood and practiced in different places, even though many or most salseros also feel they are participating in a global cultural practice and even though cosmopolitan salseros particularly value the globe-spanning connectivity the dance provides. We must therefore ask not only how globalization varies from place to place but also how the global is produced in place, through dancing in place. The chapters in this book suggest some answers to these questions.

NOTES

Acknowledgments: I thank Carol Babiracki, Birgitta Johnson, and Maurice Mengel for their comments on an earlier version of this chapter.

1. See Kapchan 2006 for a related description of interethnic salsa dancing in Texas.

2. Interestingly enough, I would later find nearly the same step pattern being taught as the "salsa step" on the Razz M'Tazz syllabus, although generally minus the small kick, or release, on count 4 (described in Chapter 2 herein).

3. See Garcia 2008 on cumbia-style salsa in Los Angeles; Ramos-Kitrell 2012 on Colombian cumbia in Monterrey, Mexico; and Chapter 8 on Mexican popular culture in Colombia.

4. Hutchinson 2007a, 2012.

5. Bosse has proposed the related term "movement dialect" to describe "dance styles as simultaneous expressions of individuality and markers of cultural affinity and difference" (2008: 48), but this is slightly different. Bosse's *dialects* are akin to the local styles (e.g., New York and Los Angeles) described here, which are shared by geographically and often ethnically delineated groups, while *accents* are the traces those dialects leave on the individual's body.

6. Dance scholar Randy Martin has also recognized the problems attendant on the institutionalization of academic disciplines in university departments, noting a tendency to obscure the interdisciplinary contexts of these disciplines' emergence as well as the ties between knowledge and power (1998: 191).

7. For further information on Fania Records' salsa productions and salsa in Venezuela, see Rondón 1980 and 2008; on gender and listening, see Aparicio 1998; on Colombian salsa and salsa fandom, see Waxer 2002a; on salsa music's transnational movements and localizations, see Waxer 2002b; on the local dance scene in Montreal, see Pietrobruno 2006; on the local dance scene in London, see Urquia 2004 and 2005; and on precursors to salsa in New York's Latin music scene, see Roberts 1999 and Glasser 1995.

8. Washburne further argues that the increasing distance between salsa and Cuban music was caused by not only the U.S. embargo, which curtailed Cuban immigration and ties between New York and Cuba-based musicians, but also the need the embargo created for Fania to distance its product from Cuban styles. This need even created the practice of adding "D.R." (*derechos reservados*, or "all rights reserved") to well-known Cuban songs on record jackets rather than the author's name (2008: 18); this practice continues today in Dominican merengue típico and other Caribbean musics, apparently as a way to avoid royalty payments to known authors.

9. In Chapter 11 Isabel Llano groups both on-1 and on-2 styles under *salsa en línea*, or slot-form salsa. Some L.A. and New York dancers might be irked to find themselves in the same category, but it makes perfect sense from an outside perspective.

10. I once attended an Afro-beat dance class in Berlin, Germany, that included West African and African diaspora dances like *funaná*, *kizomba*, and *zouk*. Noticing that salsa and *bachata* were also part of the studio's offerings, I got into a conversation with the German instructor about these styles. In the United States the salsa-origin debates generally center on the relative importance of Cuban or Puerto Rican influences; I was surprised to find that this teacher not only completely denied early salsa's ties to New York but also went so far as to discount any possibility of Puerto Rican involvement in the music's emergence. I explained that Puerto Ricans both on the island and in New York City feel very strongly that salsa is their music and added that the label "salsa" was applied to Cuban music only much later in the style's history and in the United States, but to no avail. His coinstructor walked in at that point and said, "La salsa es cubana, y punto" (Salsa is Cuban, period), thus closing off further discussion. I interpret their opinion as arising from a combination of factors, including the historical ties between East Berlin and Cuba, the absence of a Puerto Rican community in Berlin, and the increasing authenticity value attached to Cuba in globalized salsa in general. The last factor may in turn be because of (a) the international

success of Cuban nostalgia products like *Buena Vista Social Club*, (b) the heightened value given to African diaspora musics in the world music market in general (see Pacini Hernández 1998), and (c) the leftist chic attached to supporting Cuban narratives over North American ones.

11. Quintero Rivera (2009: 27) similarly explains that some Puerto Ricans start on 1, others on 2, and still others on 3, or in *contratiempo* (syncopation), although Tato Conrad, "the most historically oriented Puerto Rican professional dancer," insists on starting "*salsa cocola*," or working-class salsa, on 1.

12. Bosse's focus on small-town salsa does not disprove this fact, since the dancers she describes participate in salsa precisely because of its cosmopolitan connotations.

13. I have written elsewhere about gender relations in salsa dance (Hutchinson 2007b, 2013).

14. While essentializing, such practices of authentification can have positive economic and symbolic effects on occasion. Backstein notes, for instance, that the increased professionalization of "ethnic" dances can lead to respect for dancers of color and redress of the misperception that such dances have "no technique" (2001: 459).

15. Salsa is not part of the official set of competitive ballroom dances, but it is frequently taught in dancesport-oriented studios.

16. While "heterotopos" and "kinetopos" might seem the more correct singular forms and "heterotopia" and "kinetopia" already to be plurals, I here use the plurals "heterotopias" and "kinetopias" to match both Foucault's term "*hétérotopies*" and the related and more familiar terms "utopia" and "utopias."

17. After I drafted my chapter on the topic of kinetopias in 2009 (Hutchinson 2012), Jonathan McIntosh proposed the similar term "dance heterotopias" to describe Balinese teenagers' disco dancing practices and their appropriation and resignification of foreign dances (2010: 12–13). This is different from a kinetopia in several ways. First, kinetopias relate to all types of bodily movement, not only dance, although here I am foregrounding dance. Second, kinetopias refer to not only dance performance but also the locations themselves; the term thus emphasizes how dances are localized as well as how dances themselves contribute to the making of place.

REFERENCES

Aparicio, Frances R., and Susana Chavez-Silverman. 1997. *Tropicalizations: Transcultural Representations of Latinidad.* Hanover, NH: University Press of New England.

Appadurai, Arjun. 1990. "Disjuncture and Difference in the Global Cultural Economy." *Public Culture* 2 (2): 1–23.

Backstein, Karen. 2001. "Taking 'Class' into Account: The Dance Studio and Latino Culture." In *Mambo Montage: The Latinization of New York*, ed. Agustin Laó-Montes and Arlene Dávila, 449–472. New York: Columbia University Press.

Berríos-Miranda, Marisol. 2002. "Is Salsa a Musical Genre?" In *Situating Salsa: Global Markets and Local Meaning in Latin Popular Music*, ed. Lise Waxer, 23–50. New York: Routledge.

Bilby, Kenneth. 2011. "Africa's Creole Drum: The Gumbe as Vector and Signifier of Trans-African Creolization." In *Creolization as Cultural Creativity*, ed. Robert Baron and Ana C. Cara, 137–177. Jackson: University Press of Mississippi.

Bosse, Joanna. 2008. "Salsa Dance and the Transformation of Style: An Ethnographic Study of Movement and Meaning in a Cross Cultural Context." *Dance Research Journal* 40 (1): 45–64.

Charry, Eric. 2000. *Mande Music: Traditional and Modern Music of the Maninka and Mandinka of Western Africa*. Chicago: University of Chicago Press.

Clifford, James. 1997. *Routes: Travel and Translation in the Late Twentieth Century*. Cambridge, MA: Harvard University Press.

Delgado, Luis A., ed. 2003. "Nuestras raices/Our roots." In *Salsa Today*. 3rd ed. San Juan, Puerto Rico: Congreso Mundial de la Salsa.

Desmond, Jane C. 1997. "Embodying Difference: Issues in Dance and Cultural Studies." In *Meaning in Motion: New Cultural Studies of Dance*, ed. Jane C. Desmond, 29–54. Durham, NC: Duke University Press.

Duany, Jorge. 1984. "Popular Music in Puerto Rico: Toward an Anthropology of Salsa." *Latin American Music Review* 5 (2): 186–215.

Featherstone, Mike. 1990. "Global Culture: An Introduction." In *Global Culture: Nationalism, Globalization and Modernity*, ed. Mike Featherstone, 1–14. London: Sage.

Foucault, Michel. (1967) 2002. "Of Other Spaces." In *The Visual Culture Reader*, ed. Nicholas Mirzoeff, 229–242. 2nd. ed. New York: Routledge.

García, Cindy. 2008. "'Don't Leave Me, Celia!' Salsera Homosociality and Pan-Latina Corporealities." *Women and Performance* 18 (3): 199–213.

Gilroy, Paul. 1993. *The Black Atlantic: Modernity and Double Consciousness*. London: Verso.

Glasser, Ruth. 1995. *My Music Is My Flag: Puerto Rican Musicians and Their New York Communities, 1917–1940*. Berkeley: University of California Press.

Hall, Stuart. 1996. "The West and the Rest: Discourse and Power." In *Modernity: An Introduction to Modern Societies*, ed. Stuart Hall and Bram Gieben, 184–227. Malden, MA: Blackwell.

Hutchinson, Sydney. 2004. "Mambo On 2: The Birth of a New Form of Dance in New York City." *Centro Journal* 16 (2): 109–137.

———. 2007a. *From Quebradita to Duranguense: Dance in Mexican American Youth Culture*. Tucson: University of Arizona Press.

———. 2007b. "When Women Lead: Changing Gender Roles in New York Salsa." Paper presented at the Joint Conference of the Society of the Dance History Scholars and the Congress on Research in Dance, Paris, June 21–24.

———. 2009. "Introduction." In "Latin American Dance in Transnational Contexts," ed. Sydney Hutchinson. Special issue, *Journal of American Folklore* 122 (486): 378–390.

———. 2012. "Breaking Borders/*Quebrando Fronteras*: Dancing in the Borderscape." In *Transnational Encounters: Music and Performance at the U.S.-Mexico Border*, ed. Alejandro Madrid, 41–66. Oxford: Oxford University Press.

———. 2013. "Followers Strike Back! Backleading, Hijacking, and Role Reversal in Contemporary Partner Dance." Unpublished manuscript.

Kapchan, Deborah. 2006. "Talking Trash: Performing Home and Anti-home in Austin's Salsa Culture." *American Ethnologist* 33 (3): 361–377.

Kun, Josh. 2005. *Audiotopia: Music, Race, and America*. Berkeley: University of California Press.

Martin, Randy. 1998. *Critical Moves: Dance Studies in Theory and Politics*. Durham, NC: Duke University Press.

McIntosh, Jonathan. 2010. "Dancing to a Disco Beat? Children, Teenagers, and the Localizing of Popular Music in Bali." *Asian Music* 41 (1): 1–35.

McMains, Juliet. 2006. *Glamour Addiction: Inside the American Ballroom Dance Industry*. Middletown, CT: Wesleyan University Press.

Montes Pizarro, Errol. 2008 "Influencias del son y la salsa en el Congo y en Senegal." In *El son y la salsa en la identidad del Caribe: Memorias del II Congreso Internacional Música, Identidad y Cultura en el Caribe*, ed. Darío Tejeda and Rafael Yunén, 269–280. Santo Domingo: Instituto de Estudios Caribeños and Centro León. Available at http://

webs.oss.cayey.upr.edu/iii/sites/webs.oss.cayey.upr.edu.iii/files/u3/Errol_El_Son_y _la_Salsa-Montes-P__gina_III.pdf.

Ochoa Gautier, Ana María. 1999. "El desplazamiento de los espacios de la autenticidad: Una mirada desde la música." In *Cultura y globalización*, ed. Jesús Martín Barbero and Fabio de López LaRoche, 249–265. Bogotá: Universidad Nacional de Colombia, Facultad de Ciencias Humanas, Centro de Estudios Sociales.

Ortiz, Fernando. (1947) 1995. *Cuban Counterpoint: Tobacco and Sugar*, trans. Harriet de Onís. Durham, NC: Duke University Press.

Pacini Hernández, Deborah. 1998. "Dancing with the Enemy: Cuban Popular Music, Race, Authenticity, and the World-Music Landscape." *Latin American Perspectives* 25 (3): 110–125.

Perna, Vicenzo. 2008. *Timba: The Sound of the Cuban Crisis*. Aldershot, UK: Ashgate.

Pietrobruno, Sheenagh. 2006. *Salsa and Its Transnational Moves*. Lanham, MD: Lexington Books.

Quintero Rivera, Ángel G. 1999. *¡Salsa, sabor y control! Sociología de la música "tropical."* 2nd ed. Mexico City: Siglo Veintiuno.

———. 2009. *Cuerpo y cultura: Las músicas mulatas y la subversión del baile*. Madrid: Iberoamericana and Frankfurt am Main: Vervuert.

Ramos-Kitrell, Jesús. 2012. "Transnational Cultural Constructions: Cumbia Music and the Making of Locality in Monterrey." In *Transnational Encounters: Music and Performance at the U.S.-Mexico Border*, ed. Alejandro Madrid, 191–206. Oxford: Oxford University Press.

Renta, Priscilla. 2004. "Salsa Dance: Latino/a History in Motion." *Centro: Journal of the Center for Puerto Rican Studies* 16 (2): 138–157.

Roberts, John Storm. 1999. *The Latin Tinge: The Impact of Latin American Music on the United States*. 2nd ed. New York: Oxford University Press.

Rondón, César Miguel. 1980. *El libro de la salsa: Crónica de la música del caribe urbano*. Caracas, Venezuela: Editorial Arte.

———. 2008. *The Book of Salsa: A Chronicle of Urban Music from the Caribbean to New York City*, trans. Frances R. Aparicio and Jackie White. Chapel Hill: University of North Carolina Press.

Sachs, Curt. 1933. *Eine Weltgeschichte des Tanzes*. Berlin: Dietrich Reimer and Ernst Vohsen.

"Salsa Mubarak." n.d. *Time Out Mumbai*. Previously available at http://www.timeout mumbai.net/dance/dance_preview_details.asp?code=28 (accessed October 11, 2010).

Savigliano, Marta. 1995. *Tango and the Political Economy of Passion*. Boulder, CO: Westview.

Tomlinson, John. 1999. *Globalization and Culture*. Cambridge: Polity Press.

Turino, Thomas. 2000. *Nationalists, Cosmopolitans, and Popular Music in Zimbabwe*. Chicago: University of Chicago Press.

Urquia, Norman. 2004. "'Doin' It Right': Contested Authenticity in London's Salsa Scene." In *Music Scenes: Local, Translocal, and Virtual*, ed. Andy Bennet and Richard A. Peterson, 96–113. Nashville, TN: Vanderbilt University Press.

———. 2005. "The Re-branding of Salsa in London's Dance Clubs: How an Ethnicised Form of Cultural Capital was Institutionalised." *Leisure Studies* 24 (4): 385–397.

Washburne, Chris. 2008. *Sounding Salsa: Performing Latin Music in New York City*. Philadelphia: Temple University Press.

Waxer, Lise. 2002a. *The City of Musical Memory: Salsa, Record Grooves, and Popular Culture in Cali, Colombia*. Middletown, CT: Wesleyan University Press.

———, ed. 2002b. *Situating Salsa: Global Markets and Local Meanings in Latin Popular Music*. New York: Routledge.

2

What's in a Number?

From Local Nostalgia to Global Marketability in New York's On-2 Salsa

Sydney Hutchinson

The development of salsa music in New York has been intimately tied to dance practice from the very beginning. "Without a dance the music cannot be popular," Tito Puente asserted of mambo, salsa's precursor (Feuerstein, n.d.). Yet this dance is not singular but multiple. Alongside informal social dancing in nightclubs and family settings, New York dancers have developed a performance-oriented salsa with ties to ballroom dance, jazz, Broadway, and twentieth-century social dances. Many of these dancers prefer to call their dance mambo rather than salsa, in accordance with Puente's oft-repeated statement, "Salsa is a condiment of food. You eat salsa. You don't listen to it" (quoted in Loza 1999: 41). They further delineate the genre as on-2 mambo, referring to the musical beat emphasized in their basic step, in which they break, or change direction, on the second count of a four-beat measure.

While stepping on count 1, 2, or 3 may seem to outsiders an unimportant detail, to New York dancers it makes a world of difference. On-2 dancers believe that their rhythmic approach enables greater adherence to the clave, the rhythmic "key" of salsa music,[1] and thus a superior style and technique, which some describe as "relaxed" and "elastic looking" (Lewis, n.d., "What's Up").[2] Thus the 2 is to New York dancers what the clave is to Puerto Rican and Nuyorican musicians, a "dynamic and socially charged concept" discussed frequently and heatedly, giving rise to a kind of internally generated music theory (see Washburne 2008: 188). In fact, many on-2 dancers either cannot or will not dance with

This chapter is based on Sydney Hutchinson, "Mambo On 2: The Birth of a New Form of Dance in New York City," *Centro: Journal of the Center for Puerto Rican Studies* 16, no. 2 (2004): 109–137.

those who dance on a different count (Navarro 2000). Dancers' discussions of their "conversions" and "initiations" to the on-2 style reach near-religious levels (see Bello, n.d., "How Mike"; and Siverio 2002); many see their introduction to the style as a life-changing experience.

Developed and promoted primarily by New York Puerto Ricans, on-2 mambo or salsa was for many years understood as a distinctively Nuyorican dance genre. (I use "Nuyorican" in the sense of diasporic Puerto Ricans born and raised in New York City as opposed to those who have grown up on the island.) It was qualitatively different both from its Caribbean and ballroom dance predecessors and from other styles of salsa dance. For instance, several generations of New York dancers emphasize intricate footwork composed of named steps known as "shines."[3] They prefer a theatrical look featuring dramatic, stop-time poses with long lines, extended arms, and even occasional "jazz hands" over subtler body motion and the polyrhythmic articulation of different body parts that characterize many Afro-Caribbean dances. They also exhibit a distinctive musical feeling, stepping slightly behind the beat rather than right on it even when dancing to up-tempo music.[4] Finally, the emphasis on counting and rhythm gives New York on-2 dancers a unique relationship to their music. They often favor *salsa dura* ("hard," or old-school, salsa produced in New York during the 1960s and 1970s), which features a tightly locked rhythm section and clearly audible, repetitive percussion patterns (see Berríos-Miranda 2002).

Beyond these technical matters, since the 1980s on-2 dancers have created a subculture, or "scene," whose members consider themselves artists, "serious dancers" who "have worked very hard to learn this complicated dance" (Shaw 2013). Membership entails investing significant time and money for dance lessons, costumes, shoes, club and contest entrance fees, and travel to dance events. Yet it also entails a social commitment to the on-2 community, which maintains its bonds through websites promoting the style, online discussion groups, monthly events called socials, and yearly gatherings called congresses. Specialist DJs[5] cater to on-2 dancers, while nightclub owners make special concessions in terms of music, flooring, and lighting to attract them (see Navarro 2000; Lewis, n.d., "Club Owners"; Figure 2.1).

When I first began writing about New York salsa dancing in 2003, I was myself an on-2 dancer performing and teaching with Razz M'Tazz Mambo Company and before that with New York *salsero* Ivan Rivera. Although no longer active in this scene, I attend the occasional congress and have watched on-2 salsa spread throughout the world, as enterprising instructors cater to students eager to learn ever-more-complicated steps. In the course of such occasional visits to my former life, I have noted changes in the ethnic makeup of the scene. These changes prompted me to update my earlier article (Hutchinson 2004) and reevaluate my view of the role of place in salsa practice, one of the motivations for this book.

In this chapter, I give a brief history of on-2 mambo in New York through three generations of dancers. As sources, I use personal conversations and experiences together with dancers' websites. This methodology allows me to

Figure 2.1. Dancers at the LQ (Latin Quarters) nightclub in Manhattan, 2005. *(Photograph by Christopher Washburne, New York, 2005.)*

track key changes in dance practice. While on-2 mambo was once particular to the Nuyorican community, commercialization has de-emphasized ethnicity. While on-2 was once a local expression, directly and intimately related to its New York City surroundings, it has now moved far beyond its point of mythic origin to incorporate a transnational community of dancers. Thus, today New York salsa or mambo is defined less by its location and more by an attitude toward music and dance that emphasizes technical proficiency, precision, and commitment to a lifestyle, evidenced through adherence to a particular count. In this case "2" is much more than a number—more even than a couple, dancing—it is a way of life. At the same time, in the global salsa marketplace, New York salsa competes with numerous other styles, each of which claims to be the most "original," "authentic," or prestigious. New York–style salsa dancers—who frequently are not themselves New Yorkers nowadays—are dissolving some group boundaries while reinforcing others, transforming the terrain on which they dance.

Mambo Beginnings

New York salseros most often tie their dance's origins to the mambo, a type of music and dance from the 1930s–1950s that derived from the Cuban *dan-zón* and *son*.[6] Cubans, Puerto Ricans, and African Americans had already been collaborating musically in New York since World War I, and "Latin" dances had been popular at both black clubs like the Park Palace (Boggs 1992: 254) and white ones like the Palace Theater and the Waldorf-Astoria (Roberts 1999: 76–86). The mambo emerged as not only a pan-American dance craze but also the enabler of what, in current discourse, appears to be a kind of multiethnic utopia where, to paraphrase Rodney King, we can all get along.

Earlier Caribbean and South American dance crazes like tango, samba, "rhumba," and conga had paved the way for the introduction of mambo dancing in the North in the 1950s. Mambo arrived in New York through tours by musician Dámaso Pérez Prado (see Roberts 1999: 129–130) and others. Las Mulatas del Fuego, a Cuban dance company that "salsa queen" Celia Cruz toured with, introduced basic steps to a Manhattan audience in 1949[7] (Leymarie 2002: 161; Quintero Rivera 2009: 169). Well-known dancer Katherine Dunham later hosted Prado at her Manhattan dance school and choreographed and performed in the 1954 film *Mambo*. Mambo became more popular in New York than it had ever been in Cuba (Leymarie 2002: 161), prompting *Downbeat* magazine to announce, "Dance schools find these days that a mambo class is as essential as a credit payment plan" (October 6, 1954).

Early mambo styles are described in a *Dance Magazine* article:

The term Mambo is today used to designate two forms of Rumba which are quite dissimilar in appearance. As a foundation for either the smooth or the hectic style, however, the same or similar basic rhythm and step variations are taught. The outward differences come later, depending on the skill attained, the predominance of smooth or jazzed up band music, conservative or Jitterbug temperaments and a predilection for closed dancing or for opened up fancy steps. (Butler 1953: 52)

An Arthur Murray–style footprint chart showing the basic step on the counts of 234-678 accompanies this article. This, together with the "opened up fancy steps" of the "hectic" style, seems to describe an early version of on-2 dancing. Already, the dance was quite unlike the Cuban mambo that, rather than a back-and-forth or a side-to-side partner dance, was and is a solo step-tap step, simple but for the quick pelvic tilts that accompany it.[8] The basic North American mambo step was derived instead from the ballroom-style rumba popular since the 1930s.[9] In fact, ballroom mambo dancers of the 1950s wrote that the 234 count was also proper for rumba; however, "it [took] the jazzed-up version of the Cuban 'Son' and a new name to arouse the dance public to an acceptance of a different rhythmic counting" (Butler 1953: 52).

The Palladium Years

Dancers today trace salsa's beginnings to a ballroom rather than to the street, which would become the music's dominant topos in the 1960s and 1970s

(Washburne 2008: 18). As archetypal places, the two are near opposites: the first associated with the middle and upper classes, comprising diverse ethnicities but tending toward whiteness, and midtown Manhattan, the second associated with the lower classes, Puerto Rican and African Americans, and El Barrio (Spanish Harlem). More specifically, New York salsa dancers remember the Palladium Ballroom at Broadway and Fifty-Third Street in Manhattan, which billed itself as the "Home of the Mambo" after changing to an all-mambo format in 1952.

The Palladium house bands led by Nuyoricans Tito Puente and Tito Rodríguez reinvented the mambo by introducing jazz-influenced harmonies and arrangements, making it sound "more modern than Cuba," in Puente's words (quoted in Stephens and Randles 2000). Moreover, their music spoke to their urban setting, cosmopolitan audiences, and the multiethnic interactions particular to the New York environment. It was also informed by interaction with the dancers in attendance, as Puente noted:

> It was "in" to learn to dance the Mambo no matter what part of society you came from. And so here was a place, the Palladium, where everybody could come to dance or learn the Mambo. Dance studios sent their students to the Palladium, where they could learn and see great dancers—ballet stars, Broadway stars, expert Mambo dancers—all in one place. And I geared my music to these dancers. (Quoted in Feuerstein, n.d.)

These music-dance interactions increased the dynamism of both, for instance, when the quick tempo and impressive solos performed by instrumentalists like Puente spurred dancers to improvise complicated steps that used different body parts in polyrhythmic fashion. This characteristic also ties New York mambo to other Afro-Caribbean dances that, Ángel Quintero Rivera states, "break the sharp division between producers and 'consumers'" through improvisatory musician-dancer interactions that depend on the element of surprise (2009: 101).

A diverse array of dancers and movement styles converged in the Palladium. Today it is remembered as a kind of multiracial utopia because its integrated social scene was so unusual for the time. Dancer Eddie Torres recalls, "Tito Puente always used to say, 'We didn't know anything about ethnic groups!' There wasn't such a word as 'ethnic' [then]" (Torres 2003). Angel Rodríguez further explains:

> The most important thing about the Palladium was that's where all the Jewish and the Puerto Ricans and the Blacks got together without issues—because of this wonderful music that's a mix of everything that we've ever done! . . . That's where [the mambo] actually all got together and fused in the New York way. (Rodríguez 2003)

This nondiscriminatory atmosphere, dancers assert, allowed for the interchange of ideas and movements across cultural boundaries. For example, today's dancers are indebted to the cabaret dance team of Augie and Margo Rodríguez[10] for their blending of ballet and mambo (Craddock and Aguilar 2003), flamenco styling (Rita, n.d., "Eddie Torres"), and ballroom-derived acrobatic lifts ("Ernie Ensley," n.d.). Jazz dancer Jo-Jo Smith created a unique style of mambo jazz that influenced Eddie Torres, one of today's most prominent instructors (Torres 2003), and Puerto Rico–born Luis "Máquina" Flores borrowed moves from Cuban rumba, which he later taught to George Vascones, one of the progenitors of the Latin hustle (Rodríguez 2003). Italian American "Killer" Joe Piro drew on his extensive experience as a Savoy Lindy and jitterbug champion when he taught mambo at the Palladium (Stearns [1968] 1994: 361).[11]

Possibly the best-known Palladium dancers were the late Pedro Aguilar, better known as Cuban Pete but actually a Puerto Rican from El Barrio, and his partner Millie Donay, an Italian American from the Lower East Side. Cuban Pete[12] combined "more traditional rumba and freestyle" (Rodríguez 2003) with tap, jazz, acrobatics, "and even rock-and-roll dances" (Aguilar, quoted in Stearns [1968] 1994: 360). Donay learned to dance from her sisters and from movie musicals, winning local Lindy Hop contests as a child and a Palladium mambo contest at age fifteen (Feuerstein 1992). *Life* magazine profiled the pair as exemplars of the new dance craze (December 1954).[13]

The first mambo dance companies also date to the 1950s, evolving from the stage shows and contests held at the Palladium and the more informal presentations dancers developed and performed to the side of the stage (see Boggs 1992: 148). For instance, Augie Rodríguez and Cuban Pete teamed up to form the Mambo Devils (Feuerstein 1992), while Aníbal Vásquez, Joe Centenno, and later, Mike Ramos performed as the Mambo Aces for ten years. Ramos later performed with Andrew Jarrick and Freddie Ríos as the Cha-Cha Aces (Boggs 1992: 147; Leymarie 2002: 165), a group that combined tap dance and cha-cha with smatterings of Afro-Cuban body movement and ballet technique (Stearns [1964] 1994: 360).

Palladium mambo dancers thus drew from numerous antecedent forms and close personal interactions with musicians; they also interacted creatively with the space around them. For example, since a railing and columns enclosed the Palladium dance floor, "one of the indelible hallmarks was for a male to dance a few steps and to 'fall' against one of these structures with an outstretched arm and [right] himself . . . all the while in time with the music. The smooth execution of this movement was one clear sign that one had mastered the dance" (Stearns [1968] 1994: 360). In addition, the club's location near Broadway and the competitive environment created by so many talented—and often famous—dancers seems to have fed into the style.

Nonetheless, David García has found that the Palladium, despite its utopian function in memory, was also marked by divisions. Luis "Máquina" Flores remembers Palladium dancers grouping themselves socially and spatially, with the "trendsetters," principally those with a cultural connection to the dance, on the right of the dance floor and the "professionals," those interested in codifying, standardizing, and discovering "correct" steps, on the left. Those from the right engaged in an "embodied experience" of music, as today's street dancers likewise claim to do. Those on the left effected a quantifying, intellectualized bodily performance, a practice for which today's studio dancers are criticized (D. García 2009: 171–172). This division created an uncomfortable situation for some Latino dancers. Cuban Pete, for instance, once described the Palladium as "strange territory" compared to the Bronx and east Harlem dance halls. García suggests this "strangeness" may have been related to mambo dancers' ambivalence about the gaze of the "professional dance teachers and critics who flocked to the Palladium" to learn the dance and to criticize it (168).

The Palladium closed its doors in 1966, but it remains in dancers' memories as the mythic point of origin for on-2 dancing. Angel Rodríguez comments, "[The Palladium] is important because it was the root of New York salsa. And it's more important because that's where our masters were born. . . . Salsa is a Puerto Rican art in the United States. It was Cuban Pete, it was Augie, all the Puerto Ricans. And Cuban Pete says it, 'Mambo on-2 is as Puerto Rican as you can get'" (2003). In other words, on-2 mambo would not exist were it not for the utopian Palladium, the New York Puerto Ricans who danced there, and the mixing of people and art forms the place allowed. Yet this ideal view is only a partial truth: as noted, social divisions were not entirely erased, and many observers viewed the mambo through a racialized lens, simultaneously extolling its "primitive" qualities and worrying it would take over the Great White Way (D. García 2009: 175). Palladium dancers' combination of ballroom dance, ballet, flamenco, tap, Lindy Hop, and rumba laid the foundations for today's eclectic on-2 style, even as the spatial and racial divisions at the Palladium anticipated the later street-studio divide.

The Salsa-Hustle Years

After the Palladium closed in 1966, the dance developed in new directions, from boogaloo to hustle and finally to salsa. During this period, the place of salsa music shifted dramatically, going from the ballroom to the street. Chris Washburne believes that the emphasis on street was a strategy for distancing the new salsa from older Cuban music (2008: 18). Today, he notes, both musicians and scholars still see the street—specifically the streets of El Barrio— as an "essential quality" of salsa (110). The dance occupies a more ambiguous place, somewhere between the two poles of street and studio (the latter sometimes also associated with the related topos of the ballroom, though salseros of any type see their practice as far different from ballroom dance). Yet in narrating a history of salsa beginning in the Palladium, dancers accomplish the same task as did salsa music marketers: they assert the specificity of their practice, its local basis, and its separation from related Cuban styles.[14]

Just as during the Palladium era, Nuyoricans, like Willie Colón, Ray Barretto, Eddie and Charlie Palmieri, Ritchie Ray, and Bobby Cruz, were the most numerous and among the most influential of the new crop of Latin musicians. Stylistic innovations like Eddie Palmieri's addition of trombones to the traditional charanga ensemble, Rafael Cortijo's experiments with *bomba* and *plena*, and Willie Colón's use of jíbaro music produced a distinct musical genre, which became an important symbol of Nuyorican identity and culture (see Berríos-Miranda 2002).

Early salseros and salseras danced a basic on-1 step with a limited repertoire of simple turns (Rodríguez 2003), but many talented young dancers in the 1970s were drawn to the more demanding Latin hustle, a dance that grew out of swing and featured a slot format, fast spins, lifts, and distinctive turn patterns. Angel Rodríguez recalls:

> The hustle came out of a bunch of Puerto Ricans that didn't want to do salsa. They wanted to [dance] to English music. And they watched TV and saw Gene Kelly and stuff. The basic step came from the black hustle, which was a three-step dance, and all that influence combined with all the ballroom movies coming out at the time. That created the hustle. It was a definite Bronx street style. Some people actually say George Vascones started it. (2003)

The hustle quickly eclipsed Palladium mambo in popularity, though some dance companies, like the Latin Symbolics, tried combining the two (Rodríguez 2003). Turn combinations similar to those employed in the hustle remain a defining characteristic of New York salsa-mambo today.

By the 1980s competition from merengue, house, and hip-hop had sent salsa music into decline (Washburne 2002: 102). Nonetheless, a handful of New York dancers kept mambo dancing alive. Hustle progenitor George Vascones taught mambo—both on-1 and on-2—to many dancers at the Hunts Point Palace in the Bronx (Ortiz 2001b). Eddie Torres, who would eventually create the best-known on-2 teaching method, began dancing at this time.

Greatly influenced by Tito Puente, Torres was disappointed that the only mambo dance classes available derived from a ballroom sensibility quite different from that of the older New York mambo dancers he hoped to emulate (Ortiz 2001a). Instead, he learned from watching other dancers. After eight years of practice, Torres and his wife, Maria, approached Puente with two choreographed pieces. Impressed, Puente hired the couple in 1980 to perform with his orchestra as the Tito Puente Dancers. Having been a dancer himself, Puente understood mambo music and dance as a symbiotic pair. Torres teamed up with ballroom instructor June LaBerta, who encouraged him to put counts to his dancing, to name his steps, and to create a syllabus, an endeavor he compares to "science and poetry coming together" (Torres 2003). Around 1983 the Copacabana nightclub began hosting Tuesday salsa nights and hired Torres as their dance instructor (Rodríguez 2003).

Torres traces the mambo's revival to one historic event in 1987. Puente had hired him to choreograph numbers for an Apollo Theater tribute to legendary Afro-Cuban musician Machito that would be televised. Torres handpicked sixty of the best nightclub dancers and put them through four months of training. The show succeeded so well that Torres subsequently formed a permanent dance company of six couples, the Eddie Torres Dancers, and others were inspired to follow suit (Torres 2003). A get-together of the Mambo Society began around 1988 in what is now the East Village on Fourth Street at Second Avenue. Among others, Angel Rodríguez and his wife, Addie, taught there for about two years (Rodríguez 2003). Mike Bello, a popular on-2 instructor now located in California, recalls that the original shine list from that time contained only about twenty-five steps (Rita, n.d., "Mike Bello") in contrast to the hundreds of steps on today's syllabi.

Dancers in the 1970s and 1980s systematized the dance in an attempt to create a legitimate art form and facilitate its teaching; in the process, they altered its relationship with the clave. Eddie Torres spearheaded this movement and developed the on-2 style that is most prevalent today. Meanwhile, as Torres worked with ballroom instructor LaBerta to codify his style, Angel Rodríguez danced and taught at Paul Pellicoro's[15] Manhattan ballroom studio, Dance-Sport, where he devised an alternative school of on-2 practice that would become the Razz M'Tazz (RMT) system.[16]

Instead of simply dancing on clave, dancers now focus on counts. Torres uses a 123-567 count, with the break, or direction change, occurring on counts 2 and 6. This step is markedly different from the mambo of the 1950s (see Butler 1953), but Torres describes it as the street version of mambo (Ortiz 2001b), signaling both his attempt to replicate the style he remembers from his neighborhood and his desire to legitimize his version among dancers who disdain the artificiality of ballroom, or studio, style. Meanwhile, Rodríguez's basic step falls on counts 234-678, like Cuban son or the mambo of the 1950s; however, some RMT shines employ a 123-567 count, which Angel calls the "jazz counts" (Rodríguez 2003). Besides the different timing, RMT style, unlike Torres's, is strongly influenced by the Latin hustle.

On-2 dancers hotly debate the comparative merits of the Torres and the RMT counts. The controversy centers on which count best adheres to the clave and which is the true mambo, defined as the style most closely tied to historical dance practices located in New York, particularly in the Palladium or in that mythical street.[17] The two versions are not so very different, since, in practice, Torres dancers actually step well ahead of counts 1 and 5, pushing their count nearly a half beat closer to RMT's 234 (see Table 2.1).

Torres's timing may be tied to Puerto Rican bomba, since Quintero Rivera finds that beginning "in *contratiempo* [syncopation], a little before the first beat, [simulates] or [evokes] the dancer's anticipation of the lead drum's fill in bomba dancing" (2009: 27). Yet each version has its own pedagogical merit. Torres's is easier to learn since most students find it easier to step on the downbeat than to pause on it, while it simultaneously forces them to find the 2 because they must

TABLE 2.1   TIMING OF EDDIE TORRES BASIC STEP

Musical count	&	1	&	2	&	3	&	4	&	5	&	6	&	7	&	8
Dancers' count	(1)			2		3			(5)			6		7		

break on it (see Figure 2.2). The learning curve is steeper with the RMT count (Figure 2.3), but Rodríguez believes his students will be stronger, more versatile dancers because they understand the music (Rodríguez 2003). Both instructors teach their students to listen for the clave and the conga's slap to find the 2 count, but opinions differ on whether starting the step on count 1 (Torres) or on count 2 (RMT) best fits the clave rhythm.[18] In any case, Torres and Rodríguez set the stage for the current proliferation of on-2 dance schools and companies; both also identified and inhabited a space between street and studio.

The On-2 Era

During the 1990s, on-2 dancing became a codified, commercial product sold through lessons and congresses. From just a handful of on-2 troupes at the beginning of the 1990s, about thirty on-2 teaching and performance companies became established in the New York metropolitan area by 2003 (see Shaw 2013).[19] Moreover, by the mid-1990s, New York instructors began exporting on-2 dancing through aggressive self-promotion via websites and instructional videos and through the invitations of competitive dancers in other locales seeking new challenges. They were successful in creating a niche for the dance as far away as Europe and Asia. For instance, Angel Rodríguez moved to Milan, Italy, in 2003 and has since led RMT Italia from there. Meanwhile, dancers from elsewhere visit New York regularly to learn the style and keep up with its changes (Brown 2003; Pietrobruno 2006: 89). The circular travels of on-2 instructors like Miguel Rodríguez and Stacey López have strengthened ties between New York and Puerto Rico dance scenes as well (Renta 2008). On-2 discourse frequently emphasizes its globalizing power, as in the program for the opening day of the 2003 World Salsa Congress in San Juan, which states, "Despite differences of language, salsa dance has become a new common element of communication around the world. . . . Salsa unites the world, and the best proof is the World Salsa Congress" (Delgado 2003; my translation).

The debate over the right way to dance has become more important with commercialization, since a teacher's or performer's livelihood may depend on the public's answer to that question. Angel Rodríguez says, "[People talk about] how 'if you don't do it this way, it's not the right way' [and] 'no one in New York knows how to teach it right,' which are great business lines if you're Latino, saying, 'This is the only way'" (2003). These statements imply that many claims of authenticity are made for economic reasons. Today, each dance company produces its own syllabus of steps, turns, and shines, in which sincere commitment and commercialism are similarly intertwined. Syllabi are important for their

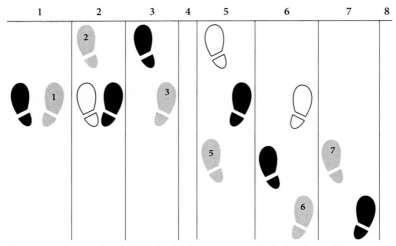

Note: 3 is sometimes placed slightly farther back than 1, and 7 further forward than 5. The steps marked on counts 1 and 5 actually occur a half beat ahead of time.

Figure 2.2. The Eddie Torres New York salsa counting system. This is the most widely known on-2 basic step system outside New York. *(Created by Sydney Hutchinson.)*

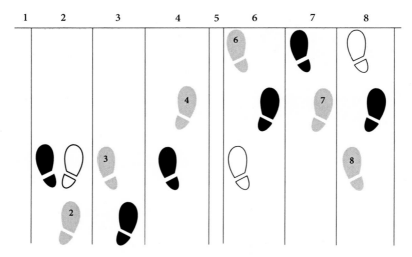

Figure 2.3. The Razz M'Tazz counting system of New York salsa. This system is also known as the Palladium 2. *(Created by Sydney Hutchinson.)*

KEY:

- Black footprints indicate the inactive foot (no motion).
- Gray footprints indicate the active foot. The number inside indicates on which musical count the motion occurs.
- White footprints indicate the previous position of the active foot.

economic value, since they ensure that students will keep coming back to learn more but also because they document important moments and figures in salsa history. Eddie Torres's syllabus includes a step called Millie Donay, which is one of that dancer's characteristic moves. Most, if not all, companies include Pachanga Taps and Pachanga Strut, recalling that 1960s dance craze. Both Torres and RMT syllabi contain tap-like shuffle steps, and Torres's Michael Jackson and RMT's Janet Jackson demonstrate the influence of pop culture as well. Named steps also encode more intimate company histories. For example, the RMT syllabus includes Konig's Grapevine, named for former instructor Carlos Konig, and Addie's Tradition, named for former company director Addie Rodríguez.

Though people of various classes do mix in a few New York clubs, on-2 salsa-mambo is primarily (and somewhat controversially) directed at the urban middle class and the upwardly mobile. Some even argue that mambo originated as a dance of the middle class, since Palladium-era mambo and Latin jazz were popular mainly with the urban, hip crowd, and clubs such as the Club Caborrojeño catered to Puerto Ricans of rural origins by programming jíbaro music instead (A. García, n.d.). Today, this class division is reflected in the rhetorical divide between street and studio.

On-2 salsa is clearly a studio-based practice, and as such it is clearly distinct from salsa as practiced in a home setting. Its devotees nonetheless both draw on and distance themselves from the street, complicating any simple division between the two realms. They pride themselves on their street style and simultaneously set themselves apart by refusing to dance with non-2 dancers in an authenticating strategy similar to that employed by salsa musicians (Washburne 2008: 42). Setting up street and studio as mutually exclusive categories thus produces a limited view of current dance practice in New York. Many on-2 dancers come from salsa's home place and from families that dance salsa at home. Many dancers adapt movements they learned from friends and relatives to the stage, an exchange hard to imagine for other studio dances like waltz or foxtrot. New York salsa thus allows for and even encourages a dialectical relationship between the street and the studio even while it enforces a social separation between the two: only studio dancers are able to teach and thus earn money from their practice.

The Magic Number: History, Ethnicity, and Dance Technique

Contemporary discourse around topics like the music-dance relationship, clave, timing, and history constitutes a community-based dance theory that justifies favored modes of bodily expression within the New York context and constructs historical continuity around a sense of place. Today's on-2 community is thus rooted in a common interest and shared beliefs. The ongoing importance of these beliefs is suggested in the many continuities between the Palladium mambo era, the salsa-hustle years, and today's on-2 dancing, from the preference for classic 1970s salsa dura and even 1950s mambo music[20] to the maintenance of particular steps, movements, and most particularly timing.

Some dancers have a near-religious devotion to salsa music or dance and especially to the clave that ties the two together. Clave, like the Palladium, is a subject elevated to magical status by such dancers. For instance, in describing his introduction to on-2 mambo, instructor Mike Bello writes:

> I have to say that almost from the moment I was first made really aware of its existence, something rang true and I GOT IT—the truth of the clave as the life force that drives the music and dance. I accepted the truth about clave kind of like one might accept religion, even without "proof" at the time, because deep down it FEELS RIGHT, and like a religion, I embraced the "word" of the clave. (Bello, n.d., "How Mike"; emphasis in original)

Such talk allows New York mambo dancers to sustain and strengthen their communities at the same time that they justify their own dance practices—specifically, breaking on 2—with appeals to emotion, spirituality, and bodily sensation.

Washburne observes that for salsa musicians clave is a "dynamic and socially charged concept . . . [that] encapsulates a continuum of ideas, beliefs, meanings, understandings, and interpretations" that go "far beyond the music structure" (2008: 188). In fact, he identifies strict adherence to an unchanging clave as a recent innovation. Earlier Cuban musicians understood the concept much more loosely, even frequently changing from 3-2 to 2-3 clave midsong in mambo (188); even today, some musicians find that the clave's direction does not always matter (Berríos-Miranda 2002: 37). Many Nuyorican musicians, however, understood clave as "bigger than any one of us," in the words of arranger Ricky González, as traceable to an African heritage and even as a musical universal (quoted in Berríos-Miranda 2002: 193–194). Paradoxically, Nuyorican and Puerto Rican salsa musicians' allegiance to Cuban forms led them to transform "originally more fluid practices into stricter forms dictated by austere guidelines" (189–190). For them, clave became a part of identity politics used to show belonging and mark themselves as different from other ethnic groups, including other Latin Americans.

Few dancers have musical training, but the relationship between music and dance is nonetheless fundamental to on-2 practice. And while New York salsa musicians transformed Cuban musics in part through their systematization of clave, New York salsa dancers have systematized dance practices, both through the standardization of steps and through the enforcement of a particular understanding of salsa music and clave. On-2 instructors teach their students to listen to specific rhythms, and dancers frequently discuss particular songs and rhythms at length and in great detail on websites devoted to the subject.[21] In fact, dance classes train students to listen to the music in a Puerto Rican way: the conga drum slap on beat two is nearly always present in Puerto Rican salsa, while in other styles, like Cuban salsa, improvisation may eliminate it (see Berríos-Miranda 2002). Former RMT dancer Ney Melo notes that while Cuban music may be better danced on the 1, "with the old-school mambo music—any Tito Puente, Tito Rodríguez music, [Eddie or Charlie] Palmieri music—I think it *should* be danced on the 2. That's just the way—the music just *sounds*, it *leads* you to the 2, so there's no way you can get away from that" (Melo 2002).

Ironically, while music is understood as central to on-2 dancing, musicians are not. Salsa New York webmaster Steve Shaw explains that live bands often play songs that are too long, too fast, or too loud for on-2 dancing or else their repertoire is simply not as good as that available on recordings. He continues:

> If the music fits our way of dancing . . . we're happy. Whether that music comes from a DJ or a live band is irrelevant to how we dance and how much we enjoy the event. When we are dancing, we are looking at our partners, not the DJ or band. And after one good song, we want another one right away. . . . So who needs a band? (Shaw 2012)

This sentiment is far different from the Palladium mambo ideal of constant interaction between music and dance; it departs from Caribbean practices in general, which are often characterized by the "creative dialogue between the dancer and the player . . . between space and time" and which set up an interaction in which "the collective *leads* and the individual *elaborates*" (Quintero Rivera 2009: 42). The recent devaluation of the musician appears to be related to two factors. In dance, the focus on globally disseminated steps and syllabi makes dancers dependent more on their memories than on their hearing. In music, salsa musicians have grown to depend on recording technologies that limit the usual interaction between performers and make impossible the reproduction of the sound in live performance (Washburne 2008: 185). One result of both factors is the increased use of recordings at dance events and the gradual disappearance of venues for live salsa music.

The emphatic character of much on-2 discourse suggests that this dance community can at times be exclusive. I have noted here that mambo dancing, as well as early salsa music, included the participation of many different groups. Since the 1970s, however, salsa increasingly became "our Latin thing" (the name of an early Fania documentary film), likely in reaction to experiences of racism. Thus, while many New York residents learned salsa, non-Latinos were sometimes subtly discouraged from performing or teaching it. Similarly, non-Latino musicians must continually "prove themselves" in ways not demanded of Latinos (Washburne 2008: 35). Dancers constantly engage in racial nicknaming, and both white and black non-Latino members of my dance troupe reported that they had felt excluded from the dance community at times.[22] Encouraging diversity among students while enforcing racial and ethnic boundaries at the professional level seems designed to protect salsa as a Latino, particularly Nuyorican, economic resource.[23] Outside the city, however, things are changing. At the Berlin Salsa Congress in 2008, I spoke with on-2 instructors of East Indian, African American, Iraqi-British, and Moroccan-French backgrounds.

As ethnicity becomes less important, new boundaries are constructed around the magic number 2. The Salsa New York website written and maintained by Steve Shaw and Manny Siverio has continually been the most vocal proponent of New York on-2 dancing and its difference from other styles, as can be observed in their description of the page as "a *pure* On 2 dancers' web site" (my emphasis). Shaw writes, "Our belief is that the only way to really understand and excel in dancing On 2 is to dance this way *only*. Because of that, we don't believe in teaching multiple timings" (2000; emphasis in original). Shaw explains further that this style "is often called 'New York,' 'club,' 'street,' 'Latino' or 'Eddie Torres' style salsa. . . . This method is technically different from other ways of dancing to salsa music, . . . such as ballroom, international, Razz M'Tazz, Cuban son montuno, as well as . . . others" (Shaw, n.d.).

The labels attached to the different styles are telling: if the Eddie Torres style is "New York" and "Latino," the others are presumably not or are not authentically so, despite their place of origin or the ethnicity of their originators. Even Cubans appear not to be Latino.

For many dancers, then, 2 is much more than just a number. It is a particular relationship to a particular style of music, one that marks these dancers with the prestige of connoisseurship. It is a demanding dance technique that earns them the additional cachet of expertise. It is membership in a worldwide community but one anchored historically and rhetorically in New York. Thus, New York on-2 dancers also gain the prestige of place-based authenticity. Nevertheless, many of those dancers most invested in establishing on-2 as a high-status style—a move that coincides with the de-emphasis of the dance's ethnic identity—are not themselves Nuyorican or Latino. The nostalgia surrounding the multiethnic Palladium dance floor as well as the simultaneous weakening of ethnic boundaries and strengthening of ones based on more abstract ideas like musical timing and dance technique must therefore be examined critically. In addition, the increased drive toward standardization in the studio—a drive that started with ballroom teachers of the 1950s who thought mambo needed to be "disciplined" to "make it acceptable" (Don Byrnes and Alice Swanson quoted in D. García 2009: 171)—is accompanied by decreased attention to street practices like musician-dancer interaction, improvisation, and use of the full body, changes that some argue signal the removal of Afro-Caribbean and working-class experience from the dance (e.g., Tato Conrad in Renta 2008: 161). Street and studio are therefore spheres charged with ethnic, racial, and classed meanings and unequal power relations.

Conclusion: From Local Past to Global Future

Judith Hamera (2007) sees dance technique as an archive that stores information about the past for those who can read its language. In this chapter, I have shown how salsa dance technique encodes a history of Caribbean dance in New York, a history that those with the requisite cultural literacy can access by watching and doing but that remains a closed book to those who learn salsa as simply a set of steps to be executed. Yet Hamera also emphasizes that dance is an everyday practice that brings people of diverse backgrounds together to create new kinds of urban communities. I have shown here that, although not free of divisions, on-2 dancing has at times accomplished this bridging of difference in New York City.

On-2 dance exists at the intersection of the global and the local. For some Nuyoricans who identify with salsa music, on-2 salsa-mambo is an important marker of ethnic identity. Yet it is also a local art form based on the ethnic diversity, interactions, and, indeed, inequalities that characterize the New York City environment. As on-2 dancing becomes globalized, an increased focus on technique, timing, and the codification of steps leads some dancers to identify it as a new art form. Yet as Priscilla Renta has pointed out (2008: 155), the professionalization of dance is a transculturating process, and transculturation always implies a loss. What is being lost in studio salsa today? Numerous long-standing salsa dance clubs in New York have recently closed, an occurrence that has further restricted the dance's practice to semiprofessional studio dancers and their students.[24] DJ Henry Knowles observes, "The people who came up in the streets and know about the music aren't dancing" (Bloom 2007); Puerto Rican dance instructor Stacey López similarly sees the "beautifying" of the dance as a counterproductive move, having observed instances where his own performances discouraged Puerto Rican aficionados from dancing themselves (Renta 2008: 163). These observations might suggest some disturbing answers.

Yet the dedication of many New York dancers is a sign of hope in the midst of this ambivalence. Whether initially motivated by nostalgia, ethnic pride, or economic gain, many on-2 aficionados are driven to dance by their love for music, movement, and cultural diversity. Dance communities may be utopian, because they provide a site in which people of diverse backgrounds can interact on more or less equal footing. At the same time, salsa is or was a dance tied to ethnic pride, an antidote to discrimination and urban poverty, and the unequal power relations from which it arose should not be ignored. Is there a way, then, to have the best of both worlds: to bridge the street and studio, to build a diverse community that simultaneously recognizes and works to counteract power imbalances and injustice?

NOTES

Acknowledgments: I thank the members and founders of Razz M'Tazz Dance Company, Barbara Craddock and the late Cuban Pete, Eddie and Maria Torres, the organizers of the Berlin Salsa Congress, and finally the editors of *Centro: Journal of the Center for Puerto Rican Studies* for allowing me to republish here much of the material that previously appeared in Sydney Hutchinson, "Mambo On 2: The Birth of a New Form of Dance in New York City," *Centro: Journal of the Center for Puerto Rican Studies* 16, no. 2 (2004): 109–137.

I also thank Katherine Borland and anonymous reviewers for their comments on this chapter.

1. "Clave" is the rhythmic pattern or timeline around which salsa and some Afro-Cuban musics like *son montuno* are structured. See Manuel 2006: 49–51 for further explanation; see also Carlo 2001 and Bello, n.d., "Salsa/Mambo Training" for dancers' views on clave.

2. New York dancers believe breaking on 2 fits with the clave because 2-3 clave "begins" on count 2. Yet 3-2 clave "begins" on count 1, as does the 3 side of 2-3 clave, so from a musician's perspective one could argue the opposite just as easily. I hypothesize that the emphasis on the 2, and thus on 2-3 clave, through the on-2 dance practice developed since the 1980s may be related to the increasing prevalence of salsa songs in 2-3 clave since the 1970s; in earlier Cuban music, Marisol Berríos-Miranda states, 3-2 clave had predominated (2002: 47n34)—as indeed it predominates in Cuban music today.

3. "Shines" are named dance steps performed solo rather than with a partner and composed of difficult, often syncopated footwork. The term is said to have come from boys who shined shoes in the street and who would perform tap dancing for a tip (Rodrí-guez 2003).

4. I base this statement on my personal experience of feeling late when I danced with local salsa or mambo dancers when I first arrived in New York. I soon realized I had been used to stepping on top of the beat, while my partners stepped behind it. See Monson 1996: 56 for a description of this phenomenon in jazz music.

5. A listing is available from Shaw 2012.

6. Cuban composer Orestes López titled one of his *danzones* "Mambo" in 1938, and in 1944 Antonio Arcaño's "Arriba la invasión" was the first tune to be named a mambo (Leymarie 2002: 111–115). The dance craze did not take effect until the 1950s, however.

7. Clearly, they could not have been partner dance steps, however.

8. Cuba's Conjunto Folklórico Nacional and Instituto Superior de Arte teach the step-tap step (called "pachanga taps" on the Razz M'Tazz syllabus and others) and a waltz-like balancé step as basic movements for mambo; Cuban social dancers also perform the step-tap when dancing to mambo music. More like on-2 mambo is the Cuban son, which is taught with the first step on count 4 and a pause on 1, effectively producing the 234 count of New York mambo (from my experience at a Conjunto Folklórico Nacional summer course in 2000 and at an intensive workshop with Instituto Superior de Arte instructors in Berlin in 2010).

9. Despite its name, ballroom rumba is actually derived from the Cuban son.

10. Cuban Pete (Pedro Aguilar) was Augie's first teacher and was responsible for introducing him to Margo (Craddock and Aguilar 2003).

11. Piro later became the "king of twist" and demonstrated popular dances on the NBC show *That Was the Week That Was* (1963–1965) (Sagolla 1999).

12. Cuban Pete later studied with Dunham (Feuerstein 1992)

13. Cuban Pete was hired as a consultant for the 1992 film "Mambo Kings," and Millie and Pete can be seen dancing in the film (Feuerstein 1992).

14. In Europe, in particular, most dancers insist that salsa is a Cuban dance (despite the fact that the term "salsa" and associated dance and music styles arrived in Cuba only recently; see Chapter 6). As noted in Chapter 1, one salsa instructor I spoke with in Germany was so vehement about salsa's Cuban origin that he refused to acknowledge any New York basis at all for either the dance or music. Eventually he made peace by asserting that "salsa is the trunk of a tree that has many roots." I wondered if this version of salsa history was an attempt to purify it by erasing its (obvious) capitalist ties, but perhaps acknowledging

many salsas, as we do in this book, rather than insisting on a single salsa trunk, could help resolve this difference.

15. Incidentally, Pellicoro notes that his dance background includes training in modern, ballet, and ballroom dance, and his "inspiration came in the 1970's as a New York Hustle street dancer" ("Paul Pellicoro" 2013), further illustrating that the line between street and studio is always a blurry one in New York City.

16. The New York branch of Razz M'Tazz is inactive as of the time of this writing, since director Angel is now living and teaching in Milan, Italy, with plans to expand into Germany. The method, however, is still used in other studios in New York and beyond and deserves to be discussed as a historical and current alternative to the Torres method, and one that shares a history, even as it draws from different dance styles, from Palladium mambo to hustle.

17. The invocation of both the Palladium, a ballroom, and the street in discourse aimed at authenticating on-2 salsa points to the dance's complicated relationship with New York City and Latinos' histories within it, as well as ambivalence about class, race, upward mobility, and what the latter means for the politics of salsa.

18. For more on how to find the clave, and how New York dancers tend to do it, see Hutchinson 2009.

19. Interestingly, Shaw (2013) purposefully excludes companies dancing the RMT count-2 method from the listing and count.

20. New York dance companies continue to use Tito Puente mambos for choreography with great frequency.

21. Articles appear on www.dancefreak.com, www.salsanewyork.com, www.salsacrazy.com, and other sites.

22. I also spent a brief time as a salsa musician in New York, playing piano with two short-lived bands there, but in that context I did not experience racial or ethnic divisions. This was probably because (1) since most of my bandmates were immigrants (largely Colombian) and monolingual Spanish speakers, my Spanish skills conferred enough insider status to override other differences and (2) my gender made me stand out from the rest far more than my ethnicity did.

23. The boundaries are not hard and fast, however: a few non-Latino instructors have had success in the city. Winsome Lee, originally from Hong Kong, has had a strong New York following for years.

24. There may be less sinister reasons for club closings, however. Many Latinos from core salsa areas in the Bronx, for instance, have been moving out of the city to Long Island, Connecticut, or other locations in recent decades (Ferris 2001). In addition, the Latino population of New York is now much more diverse than in the past, including an estimated half-million Dominicans, who often prefer merengue, and many Central Americans and Mexicans with still other regional music preferences. This has led to a proliferation of Latin American clubs around the city, although few play salsa exclusively.

REFERENCES

Bello, Mike. n.d. "How Mike Bello Became the Mambo Fello." Available at http://www.mambofello.com/articles/hmbbmf.htm (accessed January 2, 2013).

———. n.d. "Salsa/Mambo Training: The Music." Available at http://www.mambofello.com/smtm.html (accessed June 26, 2013).

Berríos-Miranda, Marisol. 2002. "Is Salsa a Musical Genre?" In *Situating Salsa: Global Markets and Local Meaning in Latin Popular Music*, ed. Lise Waxer, 23–50. New York: Routledge.

Bloom, Julie. 2007. "Salsa Spins Beyond Its Roots." *New York Times*, July 29. Available at http://www.nytimes.com/2007/07/29/arts/dance/29bloo.html?pagewanted=all&_r=0.

Boggs, Vernon. 1992. *Salsiology: Afro-Cuban Music and the Evolution of Salsa in New York City*. Westport, CT: Greenwood.

Brown, Shaka. 2003. Interview by Sydney Hutchinson. July 30.

Butler, Albert and Josephine. 1953. "The Ballroom Panorama: Mambo—Today." *Dance Magazine* 27 (12): 52–53.

Carlo, Ismael. 2001. "Space." *Planet Salsa*. Previously available at http://www.planetsalsa.com/quepasa/IsmaelSays.htm.

Craddock, Barbara, and Pedro Aguilar. 2003. Personal communications with Sydney Hutchinson.

Delgado, Luis A., ed. 2003. "Nuestras raices/Our roots." In *Salsa Today*. 3rd ed. San Juan, Puerto Rico: Congreso Mundial de la Salsa.

"Ernie Ensley: Palladium Legend." n.d. *SalsaRoots.com*. Available at http://www.salsacrazy.com/salsaroots/ernie.htm (accessed January 2, 2013).

Ferris, Marc. 2001. "For Latin Dancing, Follow the Beat and the Crowd." *New York Times*, November 11. Available at http://www.nytimes.com/2001/11/11/nyregion/for-latin-dancing-follow-the-beat-and-the-crowd.html.

Feuerstein, Alan. 1992. "Mambo Legends Cuban Pete and Millie: Architects of Excitement." *Justsalsa*. Available at http://www.justsalsa.com/culture/mambo/history/articles/alanfeuerstein/mambolegendscubanpeteandmille/.

———. n.d. "Tito Puente: Much More than a Legend." *Planet Salsa*. Available at http://web.archive.org/web/20060208091733/http://www.planetsalsa.com/quepasa/tp.htm (accessed July 4, 2013).

García, Aristides Raul. n.d. "Dancing on the '2': The Western Fluke of History." *DanceFreak*. Available at http://groups.yahoo.com/group/austinsalsa/message/2470 (accessed July 4, 2013).

García, David. 2009. "Embodying Music/Disciplining Dance: The Mambo Body in Havana and New York City." In *Ballroom, Boogie, Shimmy Sham, Shake: A Social and Popular Dance Reader*, ed. Julie Malnig, 165–181. Urbana: University of Illinois Press.

Hamera, Judith. 2007. *Dancing Communities: Performance, Difference, and Connection in the Global City*. New York: Palgrave Macmillan.

Hutchinson, Sydney. 2004. "Mambo On 2: The Birth of a New Form of Dance in New York City." *Centro: Journal of the Center for Puerto Rican Studies* 16 (2): 109–137.

———. 2009. "Listening to Salsa—for Dancers." *TucsonSalsa.com*, November 3. Available at http://www.tucsonsalsa.com/node/360.

Lewis, Edie. n.d. "Club Owners and Promoters: What Dancers Look for in a Club." *Edie the Salsa Freak*. Previously available at http://www.dancefreak.com/stories/clubown.htm (accessed March 17, 2003).

———. n.d. "What's Up with the New York 'Two'?" *Edie the Salsa Freak*. Previously available at http://www.dancefreak.com/stories/new_york_difference.htm (accessed March 17, 2003).

Leymarie, Isabelle. 2002. *Cuban Fire: The Story of Salsa and Latin Jazz*. New York: Continuum.

Loza, Steven. 1999. *Tito Puente and the Making of Latin Music*. Urbana: University of Illinois Press.

Manuel, Peter. 2006. *Caribbean Currents: Caribbean Music from Rumba to Reggae*. Philadelphia: Temple University Press.

Melo, Ney. 2002. Interview by Sydney Hutchinson. July 2.

Navarro, Mireya. 2000. "Battle of the Mambo Is Bruising Some Toes." *New York Times*, September 3.

Ortiz, Angel. 2001a. "Freddie Ríos—Palladium Mambo Legend." *Rhythms and Soul*, October 13. Available at http://www.rhythmsandsoul.com/articles4.html.

———. 2001b. "Interview: Eddie Torres, 'the Mambo King.'" *ToSalsa.com*, October 21. Available at http://www.tosalsa.com/forum/interviews/angel_ortiz/article011021ed dietorrespart1.html.

"Paul Pellicoro." 2013. *Paul Pellicoro's DanceSport*. Available at http://www.dancesport .com/paulpellicoro.

Pietrobruno, Sheenagh. 2006. *Salsa and Its Transnational Moves*. Lanham, MD: Lexington Books.

Quintero Rivera, Ángel G. 2009. *Cuerpo y cultura: Las músicas mulatas y la subversión del baile*. Madrid: Iberoamericana and Frankfurt am Main: Vervuert.

Renta, Priscilla. 2008. "Migración de retorno y decisiones estéticas: Bailando salsa entre Nueva York y Puerto Rico." In *El son y la salsa en la identidad del Caribe*, ed. Darío Tejeda and Rafael Emilio Yunén, 155–165. Santiago: Centro León and INEC.

Rita. n.d. "Eddie Torres: Modern Day Mambo Legend." *SalsaRoots.com*. Available at http:// www.salsacrazy.com/salsaroots/eddietorres.htm (accessed January 2, 2013).

———. n.d. "Mike Bello: L.A.'s Mambo Fello." *SalsaRoots.com*. Available at http://www .salsacrazy.com/salsaroots/mike_bello.htm (accessed January 2, 2013).

Roberts, John Storm. 1999. *The Latin Tinge: The Impact of Latin American Music on the United States*. 2nd ed. New York: Oxford University Press.

Rodríguez, Angel. 2003. Interview by Sydney Hutchinson. January 5.

Sagolla, Lisa Jo. 1999. "Frank 'Killer Joe' Piro." In *American National Biography*. New York: Oxford University Press.

Shaw, Steve. 2000. "About Salsa-Dancing—The Story of This Web Site—Acknowledgements." *Salsa New York*. Available at http://www.salsanewyork.com/guide/this_web_site.htm.

———. 2012. "Good Salsa Dance Songs and Guidelines for DJ's." *Salsa New York*. Available at http://www.salsanewyork.com/guide/song_list.htm.

———. 2013. "Directory of 'On 2' Mambo Performing Groups." *Salsa New York*. Available at http://www.salsanewyork.com/guide/performers1.htm.

———. n.d. "Web Site Description." *Salsa New York*. Available at http://www.salsanewyork .com/guide/description_newsletter.htm (accessed June 5, 2013).

Siverio, Manny. 2002. "Cyber-Interview of the Month: Rodney Lopez." *Salsa New York*. Available at http://www.salsanewyork.com/magazine/articles/interview_rodney _lopez.htm.

Stearns, Marshall, and Jean Stearns. (1968) 1994. *Jazz Dance: The Story of American Vernacular Dance*. New York: Da Capo.

Stephens, Dave, and Susan Randles. 2000. "Talking with Tito Puente." *Jazzreview.com*, January 29. Available at http://www.jazzreview.com/index.php/reviews/jazz-artist-interviews/item/12883.

Torres, Eddie. 2003. Interview by Sydney Hutchinson. August 27.

Washburne, Chris. 2002. "Salsa Romántica: An Analysis of Style." In *Situating Salsa: Global Markets and Local Meaning in Latin Popular Music*, ed. Lise Waxer, 101–132. New York: Routledge.

———. 2008. *Sounding Salsa: Performing Latin Music in New York City*. Philadelphia: Temple University Press.

3

From Hip-Hop and Hustle to Mambo and Salsa

New Jersey's Eclectic Salsa Dance Revival

Katherine Borland

I think one of the things that makes us really unique is that connection that we have to New York. . . . And you know, we've been able to draw on that influence and really . . . make a name for what [New] Jersey is doing in the salsa map. (Alex Díaz)

I say the trick is to recognize New York's influence without getting engulfed in it. (Johann Pichardo)

We all have to be realistic and understand that New Jersey will always be in the shadow of New York . . . but there's no reason why New Jersey can't compete, at least as second place to New York. (Mario B.)

I don't think we're trying to compete with New York. I think we're trying to be Jersey, stand on our own. (Griselle Ponce)

On July 18, 2006, thirteen accomplished New Jersey *salseros* attended a focus group designed to document their local dance scene.[1] Participant Jossué Torres called the meeting a historic occasion, because it was the first time this group of instructor-performers had sat down together to discuss the scene. Nevertheless, as demonstrated by some of the comments quoted above, these dancers struggled to define themselves as a distinct stylistic community, a consequence of their proximity to New York as well as their own internal divisions. Their story provides a useful counterpoint to narratives of localization, particularly those emanating from New York City. It reminds us that while all scenes are local, not all locales produce the conditions for the development of a place-specific style.

Over the past decade scholars have attended closely to the ways that the internationally disseminated music and dance complex called salsa, which developed from a New York–Cuban–Puerto Rican axis, has adapted to diverse areas throughout the world and created distinctive regional styles (Arias Satizábal 2002; Waxer 2002a, 2002b; Rondón 2008; Román-Velásquez 1999, 2002; Hosokawa 2002). Moreover, with the rise of new consumers and producers, the music has accreted new and sometimes contradictory meanings (Waxer 2002b). Whereas it remains a potent symbol of national and ethnic identity among Puerto Ricans residing in New York and Puerto Rico (Berríos-Miranda 2002; Flores 2004; see also Aparicio 1998), it expresses a deterritorialized identity for Spanish-speaking migrants to English-dominated social spaces (Quintero Rivera 1999). In South America the music accrued a cosmopolitan value associated with the metropolitan centers from which it emanated, and connoisseur communities of listeners developed (Waxer 2002a).[2] In the hands of Orquesta de la Luz, a Japanese salsa band that received considerable international attention in the 1990s, the music returned to its roots in the *salsa dura* (heavy salsa) of the 1970s. Yet Orquesta de la Luz's concern for retaining the purity of a foreign form through hypersimulation betrays a thoroughly Japanese aesthetic sensibility (Hosokawa 2002).[3]

With regard to the dance, Priscilla Renta (2004) and Sydney Hutchinson (2004) have documented the rise and spread of the New York mambo, or on-2, style, which on the one hand borrows heavily from tap, theatrical, hustle, and ballroom traditions and on the other represents a specifically Nuyorican[4] project for cultural recovery and artistic expression. New Jersey salseros both benefit and suffer from their proximity to salsa's creative center. A steady stream of talented dancers from New Jersey enriches the burgeoning New York and transnational scenes. Yet local clubs and venues change from year to year, offering no fixed locales to rival either Jimmy Anton's famed salsa social or the Corso, Copacabana, and Palladium nightclubs of earlier eras in New York.[5] The New Jersey Salsa Congress of 2003, in fact, survived for only one year before being relocated to New York and rebranded as the New York/New Jersey Salsa Festival. Since 2004 Johann Pichardo's website jerseysalsa.com has attempted to establish an identity for New Jersey. It provides a weekly listing of local classes and clubs and a photo and video gallery of events, but it remains unelaborated compared to websites serving the New York on-2 community.

Nevertheless, the dance scene in New Jersey provides a useful contrast to New York–origin narratives. In contrast to the strong ethnic specificity of on-2 histories, New Jersey salseros articulate a message of cultural inclusiveness, which embraces the ethnic diversity of the salsa dance community under the rubric of *latinidad*, an ethnic specificity founded on notions of hybridity. Latino/a and non-Latino/a participants in this scene articulate a desire to transcend limiting social milieus and identity categories even as they use the dance to develop a deeper understanding of Latino/a culture (Borland 2009). While these cosmopolitan attitudes may also exist among dancers in New York and other regional centers, narratives of localization work to ascribe ownership and agency in ways that erect lines of ethnic and place-based difference. In the absence of a strong localizing narrative, New Jersey dancers emphasize the cosmopolitan dimensions of their scene.

The term "cosmopolitan" has been used in a variety of ways in the social sciences and cultural studies to describe extralocal group formations (characteristic of but not limited to contemporary societies) that create an imaginary bond among people who do not necessarily share a territorial or cultural identity (Nowicka and Rovisco 2009). Cosmopolitan formations register the increasingly hybrid nature of local cultures and the important transnational component of group identities as a consequence of migration and mobility (Gupta and Ferguson 1997). Emphasizing the voluntary nature of cosmopolitan affinities, White suggests that "unlike 'globalization' or 'modernity,' cosmopolitanism is not something that happens to people, it is something that people do" (2002: 681).[6] Thus, Magdalena Nowicka and Maria Rovisco suggest, we should be asking, "How are ordinary individuals and groups making sense of their identities and social encounters in ways that can be said to be cosmopolitan?" (2009: 1). Bearing in mind that continuing social and legal inequalities result in very different senses of entitlement to shared cultural space, we might characterize cosmopolitanism as an attitude or disposition of individuals and groups to not only tolerate but also engage with people and forms they view as culturally different from themselves (Nowicka and Rovisco 2009; Donald, Kofman, and Kevin 2009).

These open and inclusive cultural attitudes are not necessarily restricted to members of privileged groups. Instead, the boundaries of a cosmopolitan cultural scene remain porous to outside influences even as a central set of values and tastes provide a stable core across dispersed locales. Thomas Turino (2003), for instance, identifies Zimbabwean popular music as a project of middle-class cosmopolitans who first imitated, then internalized, and ultimately reshaped internationally circulating cultural forms. When this popular music was transnationally circulated, it encountered audiences who recognized both its similarity to a shared model and a valued "otherness" characteristic of cosmopolitan tastes. I add that since the "otherness" of cosmopolitanism often draws on traditional cultural forms, it can provide a sense of heritage for culturally uprooted individuals who identify with the donor tradition. Moreover, the degree of cosmopolitanism in any given cultural scene may intensify or diminish according to the experiences of its members and the social work the scene performs vis-à-vis other associated or competing scenes.

From the mid-1990s, for instance, New Jersey dancers simultaneously embraced and reformulated the New York salsa revival. In Jersey City Ismael Otero disseminated his own hip-hop-inflected version of dancing on-2 through his company Caribbean Soul. In contrast, Juan Calderón understood the salient feature of the New York style to be its elaborate turn patterns borrowed from the Latin hustle of the 1970s.[7] He identifies his primary teaching-performing style as nightclub, or on-1, salsa.[8] This stylistic division makes describing the New Jersey dance scene in a unified way impossible; however, the July 2006 focus group participants concurred that Otero and Calderón were early, influential promoters of salsa dancing in New Jersey.

Moreover, the development of these and other New Jersey dance companies foregrounds the importance of in-migrating Latin Americans to the local dissemination of salsa dancing from the 1990s to the present. Afro-Peruvian Luis Zegarra, Dominican Smiling David, and Puerto Rican–born Juan Calderón, Griselle Ponce, and Jossué Torres have provided a cultural bridge to second-generation Latino youth who initially rejected the music and dance of their parents in favor of a commercially disseminated, English-language youth culture. This peculiarity of New Jersey studio instruction accentuates its cosmopolitan character.

The development, decline, recovery, and repopularization of the New York mambo has been well documented by Sydney Hutchinson (2004 and Chapter 2 herein) and Priscilla Renta (2004). But the on-2 revival also constituted part of a broader revival of salsa dancing across the United States that gained momentum in the early 1990s, sparked by a return of Latin rhythms and Latino artists to the commercial airwaves (Cepeda 2000). What made this broader revival distinctive was the predominantly Latino clientele at dance studios. Instructors comment that studio instruction had historically been a way for cultural outsiders to learn Latin dances. Now, Latinos were also attending classes to learn technically elaborated styles of partner dancing. In 1997 the first Puerto Rico Salsa Congress brought dancers from the East and West Coasts together to teach, perform, and dance on the island. In the beginning, New Jersey dancers volunteered at the congresses in exchange for plane fare, hotel accommodations, and the excitement of participating in the revival.

Salsa congresses (along with cruises and dance festivals) quickly developed as a niche tourist market and proliferated: by 2006 one could find a salsa congress somewhere in the world on any given weekend. These events offer dance enthusiasts the opportunity to stay at a nice hotel, take classes from well-known instructors, and attend performances and social dances. While dancers generally bemoan the resulting commercialization of the salsa scene, the congresses have provided professional opportunities for New Jersey salseros—Griselle Ponce, Ismael Otero, and Candy Mena, for instance—who quit their day jobs to work full time on the international circuit.

Caribbean Soul

Whereas the development and revival of on-2 salsa in New York is strongly associated with Puerto Rican musicians and dancers, in New Jersey, in-migrating

Latin Americans played an important role in revaluing salsa music and dance and transmitting it to second-generation Latino youth. Second-generation Latinos I interviewed commonly narrated a personal journey from ignorance, indifference, or hostility with respect to Spanish-language music and dance during their youth to a newfound appreciation of the pleasures of partner dancing as young adults.[9] The dynamics of this cultural realignment is well illustrated in the story of Caribbean Soul.

Afro-Peruvian Luis Zegarra is credited with having brought the on-2 style of dancing to New Jersey in 1994. Now a promoter engaged in organizing salsa congresses, he arrived in Jersey City in 1986. Zegarra remembers that salsa music and dance constituted an important element in Lima's popular culture during his youth. All the radio stations played salsa, salsa concerts and documentaries frequently aired on television, and international salsa bands provided the biggest draw at the annual Lima fair. He explains, "The people there in South America educate themselves more in the music, the bands, the artists, than the people here" (Zegarra 2007). As a consequence of salsa's continuing popularity and of the development of connoisseur groups, Peruvian youth had a kind of cultural knowledge Zegarra found lacking in his English-speaking, Puerto Rican peers. He therefore struck up a friendship with an older Jersey City neighbor named Iris, who was an avid salsera. Her children, Ismael and Irene Otero and Yesenia Peralta, were all accomplished hip-hop dancers, uninterested in the music and dance of their mother's era. Despite being underage, Zegarra had set out for New York City to dance at the Corso and Copacabana. In 1989 he won a dance contest at the Palace in Elizabeth, New Jersey, but encountered dismissive attitudes when he entered a contest at Sidestreet, an on-2 club in the Bronx. He reports:

> The people were very closed-minded. If it was on-2, it was on-2, and nobody else could dance! But I came in third. . . . That was the point at which I said, "Well, we're going to look for someone to train us." . . . So I found a woman to do this. . . . She said, "I'm going to do an on-1 choreography, because that's what you dance. But if you win, I want you to come to my classes. . . . Because you're a good dancer, but I think if you dance on-2, you're going to be better." (Zegarra 2007)

Locally, on-2 was the prestige style for serious dancers, so Luis learned the new timing.[10] Subsequently, he competed in and won numerous local contests. By 1993 he was teaching on-2 classes at DanceSport in Manhattan. Then the owner of Foxes, a Jersey City club, invited him to teach. Luis recalls that people initially came because of the novelty, but interest spread quickly, leading him to open schools in North Bergen, Jersey City, and Elizabeth and to put together performance groups for area festivals. Dancing on-2 was not only the hot, new thing; it also had heritage status and was showcased at displays of Latino culture, such as the annual Puerto Rican Day Parade.

By 1994 Zegarra had formed his own performance group with five female dancers called Fuerza Latina. In 1995 he was dancing for Jerry Rivera, a popular *salsa romántica* singer, and in April of that year he returned for the first time to Peru as a dancer with Rivera's international tour. Of his younger neighbor, Ismael Otero, Zegarra recalls, "Iris always asked me to take Ismael . . . and he didn't want to take classes. He didn't like salsa. . . . He had the hip-hop style" (Zegarra 2007). For his part, Otero recalls living in a neighborhood where his second-generation group shared the same social space with in-migrating Latinos but exhibited a distinctive cultural style:

> We would wear clothes and look like thugs, and they would be all dresses with shirts and ties and things. . . . Every time you'd go to a Latin party they would play English and Spanish, and every time they would play something English, I would get up and dance all night. But whenever the Spanish music [came on], I would sit down, and another guy would come up and start dancing. . . . And one day, I realized . . . I'm dancing against guys; he's dancing with women. I'm in the wrong kind of dance here! (Otero 2007)

Even after this revelation, Otero was embarrassed to admit an interest in salsa, because it conflicted with his image as a tough, streetwise Latino. He finally succumbed to Zegarra's pressure to attend classes by accompanying a girl who said she wanted to learn. Soon he was teaching Zegarra's beginners and by 1998, he had formed his own dance team, Caribbean Soul, a group that included, among others, his older sister Irene, Griselle Ponce, and Candy Mena.

Otero describes the late 1990s as a period of intense creativity and experimentation. He recalls New York luminary Eddie Torres telling him he most admired originality in dancers, which inspired Ismael to try out his own new moves with his sisters and then at Latin Quarter nightclub in Manhattan, where they attracted attention. Edie "the Salsa Freak" Lewis, creator of the bicoastal Salsa Web website, christened him the "Million Moves Man" after dancing with him there. Otero remarks, "Right there I have a title, so now I have to live up to it. My style shot up through the stratosphere. Now people have expectations" (Otero 2007). Otero thus distinguishes his own creative approach to learning salsa from the uniformity of New York on-2 dancers, while acknowledging his New York elders for stimulating his creativity.

Otero correspondingly encouraged those who studied and performed with him to develop a personal style. For instance, Griselle Ponce, who had grown up in a small town near Ponce, Puerto Rico, dancing Puerto Rican–style salsa, *bomba*, and *plena*, excelled at body movement. Candy Mena, a Dominican American whose high school passion had been cheerleading, practiced and became known for her distinctive hand styling. Jesse Yip, a Peruvian American who studied with Otero sometime later, concentrated on developing elaborate turn patterns. Ismael explains, "I tell all my students that I don't teach [style]. I bring it out. And in the beginning it's okay to mimic somebody, but once you start getting into your own body, your own natural style comes out" (Otero 2007).[11] Initially, Caribbean Soul dancers were short on technique and long on creativity, according to Otero. They borrowed from hip-hop and relied on "shaking your body and whipping your hair" to present a look that departed from the New York on-2 emphasis on elegance.[12] Moreover, they opted for sleeveless shirts as opposed to the suit and tie costuming of the more established salsa performers. As Otero sought to update the New York style by inserting a hip-hop sensibility, his neighbor Juan Calderón was engaged in a different kind of imaginative refashioning.

Cultural Explosion

Puerto Rico–born Juan Calderón first learned to dance at home; at age seven he won second place in a dance contest on a ferry to the Dominican Republic. He moved to New Jersey as a teenager and attended Seton Hall University in Newark, majoring in business. At that time, he recalls, Latino students were trying to get in touch with their cultural roots, and he began informally teaching salsa dancing to his friends. For a brief time Calderón also worked as an instructor at a nearby ballroom studio. However, he resisted the studio's exploitative wages as well as its gradualist approach to teaching, which he viewed as exploiting the clients. Nevertheless, Calderón recognized a potential market and set himself the task of learning several different styles of salsa dancing: nightclub, or on-1; on-2; and the *rueda de casino* style from Miami. Offering classes five nights a week at different clubs, bars, and ethnic halls in and around the Elizabeth area, Calderón quickly developed a student following. In 2001 he produced the *New York Salsa* series of instructional videos with his then partner Diana Diappa, in which he demonstrated turn patterns using both the on-1 and on-2 counting systems.[13] Rather than referring to a specific timing, Calderón explained, the New York label accentuated the smoothness in the turn patterns in comparison to Los Angeles style. The DVDs aimed to evoke "the Copacabana, old-style grandfather dancing, who dances his own style that he learned at home to no structure, no timing, but his turn patterns are influenced by another era, usually the seventies or eighties and the strong hustle influence that was at that time" (Calderón 2007).

Calderón's understanding of earlier dance styles in New York diverges from the on-2 history of the dance, which locates the important creative moment at the Palladium Ballroom of the 1950s rather than the Copacabana of the 1970s. His "grandfather" is of a different generation from the "grandfather" of Eddie Torres. One consequence of this alternative reading of New York (and therefore New Jersey) style is a social and stylistic separation of Calderón's dancers from those studying at on-2 studios. Calderón asserts that the concept of timing is divisive, so his school encourages "being bilingual, knowing different styles" through teaching both and prioritizing neither. This perspective defends the equal artistic worth of all styles against on-2 instructors' assertions that theirs is the more elegant, more adept, and more musically perceptive prestige style (Hutchinson 2004).

Whereas Otero earns a living primarily as an instructor-performer on the international circuit, Calderón has succeeded in building an impressive local following through an instructional model that links formal classes with opportunities for students to dance socially and participate in amateur salsa stage shows. Most of Calderón's classes are held in bars and clubs, rather than in studios, so students can immediately practice the dance. In contrast to on-2 instructional venues, where a marked emphasis on the mastery of timing results in repeated drilling of the basic steps,[14] Calderón's school has the goal of getting people dancing as quickly as possible. The first half of a two-hour class is dedicated to basic footwork or shines, the second half to partner work. Beginning students are required to master eight turn patterns[15] to move to the next level of instruction. In the intermediate class, Calderón walks students through a seemingly limitless set of turn pattern combinations. This approach to dance instruction provokes critiques by on-2 instructors that he is teaching steps, not dancing. However, aficionados appreciate the faster pace and novelty of the classes, as well as Calderón's students' ability to dance with any partner.

Calderón and his dance partner Christina Piedra point out that everyone comes to classes for different reasons: some to socialize, some for romance, some to get in shape, some for cultural exploration. Therefore, to insist on perfect technique from everyone would be a mistake. At the same time, Piedra notes, people who begin with only a casual interest in the dance often get hooked:

> I think by the third lesson a student can . . . say, "I would like to be advanced," but they can see that what the advanced people are doing took them two or three years [to learn]. I think that's what tends to happen. It takes over people's lives. (Piedra 2007)

Even at a school that works to avoid overtechnical instruction and preserve a home-style flavor, many students develop serious aspirations to dance.

Many other instructors active in the scene have trained with Calderón or Otero. Nevertheless, each studio and each dance company has its own way of understanding the tradition, its own particular style. If the New York style is marked by conformity to a particular model (a preference for a specific timing, footwork, music, and dress) and ethnically inflected, stylistically based exclusionary practices, New Jersey dancers, perhaps as a consequence of their permanently peripheral location, have emphasized the drive toward innovation and a culturally open attitude that has arguably also long been part of salsa's tradition as a musically and socially hybrid form.

Diversity and Latinidad

By 2006 salsa studios in New Jersey had changed from almost entirely Latino to about 60 percent Latino; the rest were blacks, whites, East Asians, South Asians, Filipinos, and members of other immigrant groups. An almost entirely Latino group of instructors recognize they benefit from their students' desires to learn salsa from authentic Latinos; nevertheless, they are unanimous in challenging essentialist notions, arguing that with practice and perseverance, anyone can learn to dance. These arguments serve the commercial interests of dance instructors to cultivate paying students. Yet instructors also draw on their own experiences as in-migrating Latinos who had to learn the local on-2 style (or, as in the case of Calderón, have been marginalized because they have not preferred that style) or as second-generation Latinos who had to study salsa to reacquaint themselves with their heritage. Latino and non-Latino dancers in the studio setting, then, share an experience in which mastery of the form is not a cultural given, something soaked up in the home environment, but rather a bodily accomplishment based on training.

In this setting, stories of dancing ability based on cultural immersion are interlaced with stories of the difficulty of perfecting fundamentals to develop cultural competence and, eventually, a personal style.[16] For instance, Puerto Rican–born Wil Cuba remembers a traumatic first experience in 1996 when his partner left him on the dance floor because he repeatedly stepped on her foot. Three years later he started training in the on-2 style and progressed rapidly. Nevertheless, he discovered that he was arrhythmic. So Cuba enrolled in several basic music classes at the local community college in addition to training with Javier and Sweety's salsa company. He says, "I had lots of trouble. It took me two years to finally learn and to hear the beat" (Cuba 2007). Cuba claims improvisational ability based on his Puerto Rican home life, where everyone danced freestyle salsa; at the same time, lessons and study taught him to dance to the rhythm of the music. This narrative displaces the centrality of rhythm in arguments about a natural or authentic connection to Caribbean culture based on heritage.

Moreover, non-Latino dancers who participate in the salsa scene find that training in other kinds of dance assists them in learning salsa, and they use their dancing competence to resist ethnic stereotyping. For instance, African American Ivan Taylor studied ballet, modern dance, jazz, and capoeira before he started salsa. He asserts, "I believe I have the ability to adapt to any culture. I don't want to just be limited to, you know, black culture" (Taylor 2007). Dancer Alexis Madill, who is white, came to salsa from competitive ballroom dancing. In salsa studios and clubs, she finds that her dancing ability renders her ethnicity ambiguous so that she is often taken for a light Cuban despite her Irish, English, and Cherokee heritage. She reports, "I've never felt discriminated [against]. If anything, it just gave people hope. They're like, 'Wow! All right, we can't use this as an excuse why we can't dance.' You gotta go out there.

It doesn't matter what background you come from" (Madill 2007). Madill's narrative simultaneously exposes and challenges racial stereotypes operating in the studio salsa scene. In fact, she believes that other dancers appreciate her commitment to the dance precisely because she came from another culture. Marciarie Rodríguez, a Nuyorican dancer with Pzazz in Newark, supports Madill's claim to inclusion, stating that even though she considers salsa part of her Nuyorican heritage, its popularity among a diverse group of dancers is a source of cultural pride for her.

Of course, even in settings that consciously embrace diversity, lines of difference continue to be drawn. In London, Patria Román-Velázquez (2002) found that the apparent diversity of musicians in salsa bands belied patterns of ethnic (and gender) distinction by instrument that conformed to common stereotypes identifying rhythm as the African and melody as the European contribution to contemporary music. Hutchinson (Chapter 2) identifies Nuyorican dancers as holding a virtual monopoly on instruction in New York; in New Jersey, other Latino instructors predominate. Moreover, among the highly trained dancers in New York performance companies, Hutchinson notes a continuing insistence on the phenotypical specificity of dancers—describing some as "vanilla" and some as "chocolate"—that reasserts the primacy of ethnic/racial categories (2007).

Hence, it would be unwise to proclaim the studio salsa scene an idyllic haven for individuals seeking to transcend fixed identity categories. More realistically, the scene represents a Latino-dominated space that, at least at the entry level, welcomes non-Latinos. This openness provides an opportunity for highly competent non-Latino dancers to challenge existing stereotypes, and because latinidad itself is a hybrid category, many non-Latinos pass as Latino to varying degrees. For instance, Filipina Geraldine Pagaoa of Pzazz asserts that when she dances socially, people rarely realize she is Asian. Nevertheless, she sometimes confronts a linguistic barrier in her dance company: "I missed things sometimes. Even in practice, they laugh at me. . . . They make jokes, and I don't understand, or they make jokes about the songs, and I just don't get it" (Pagaoa 2007). Several scholars have emphasized the importance that Spanish-language lyrics came to have in salsa music despite early experiments in English and the emergence of salsa bands in non-Spanish-speaking areas (Rondón 2008; Román-Velázquez 2002; Hosokawa 2002). In the social environment of the studios, as well, Spanish can be important, even though classes are conducted in English.

Japanese Tsuyoshi Miyajima, a long-time student at Cultural Explosion, had no previous dance training. He enjoyed dancing salsa, even though he felt he would never be able to move his body in a Latino way (Miyajima 2007). Chinese Bin Bin Zhang felt Asians progressed more slowly in the classes because they are shy and have difficulty asking people to partner with them (Zhang 2007). Both were initially drawn to other Asians in the scene because they felt they confronted a shared set of obstacles. Over time, as their skill and confidence grew, they began to dance and socialize with Latinos and other non-Asian dancers. Zhang emphasizes that salsa allows ordinary Asians an opportunity to express themselves through dance, something that traditional Asian dance forms, which require intensive body training, do not. On the whole, student attitudes echo those of their instructors, who claim that with enough practice and commitment, anyone can learn to dance.

Cosmopolitanism and Social Class

The critical literature privileges a perspective on salsa as a means to maintain a defiant alterity rather than reaching for the artistic respectability associated with a middle-class status (Delgado and Muñoz 1997; Berríos-Miranda 2004; but see Renta 2004). This scholarly preference derives from the emphasis in cultural and anthropological studies on subaltern forms of resistance, an emphasis that sometimes runs the risk of romanticizing poverty. Moreover, by locating authenticity as a quality of the streets, this perspective ignores the dynamic give and take of stylistic influences from home, the media, and club and studio environments and from one ethnic group to another (Desmond 1997; Chapter 2 herein; López 1997). Additionally, it obscures women's contributions to stylistic innovation (Borland 2009). In his work on Zimbabwean popular music, Turino (2003) implies that cosmopolitanism itself represents a middle-class set of values and concerns that contrasts with the traditional Shona music and culture rooted in the countryside. In First World contexts, however, commercial and popular influences penetrate all classes. Moreover, successive waves of migration combined with shifting class affiliations between first- and second-generation migrants add considerable complexity to the relation between a cosmopolitan outlook and a particular class standing.

The New York dance scene has been characterized by some as a middle-class professional environment (see Hutchinson 2004: 129), yet New Jersey dance instructors emphasize their students' varied class backgrounds. Particularly in the smaller studios, the idea that the dance studio provides a haven for community members sometimes interferes with the reality of the studio as a business. Griselle Ponce and Jossué Torres, for example, have organized several children's performance teams over the years. They complain that struggling parents often neglect to pay for the children's training, trusting (correctly) in the instructors' motivation to pass on their tradition to a new generation of dancers. Indeed, several New Jersey studios represent enterprises that are in many ways labors of love. Torres, Mario B, Smiling David, Alex Díaz, Jesse Yip and Joanna Sánchez, and Javier Almeida all hold full-time jobs and practice salsa in the evenings or on weekends. They depend on long-time students and company members to help organize socials, performances, and rehearsals. Thus, studios often feel more like clubhouses than commercial enterprises. They perform a social as well as an artistic function.

Moreover, salsa remains an important element of heritage, particularly for Puerto Ricans but also for Latinos in general. Griselle Ponce and Mario B noted they prepared salsa dance routines for *quinceañeras*, the elaborate birthday parties that mark a young girl's coming of age in Latino families. Ponce identified the *quinceañera* as an ideal vehicle for introducing salsa to a sometimes resistant younger generation, because parents will not allow routines based on *reggaetón*, the dance music currently popular with the Latino youth. In this frame, and despite its sexy image, studio salsa represents a positive, uplifting, safe cultural activity that offers an alternative to crass, commercial youth culture.

It also provides safety from sometimes violent street life. Ivette Ramírez, for instance, credits Smiling David's Broadway Dance Studio in Newark with providing an alternative to hanging out in the streets during her adolescence. Ivette had initially contacted Smiling David to teach on-2 salsa to a high school dance team she had organized as a way to explore her Puerto Rican heritage. When I met her eight years later, she was working full time as a secretary but remained a permanent member of Smiling David's Pzazz dancers and taught salsa classes with him four or more evenings a week. She was proud to have successfully guided several other girls through adolescence by means of her dance performance groups (Ramírez 2007).

Yesenia Peralta's salsa story depicts the current salsa revival as a route to self-determination through social mobility. In high school, Peralta was immersed in gang culture in a neighborhood she describes as permeated by drugs and violence. The consequences of this lifestyle for Peralta were early pregnancy and motherhood followed by social isolation: a jealous boyfriend confined her to home and child care, preventing her from visiting her family and friends. She explains, "You usually think your destiny is written: you're sixteen years old, you've dropped out of high school, you have no education, no work experience, you're gonna have to go on welfare, he's gonna leave you, you're gonna have to move back in with your parents, and you ain't gonna amount to much" (Peralta 2007). Determined that her story would be different, Peralta left her boyfriend when she was twenty-one and moved in with her older brother, Ismael, and sister, Irene. It was 1999, and Otero was having trouble meeting the demand for his salsa classes, so he drafted his two sisters to teach. Both had been break dancing for many years, but neither knew how to dance salsa. Within a few months, however, they were not only teaching but also touring with Caribbean Soul. Peralta continues:

> And then salsa came along. It was meeting new people and being creative and traveling to Washington, and I would never have thought that would have been my life when I was in high school. I mean, I liked to dance; we all liked to dance, but to actually make a career out of it? How am I going to do that with no money—no credit—I'm living paycheck to paycheck? What are the possibilities of me opening up a dance school? (Peralta 2007)

For Peralta, salsa provided a space for self-definition and professionalization after a prolonged period of confinement and passivity. Distancing herself from a world of restricted choices and violence, Peralta embraced the broader horizons and new social opportunities that an increasingly diverse and internationally connected salsa scene offered. This new orientation does not mean that Peralta no longer identifies with hip-hop style. Both she and her brother feel they bring a valuable street flavor to an increasingly technical dance scene. However, they do not feel limited to dancing and performing an underclass identity.

Otero understands the salsa studio as a place where social class no longer divides people:

> Most people come to my class because I look like a street person, so people come to my class thinking they can look cool and dance salsa. . . . You dance with someone; you suddenly realize you're dancing with a doctor or a poet. When you dance, you're just another dancer. They don't see you as a street person, just another dancer. An equal. (Otero 2007)

For Otero, salsa scenes are inhabited by a diverse group whose easy interchange offers the possibility of redemption for those who have lost their way in economic hard times. Others who have entered the scene from more secure economic conditions narrate escapes from the boredom and passivity of desk jobs or the solitude of long evenings in front of the television.

Juan Calderón identifies salsa congresses as attracting a certain quality of person who is "cultured," "worldly," and interested in dancing with others, rather than sticking to his or her own group:

> It's really a way to come together with different people, which we don't have an opportunity to do in everyday life—to socialize with people from other countries, you know, people from different cultures that have nothing in common other than, in this case, the love for music and dance. (Calderón 2007)

Taken together, these descriptions construct serious salseros as a subset of people crosscutting class and ethnic categories who are interested in people different from themselves.

Calderón's emphasis on being "bilingual," on being able to dance both on-1 and on-2, conforms to his understanding of salsa's social space as an open and inclusive one rather than a private club to which one must gain entry through stylistic discernment. He adopts the language of tourism to market this inviting space:

> So it's a way to explore an exotic, tropical place while being in cold New Jersey. So tonight, Monday night, salsa night at Terminal One, although it's cold outside, inside we have a tropical environment of not only music but people. So the people are very warm and friendly, and when we say hello to each other, we give each other a kiss on the cheek, something that outside of Terminal One might be looked upon as weird.

> When we're here in the salsa community, it's almost like we're another
> country inside the country. And that country is welcoming of all coun-
> tries and cultures of people. (Calderón 2007)

The social space Calderón constructs is an imaginary world—a country within
a country, which is both a nostalgic invocation and a utopian vision, set apart
from a cold, uncaring world populated by alienated individuals. He and other
New Jersey instructors offer their students a nightlife fantasy that blends exoticism with heritage in a safe and welcoming environment that is also charged
with sensuality and energy. In this sense the actual location of the club, studio,
or ethnic hall becomes irrelevant as dancers nightly repeat their escape to geographically, socially, and affectively warmer climes. One might argue that the
tourism at home offered by the New Jersey salsa studio replicates the situation
one might find on Caribbean islands, where Latino "locals" cater to the desires of culturally "other" paying guests.[17] And yet as long-time guests become
members of companies and teach classes alongside their mentors, and a steady
stream of Latino and non-Latino newcomers line up to pay for beginning dance
lessons, these lines of difference are blurred.

Transcending limiting identity categories through dance remains attractive to Latino and non-Latino, affluent and not-so-affluent dancers. Yet one
might argue the resulting scene provides an intimacy without depth. Sixty-
year-old white dance student Joanne Reynolds enjoys the generational, racial,
and cultural diversity of the scene but adds:

> What surprises me is that there is very little talk about what people do
> for a living. There are some people I know there whom I see every week
> since last March, and I haven't a clue what they do for a living because
> nobody talks about the things you think people would talk about in the
> more traditional type settings. (Reynolds 2007)

The New Jersey salsa scene thus accomplishes its projection of an idealized
cosmopolitan space by avoiding talk that might lead to social differentiation.
While social alliances are built across ethnic, class, and age differences, the
promise of community is largely sustained *and* contained by participants'
shared passion for the dance.

As New York salseros developed an ethnically and regionally specific style
during the salsa dance revival of the 1990s, New Jersey instructors emphasized
the increasingly cosmopolitan nature of their clubs and studios, embracing difference under the sign of latinidad. Actual places became irrelevant in this construction of studio-based salsa, because the tropical illusion could be replicated
in any space. Studio instructors who have worked over the past fifteen years to
construct a local scene embrace cosmopolitanism partly as a defensive response
to the exclusivity of on-2 New York dancers. The scene has also been shaped
by in-migrating Latin Americans who understood salsa music and dance as a

cultural practice broadly shared across the Spanish-speaking world. This alternative perspective does not challenge New York's centrality in inventing a regionally specific style of salsa and nurturing its more recent revival. Nevertheless, New Jersey's stylistic eclecticism and broad embrace provide a useful counterpoint to the connoisseur tendencies evident in the New York scene.

NOTES

Note: This chapter expands one of a number of arguments I developed in "Embracing Difference: Salsa Fever in New Jersey," *Journal of American Folklore* 122, no. 486 (2009): 466–492. Both essays draw from five months of field research conducted in the summer of 2006 and the winter of 2007, supported by a Faculty Assembly Research Grant from the Ohio State University, Newark, and a travel grant from the Ohio State University Center for Latin American Studies.

1. My research concentrated on dancers in northern New Jersey, in Essex, Hudson, and Union Counties. However, a vibrant scene also exists in southern New Jersey and is strongly connected in particular with Cultural Explosion Dance Company in the northern part of the state. Attending the focus group meeting were Ismael Otero of Caribbean Soul; Juan Calderón of Cultural Explosion; Griselle Ponce; Smiling David of Pzazz Dancers; Mario B (Mario González), owner of Salsa Fever On2 Dance Academy; Jossué Torres, owner of J. Bonilla Dance Studio; Sweety Vélez of Javier and Sweety; Jesse Yip and Joanna Sánchez of Tumimambo; and Alex Díaz. Also participating were Ray Colón, salsa DJ; Johann Pichardo, webmaster for jerseysalsa.com; Winsome Lee of Tormenta Oriental in New York; and Susan Tel, former salsa promoter and aficionada. I also conducted private interviews with several who could not attend (promoter Luis Zegarra, Irene Otero, Yesenia Peralta, and Candy Mena, all formerly of Caribbean Soul; Christina Piedra of Cultural Explosion; Javier Almeida of Javier and Sweety; and Amanda Estilo). All of them agreed that they were the established leaders in the local dance scene in 2006. However, some individuals who were either new to the dance scene or less connected to this core group of dancers were missed.

2. In the Congo, Cuban-derived music became popular in much the same way, producing an alternative to European cosmopolitanisms (see White 2002).

3. Salsa dura style has also been revived in New York and New Jersey, but in contrast to Orquesta de la Luz's depoliticized sound, Jimmy Bosch and others attempt to recapture the connection between salsa, cultural liberation, and community uplift.

4. People of Puerto Rican descent residing in New York.

5. For a list of New Jersey salsa clubs popular with dancers in the 1990s, see Washburne 2008: 210.

6. James Clifford (1998) prefers the term "cosmopolitan" to "multicultural," because, as an imaginary association, it avoids the latter's essentialism.

7. I spell the last name Calderón with an accent mark for consistency; however, on the web and in promotional materials, he and other dancers typically drop the accent marks from their names.

8. Calderón's Cultural Explosion Dance Company is located farther south in the Elizabeth area. His social and professional networks are oriented away from New York toward the on-1 Philadelphia and Chicago salsa scenes.

9. Mario B, Johann Pichardo, Candy Mena, Alex Díaz, Christina Piedra, Jesse Yip, Joanna Sánchez, Ismael Otero, Irene Otero, Yesenia Peralta, Ray Colón, and many students at salsa studios employed this trope in their interviews.

10. Smiling David of Newark reports a similar experience when he first arrived from the Dominican Republic. Although he was a talented dancer, his friends refused to take him clubbing because he did not know the on-2 style. David was eventually enticed to study on-2 style formally with his friend and fellow Dominican Victor Mayovanex.

11. Otero's emphasis on improvisation and play contributed to the development of a humorous tradition at salsa congresses. Together with Los Angeles dancer Al Espinosa, he formed a salsa comedy duo called Electric Beat on Two and a Half, which clowned around on stage at congresses (Otero 2007).

12. Chris Washburne (2008) identifies this blending of salsa with hip-hop style and sensibilities in salsa singer La India's professional trajectory and stage self-presentation, indicating that the trend was musical as well as dance-related.

13. *New York Salsa* 2002.

14. For instance, Mario B at his Salsa Fever On-2 studio in Jersey City provides students with timing CDs for learning the on-2 count and requires students to attend music appreciation classes.

15. The required sequence is as follows: cross-body lead, break back right turn, right turn (three stylings), inside turn (three stylings), shoulder turn behind the back, body roll, out of the way, and frisbee (revolving doors). For an explanation of these elementary steps, see his instructional DVD.

16. See Fraleigh 1994 for a succinct discussion of the relation between freedom and control and between improvisation and training in dance.

17. Deborah Kapchan (2006) identifies a comparable dynamic in Austin, Texas, salsa clubs, where non-Latina women professionals connected with Latino working-class men to construct both a space of difference and a sense of home. In New Jersey studios, however, lines of difference are less clearly drawn.

REFERENCES

Aparicio, Frances. 1998. *Listening to Salsa: Gender, Latin Popular Music, and Puerto Rican Cultures.* Middletown, CT: Wesleyan University Press.

Arias Satizábal, Medardo. 2002. "Se Prohíbe Escuchar 'Salsa y Control': When Salsa Arrived in Buenaventura, Colombia," trans. Lise Waxer. In *Situating Salsa: Global Markets and Local Meaning in Latin Popular Music,* ed. Lise Waxer, 247–258. New York: Routledge.

Berríos-Miranda, Marisol. 2002. "Is Salsa a Musical Genre?" In *Situating Salsa: Global Markets and Local Meaning in Latin Popular Music,* ed. Lise Waxer, 23–50. New York: Routledge.

———. 2004. "Salsa Music as Expressive Liberation." *Centro: Journal of the Center for Puerto Rican Studies* 16 (2): 159–173.

Borland, Katherine. 2009. "Embracing Difference: Salsa Fever in New Jersey." *Journal of American Folklore* 122 (486): 466–492.

Calderón, Juan. 2007. Interview by Katherine Borland. March 12.

Cepeda, Maria Elena. 2000. "Mucho Loco for Ricky Martin; or the Politics of Chronology, Crossover, and Language within the Latin(o) Music 'Boom.'" *Popular Music and Society* 24 (3): 55–71.

Clifford, James. 1998. "Mixed Feelings." In *Cosmopolitics: Thinking and Feeling beyond the Nation,* ed. P. Cheah and B. Robbins, 362–370. Minneapolis: University of Minnesota Press.

Cuba, Wil. 2007. Interview by Katherine Borland. February 10.

Delgado, Celeste Frasier, and José Esteban Muñoz, eds. 1997. *Everynight Life: Culture and Dance in Latin/o America.* Durham, NC: Duke University Press.

Desmond, Jane C. 1997. "Embodying Difference: Issues in Dance and Cultural Studies." In *Meaning in Motion: New Cultural Studies of Dance*, ed. Jane C. Desmond, 29–54. Durham, NC: Duke University Press.

Donald, Stephanie Hemelryk, Eleonore Kofman, and Catherine Kevin. 2009. "Introduction: Processes of Cosmopolitanism and Parochialism." In *Branding Cities: Cosmopolitanism, Parochialism, and Social Change*, ed. Stephanie Hemelryk Donald, Eleonore Kofman, and Catherine Kevin, 1–13. New York: Routledge.

Flores, Juan. 2004. "Creolité in the 'Hood: Diaspora as Source and Challenge." *Centro: Journal of the Center for Puerto Rican Studies* 16 (2): 283–293.

Fraleigh, Sondra Horton. 1994. "Good Intentions and Dancing Moments: Agency, Freedom, and Self-Knowledge in Dance." In *The Perceived Self: Ecologica and Interpersonal Sources of Self-knowledge*, ed. Ulric Neisser, 102–111. Cambridge: Cambridge University Press.

Gupta, Akhil, and James Ferguson. 1997. "Beyond 'Culture:' Space, Identity, and the Politics of Difference." In *Culture, Power, Place: Ethnography at the End of an Era*, ed. Akhil Gupta and James Ferguson, 33–52. Durham, NC: Duke University Press.

Hosokawa, Shuhei. 2002. "Salsa No Tiene Fronteras: Orquesta de la Luz and the Globalization of Popular Music." In *Situating Salsa: Global Markets and Local Meanings in Latin Popular Music*, ed. Lise Waxer, 289–312. New York: Routledge.

Hutchinson, Sydney. 2004. "Mambo On 2: The Birth of a New Form of Dance in New York City." *Centro: Journal of the Center for Puerto Rican Studies* 16 (2): 109–137.

———. 2007. Personal communication.

Kapchan, Deborah. 2006. "Talking Trash: Performing Home and Anti-home in Austin's Salsa Culture." *American Ethnologist* 33 (3): 361–377.

López, Ana M. 1997. "Of Rhythms and Borders." In *Everynight Life: Culture and Dance in Latin/o America*, ed. Celeste Fraser Delgado and José Esteban Muñoz, 310–344. Durham, NC: Duke University Press.

Madill, Alexis. 2007. Interview by Katherine Borland. February 2.

Miyajima, Tsuyoshi. 2007. Interview by Katherine Borland. February 8.

New York Salsa. 2002. DVD. Directed by Media Plus Entertainment.

Nowicka, Magdalena, and Maria Rovisco. 2009. "Introduction: Making Sense of Cosmopolitanism." In *Cosmopolitanism in Practice*, ed. Magdalena Nowicka and Maria Rovisco, 1–14. London: Ashgate.

Otero, Ismael. 2007. Interview by Katherine Borland. February 9.

Pagaoa, Geraldine. 2007. Interview by Katherine Borland. January 28.

Peralta, Yesenia. 2007. Interview by Katherine Borland. January 27.

Piedra, Christina. 2007. Interview by Katherine Borland. January 25.

Quintero Rivera, Ángel G. 1999. *¡Salsa, sabor y control! Sociología de la música "tropical."* 2nd ed. Mexico City: Siglo Veintiuno.

Ramírez, Ivette. 2007. Interview by Katherine Borland. January 28.

Renta, Priscilla. 2004. "Salsa Dance: Latino/a History in Motion." *Centro: Journal of the Center for Puerto Rican Studies* 16 (2): 138–157.

Reynolds, Joanne. 2007. Interview by Katherine Borland. February 3.

Román-Velázquez, Patria. 2002. "The Making of a Salsa Music Scene in London." In *Situating Salsa: Global Markets and Local Meaning in Latin Popular Music*, ed. Lise Waxer, 259–288. New York: Routledge.

Rondón, César Miguel. 2008. *The Book of Salsa: A Chronicle of Urban Music from the Caribbean to New York City*, trans. Frances R. Aparicio and Jackie White. Chapel Hill: University of North Carolina Press.

Taylor, Ivan. 2007. Interview by Katherine Borland. January 31.

Turino, Thomas. 2003. "Are We Global Yet? Globalist Discourse, Cultural Formations and the Study of Zimbabwean Popular Music." *British Journal of Ethnomusicology* 12 (2): 51–79.

Washburne, Chris. 2008. *Sounding Salsa: Performing Latin Music in New York City.* Philadelphia: Temple University Press.

Waxer, Lise. 2002a. *The City of Musical Memory: Salsa, Record Grooves, and Popular Culture in Cali, Colombia.* Middletown, CT: Wesleyan University Press.

———, ed. 2002b. *Situating salsa: Global Markets and Local Meanings in Latin Popular Music.* New York: Routledge.

White, Bob W. 2002. "Congolese Rumba and Other Cosmopolitanisms." *Cahiers d'Études Africaines* 168 (42): 663–686.

Zegarra, Luis. 2007. Interview by Katherine Borland. February 8.

Zhang, Bin Bin. 2007. Interview by Katherine Borland. February 8.

4

Contextualizing Content and Conduct in the L.A. Salsa Scene

Jonathan S. Marion

Background

Although it is largely in jest that I occasionally refer to salsa as "my other religion," Robert Redfield's (1956) distinction between a religion's "Great Tradition" versus its "Little Tradition"—the official version of a major world religion versus its local iteration—provides a useful lens for viewing salsa. Just as a religion's shared underlying belief system and structure allow for broad participation, so too with salsa's relatively common underlying structure of music and movement. But as a religion's canonical beliefs and practices are enacted only in particular ways in specific places, so too for salsa. If the underlying patterns of movement and partnering allow shared participation, still, the vast majority of salsa takes form according to local shapes, circumstances, and nuances.

I first saw salsa dancing in Toronto in 1998, started lessons in San Diego soon thereafter, and attended my first congress in Los Angeles in 2000.[1] During my first few workshops at the congress, I danced with women from five continents. Since then I have visited and danced at salsa venues in California, around the United States, and outside the United States (including Denmark, Mexico, and Canada). It is no accident that the thousands of dancers attending numerous salsa congresses and festivals around the world can all dance with each other: the shared codes of bodily conduct and practice serve as the foundation of a translocal activity-based culture and community (see Marion 2006, 2008, 2012).

Much of my previous work has focused on the translocality of dance cultures. Yet the globalization of salsa dancing—including its embodied customs and practices—is only part of the picture. Indeed, despite an ever-expanding calendar of local, national, and international salsa festivals, the vast majority of salsa dancing takes place within the local contexts of specific opportunities, situations, settings, and venues. Salsa's status as a global product, process, and commodity does not negate its local iterations, nuances, and practices.

While it is certainly true that salsa can be fully understood or appreciated— historically, musically, or culturally—only in relation to its "roots in the Cuban and Puerto Rican cultural diaspora of New York City" (Waxer 2002b: 3),[2] it is equally true that, as a now worldwide phenomenon, "salsa no longer points to just New York, Cuba, and Puerto Rico" (Waxer 2002a: 18). Every salsa scene represents its own intersection of local and global dynamics, and the L.A. salsa scene is no exception. With this in view and drawing on (a) formal and informal interviews with both regulars and visitors to the L.A. salsa scene, (b) my experience dancing at salsa venues in Los Angeles, Orange County, Riverside, San Diego, San Francisco, and San Jose, and (c) archival research in print and online, I examine in this chapter the "Little Tradition" of the Los Angeles– based West Coast salsa scene from three interrelated perspectives:

1. The confluence of sociocultural factors and dynamics—especially those pertaining to population size, performance teams, and competitions—shaping the L.A. salsa scene
2. How it is seen and experienced by salsa dancers
3. The role of L.A.-style salsa in the globalization of salsa dancing, especially in relation to salsa festivals, videos, and the Internet

What, however, is L.A. salsa? To answer this central question, I begin by noting some of the problems with defining L.A. salsa and provide some key musical history.

Multiple Realities: Some Problems with Defining "L.A. Salsa"

It is important to realize that there is not *an* "L.A. salsa" scene. U.S. Census Bureau statistics for 2010 put the population of Los Angeles County in the vicinity of ten million, Orange County and San Diego Counties at over three million apiece, and Riverside and San Bernardino Counties each at over two million (U.S. Census Bureau 2010). This large population makes it nonsensical to think of L.A. salsa in the singular. In reality, a tremendous range of overlapping scenes falls under the umbrella of "L.A. salsa." To understand how significant this dynamic is, consider the listings of salsa dance venues that were posted at VidaSalsera.com[3] for the greater L.A. vicinity throughout the week of July 16, 2009. On Monday, seven venues held salsa events; on Tuesday, twelve; on Wednesday, seventeen; on Thursday, thirteen; on Friday, twenty-three; on Saturday, sixteen; and on Sunday, thirteen. Separate from any studio-based social dance parties, then, as of July 16, 2009, there were 101 different salsa nights that a dancer could attend in a single week in the larger L.A. area. Even if a dancer attended two different clubs each night for a full week, this would still be only fourteen club nights, or roughly one-eighth of the possibilities in Los Angeles. Factor in all the different permutations of clubs a dancer might go to on any given night, let alone personal preferences and geographic distances, and it should be clear how absurd it is to think of *the* L.A. salsa scene.

It is equally important to recognize that culture and community are never static but continuously changing because of the wide array of people and practices involved in L.A. salsa. Additionally, each person's experiences are inherently subjective, and two hours in a salsa club does not—indeed cannot—mean the same thing to the first-time club attendee as it does to the experienced dancer, the person who grew up learning to dance at family gatherings in the backyard, or the studio-trained dancer, or mean the same thing to the native Spanish speaker as it does to the person who does not understand most salsa lyrics. It is not that there is *no* such thing as "L.A. salsa" but rather that this label means many things.[4]

Common Understandings of "L.A. Salsa"

Although some salsa scholars have recognized the inextricable links between salsa music and dance (e.g., Wade 2000; Waxer 2002a), the vast majority of salsa scholarship concerns the origins and development of salsa music beginning in 1960s New York. Certainly, there would be no salsa dancing without salsa music, but while particular musicians and musical styles are at the heart of other salsa scenes, "L.A.-style salsa" is almost universally used to refer to a particular style of dancing. Indeed, as the popularity of salsa music and dancing spread—especially among West Coast populations less familiar with Afro-Cuban rhythms—the dancing (like much of the music) changed, with the footwork and timing patterns developing in several different directions.

What is now most commonly known as L.A. style retained the original Palladium footwork (see Chapter 2), with the difference that dancers were breaking (changing direction) on the first and fifth beats and stepping on counts 1, 2, 3, 5, 6, and 7 of an eight-beat measure.[5] Similarly—and in no small part because of the dearth of Puerto Rican and Cuban émigrés (compared to New York and Miami)—early versions of Los Angeles–style salsa were more heavily influenced by West Coast swing and Latin ballroom dancing, and they evolved through crossing these influences with *cumbia*, the musical and dance tradition of the area's Mexican-, Central American–, and Colombian-origin populations. Indeed, the Colombian and Mexican[6] (and to a lesser extent Cuban) musical influence led to the on-1 timing of L.A. salsa dancing, one of the key features said to differentiate L.A. style from New York's on-2 dancing, derived from the Latin jazz influences in New York.

Originally danced more like cumbia's side-to-side motion as described by Laura Canellias (Torres et al. 2010), since the first world salsa congress in 1997,

L.A.-style salsa has been conceptualized as a flashy cross-body style[7] (based on linear forward and backward breaks) that breaks on the count of 1 and prioritizes fast speeds and tricks instead of intricate footwork (shines). Josie Neglia, world-renowned instructor and performer, describes the Los Angeles–salsa style danced at the Puerto Rico congress:

> Los Angeles—mostly partnering, danced to every song, many turns, dips and drops. Very flashy and accenting all the hits in the music with a large movement with their partner. Little or no shines and little or no torso undulations. Danced on 1. (Neglia 2002)

While critics and detractors described L.A. salsa as "flash and trash," proponents and fans raved about the style's impressive speed, power, and tricks. Indeed, as noted by Francisco Vázquez, even while criticized for using "tricks, tricks, tricks," he has also "flown around the world because of" the popularity of the style (Torres et al. 2010). Before exploring the multiple realities of L.A. salsa, however, it is important to understand how the various musical and dance traditions involved came to be recognized as "L.A.-style" salsa.

Becoming "L.A. Style" Salsa

In the same way that "salsa music" was originally a marketing label, the same can be said of "salsa dancing." When the studio Let's Dance L.A. opened in 1992, its instructors were still teaching on-2 ballroom mambo. But the early 1990s also saw Albert Torres—today the most prominent salsa promoter in the world—take charge of the salsa events at the Sportsmen's Lodge on Ventura Boulevard in Studio City. Torres brought live salsa music to Los Angeles, hiring numerous bands from New York and Puerto Rico, and had Joe Cassini, Laura Canellias, and William Ochoa give dance lessons. After Cassini organized a performance for his own birthday, participants Enio Cordoba and Terryl Jones were inspired to put together a show at the Country Western World Championships, which received rave reviews. The dancers involved included those with ballroom training—such as Cordoba and Jones, Melissa Dexter, and Steve Vasco—as well as up-and-coming salsa dancers, including Luis and Francisco Vázquez, Joby Martínez, Monica González, Edie Lewis, Tony Welch, and Thomas Montero.[8] Some of these dancers in turn formed the original and best-known salsa teams in Los Angeles: Salsa Brava (founded in 1994 by Luis Vázquez, Joby Martínez, and Janette Valenzuela) and Los Rumberos (founded in 1996 by Francisco Vázquez, Johnny Vázquez, and Monica González). Learning tricks and flips for shows, many of the young performers were (as one of the earlier L.A. instructors worded it) "like kids with a new toy," taking these moves to clubs like Sportsmen's Lodge, the Conga Room, the Mayan, Century Club, Mama Juana's, and Steven's Steakhouse.

L.A. Style Goes Global

Teaching larger and larger international workshops, Luis Vázquez, Francisco Vázquez, Martínez, González, and others were internationally promoted and marketed as teaching L.A. salsa, and their version of it—including neck drops, dips, and flips—thus started to be recognized as definitive. In much the same vein and adding to this process was the first World Salsa Congress in Puerto Rico, organized by Elí Irizarry in 1997, where this emerging generation of salsa dancers represented L.A. style on the international stage. Indeed, these dancers traveled widely to places that could not afford more established instructors, thus exposing ever-broader populations to Los Angeles–based dancers. Ultimately, such exposure proved instrumental in establishing the careers of many of these early proponents of L.A. salsa, spreading the style, and cementing the definition of L.A.-style salsa. The marketing of salsa videotapes, the Internet, population dynamics and musical predispositions in Europe, and the start of the West Coast Salsa Congress also aided in these processes. In this way, what had been considered simply choreography up until that point came to be recognized as the particular and distinctive variant of salsa dancing labeled "L.A.-style salsa."

As Salsa Brava, Neglia, and others started teaching more widely and marketing videos,[9] another element came into play: precursors to the salsa scenes in Europe mostly came by way of Cuba. Whereas only small pockets of Puerto Ricans were in Europe, many Cubans went there, since most could not legally come to the United States. This demographic variable played out in important ways, since Cuban-style salsa dance timing, although very different, predisposed Europeans to the on-1 timing of L.A. salsa.

The West Coast Salsa Congresses Albert Torres has run since 1999 were also significant in L.A. salsa's globalization. In many ways modeled after the nine Mambo Manias[10] (workshops during the day, competitions and performances at night, with an array of teachers and a band), Torres's congresses, in contrast to the first Puerto Rican congresses, showcased dancers instead of bands. The best performers were thus recruited to do shows, compete, and teach, and through Torres's active promotion, more and more dancers were exposed firsthand to L.A. salsa performers. Performances by the top L.A. dancers on videos and the Internet also drew attention and interest, since these dancers' power, speed, and tricks did not require specialized, technical knowledge to be appreciated.

Represented *As* versus Representative *Of*

Amid the discussion of how L.A.-style salsa went global, it is important not to confuse "representation" with "representativeness." Just as "salsa" was originally a marketing label, so was "L.A. style" for the performers and instructors involved in promoting themselves and their style. If the dancing being marketed—and consumed—was represented *as* L.A. salsa, this does not make it representative *of* the L.A. salsa scene. Although the two are tightly intertwined, the reputations arising from "represented as" are always oversimplifications. Thus, while the performances by L.A. salsa teams like Salsa Brava and Los Rumberos represented L.A. salsa *as* being danced with on-1 timing, this was not representative *of* Los Angeles–based instructors (such as Josie Neglia) and dancers who danced both timings—or even exclusively on-2. Conversely, many erroneously believe that San Diego is primarily an on-2 town even though the vast majority of salsa dancing in San Diego is on-1 style.

The Impact of Salsa Teams

Teams played a large role in the early development of the current salsa scenes in Los Angeles and San Diego. First, teams presented salsa as not just a social dance in Los Angeles but something to be performed. Endeavoring to establish themselves, their reputations, and their financial stake in the rapidly expanding commercial pie, early teams on the L.A. scene, like Salsa Brava, Los Rumberos, Sabor y Caché, and Royalty Salsa, were continually trying to one-up each other's performances.[11] Trying to attract students and attention, and also just having fun with what they could do, the team members brought their performance-based moves into the clubs.

On the positive side, this fueled a period of innovation and dedication, albeit one where the Colombian[12] roots of L.A. salsa all but disappeared. On the downside, however, many club dancers started trying to emulate, without proper training or practice, every trick they saw, producing a heyday of flash-and-trash salsa in Los Angeles over roughly three years in the late 1990s. One example is the neck drop, first executed in the United States by dancers Miriam (Larici) and Sandor of Forever Tango (a company born in San Francisco in 1994), where the woman drops backward toward the ground, the man catching and supporting her by the back of her neck. As executed by Miriam, the neck drop produces an elegant line based on core strength and balance. Yet less skilled dancers attempted to copy this move without the requisite training; Terryl Jones explains:

> For several years wannabes have been doing this drop on two legs, thighs wide open, crotch to the audience. Ladies get a clue!! Do we really need to be in these gynecological positions? Not only is this a lower skill level[;] it is just low class. (Jones, n.d.)

In an online discussion at SalsaForums.com, L.A. *salsera* "Brownskin818" further describes how teams affected the character of L.A. salsa:

> L.A. is majorly different from NY in that the schools/studios are mostly separate from teams. The studios never seem to put together reputable

teams, and the "reputable" teams never seem to offer classes. It seems that in NY, reputable teams are a product of the schools' classes. ("Brownskin818" 2009)

As she went on to note, this atmosphere engendered (a) a general separation between the teams and the salsa schools and studios, (b) little long-term loyalty to a particular instructor, and (c) a relative dearth of advanced classes because of the lack of long-term students.

Given the sheer number of dancers in the L.A. area, only a small fraction ever ended up dancing on a team. In contrast, the introduction of teams into smaller salsa scenes often profoundly altered the social dynamics of the local scene. For example, the current shape of salsa in San Diego cannot be understood save in reference to the impact of the team Salsa y Fuego, the first dance company in San Diego and the first on-2 team in California. From a marketing perspective, the on-2 emphasis set Salsa y Fuego apart from all the other salsa instructors in San Diego at the time. The team's 2001 Red and White routine, performed at the third annual West Coast Salsa Congress, was structured as a showdown between on-1 "salsa" and on-2 "mambo," showcasing both timings.[13] As noted by former team member Raquel Gómez, this routine "put San Diego on the map" (2011). Salsa y Fuego's legacy includes (1) the style of salsa danced in San Diego, (2) the lineages of San Diego salsa, (3) San Diego's salsa reputation, and (4) a shift in the social dynamics between local dancers.

The most immediate and obvious impact of Salsa y Fuego was the introduction of Eddie Torres–style on-2 dancing to San Diego, including bringing in guest instructors like Seaon Stylist. Its offspring, Majesty in Motion, has since proved a training ground for many of San Diego's top dancers, including Deseo Dance Company founder Serena Cuevas and Alma Latina dance company cofounder Sergio Jasso. Thus, many of the most visible San Diego dancers trained in and performed on-2 style, leading to San Diego's reputation as an on-2 town—even though, as noted, the majority of salsa in San Diego has always been on-1 style.

Perhaps most significant of all, however, was the tectonic shift in the social landscape. The introduction of teams to San Diego introduced "class" differences between local dancers; now there were those who had made it onto teams and everybody else. Teams continued to expand, split, and inspire others, and they made a larger impact in San Diego, with its relatively small participation base, than in Los Angeles.[14] Nonetheless, the competition scene in Los Angeles amplified the performance-driven mentality of L.A. salsa many times over.

Competitions

The major impact of teams in Los Angeles involved shifting salsa from being a social activity to being performance oriented, and this tendency found its culmination in salsa competitions. Competitions ultimately drove the salsa scene in Los Angeles in a way that seems to have occurred nowhere else in the world, not simply because of their presence but because of their scale and scope. While other locations may draw more contestants and spectators—such as the one thousand contestants and fifteen thousand spectators reported at the world qualifying event in Cali in 2007 (Pratt 2007)—the prize money available in Los Angeles means that this city regularly draws more top competitors than any other. Prizes range from the $5,000 offered by the Mayan World Salsa Competition to the $10,000 awarded by Steven's Steakhouse and the Granada in each of their competitions.[15] Inspiring competitiveness and greater technical proficiency through their financial incentives, these competitions also draw in many spectators—and generate large online followings of interested dancers from around the world, who eagerly await video clips and then discuss and debate them in online forums such as www.SalsaForums.com.

The first Mayan competition, in 1996, demonstrates the impact of such events. The winners, Steve Vasco and Natalie Mavor, were relative outsiders to the salsa scene but had ballroom training, as did the second-place couple. That these two couples placed ahead of L.A. salsa teachers cast the perceived cleanliness of ballroom-trained technique[16] as the pinnacle of competitive success. This increasing awareness of image (lauded by many) led on the one hand to more defined technique and more precise performances but on the other to what many see as a more sterile performance, ever more removed from salsa's Afro-Caribbean roots.

What is viewed as "clean" and "professional" by some is regarded as overly "produced" and "affected" by others. Increased standardization means most L.A. dancers have come to dance in the regimented slot pattern, and while the increasingly complex wraps and patterns adapted from hustle and West Coast swing are applauded by some, they are lamented by those who feel today's dancers rush through steps with little, if any, rhythmic body action. Salsa Brava cofounder Janette Valenzuela, for instance, offered the following critique after judging the 2009 Granada amateur semifinals and the 2009 Mayan Amateur Finals:

> Who ever [sic] got the message that if you are in the amateur category you should be doing nothing but spins, poses, and tricks and to try to do them like the professionals? . . .
> After the contest, the other judges and I were deliberating the results. Joe Casini (one of the judges) said it best and I do quote him. "Where did these kids think they were supposed to do tricks in an amateur contest? None of them danced salsa. They were dancing adagio. What they did was adagio to salsa music. The professional moves they were attempting takes [sic] years of training and years to perfect." (Valenzuela 2009)

The problem is that the professional divisions serve as the model of the best salsa dancing for amateur competitors.[17] Most telling, however, is the implicit acceptance of salsa dancing as appropriate for competition. The Mayan competition thus had long-lasting significance for salsa in Los Angeles.

Continuing Consequences

Competitions have established certain stylistic expectations and norms because the most extreme performances—those with the fastest, sharpest, biggest dips, tricks, and risks—received the greatest accolades from audiences and, often, the highest judges' marks. Impetus for excellence and inspiration for some, this same climate has proven intimidating and alienating for others. Because of the performance-based tradition set by the early teams and competitions, combined with the influence of nearby Hollywood and the possibility that each person entering the club might be a promoter or producer, dancers started trying to stand out. As Edie "the Salsa Freak" Lewis noted at the 2010 L.A. Salsa Congress, Los Angeles has always been one of the few places where someone could ultimately make anywhere from $100 to $100,000 by doing one flip at a club (Torres et al. 2010).

At its best, this practice translated into the performances that made L.A. style a hot commodity at salsa congresses around the world. At its worst, it translated into a view of "salsa as spectacle," in which being seen emerged as an implicit cornerstone of going out to clubs, and many club-goers gave little or no thought to those around them on the dance floor. Indeed, the first thing I saw upon walking into the social dancing in the main room at the 2009 L.A. Salsa Congress was a local salsera suspended in a "fish lift," wherein her partner held her inverted, with her head at other dancers' knee level and her high-heeled shoes at other dancers' face level. Like even riskier aerial lifts, flips, and tricks, such moves were designed for staged performances and are hazardous when executed on the social dance floor. While some salsa observers (e.g., García 2007) have decried this prevalence of dips and tricks in L.A. salsa as structurally misogynistic, I find this a problematic oversimplification[18] given both the complex backstory from which such performance-rooted materials arose and the prohibition of lifts, dips, and tricks by popular L.A. venues such as the Granada—regularly attracting well over 500–650 people every Friday and Saturday night.

Appearance, Clothing, Gender, and Ethnicity

L.A. salsa is further characterized by interrelated issues of appearance, dress, gender, and ethnicity, especially as these arise amid the highly body- and image-conscious aesthetics of Southern California, Hollywood, and performance-driven L.A. salsa. Since "dress is both an indicator and a producer of gender" (Barnes and Eicher [1992] 1997: 7), attire on the L.A. salsa scene not only reflects cultural norms informed by "Hollywoodized" versions of overtly gendered and explicitly sexualized identities and appearances but also constructs them, as dancers concomitantly meet and model local standards. "Young, thin, tan, and in" is a description of how one should look in Southern California that has carried across into salsa (especially for women, paralleling larger social dichotomies), and this standard is deeply and insidiously pervasive at all levels. Grooming and clothing are then layered over these bodily standards, and taking them together, appearance plays a tremendous role in setting the social salsa stage—at least until one's salsa skills have had the chance to "speak" for themselves.

Nonetheless, it is important to note that all such dynamics are subject to the multifarious nature of the salsa scene in Los Angeles. One version of L.A.-style salsa, for instance, involves exaggerated flips, dips, and tricks and uses as the uniform of choice what I have heard many dancers refer to as ghetto-style clothing.[19] Yet while this style is popular among some L.A. dancers, it would be erroneous to say that this style is representative of either L.A. dancing or grooming since neither are even allowed at the Granada, one of the busiest salsa clubs in Los Angeles since it was first opened in 2003.[20] Opinions on the Granada's policies vary, but their very existence makes sense in the context of such practices at other local venues and further illustrates the scale and scope of participation and practices that make it impossible to paint the L.A. salsa scene with a single brush.

As with gender, the topics of race and ethnicity must also be contextualized within the larger Los Angeles–Hollywood scenes framing L.A. salsa standards and practices. Here too the complex nature of L.A. salsa is significant: different socioeconomic and ethnic groups typically live in different areas and frequent different clubs, thus experiencing very different versions of L.A. salsa. Cindy García, for instance, offers the following critique: "To be considered desirable pan-Latina dance partners . . . salseras must dislocate their dance techniques from Mexico . . . or be accused of 'dancing like a Mexican,'" and she goes on to suggest that "many salseras attempt to disguise bodily features that could locate them as unskilled, Mexican immigrant labor" (García 2008: 201). Certainly, the highly racially charged atmosphere and larger social tensions regarding immigration in Los Angeles cannot be entirely divorced from attitudes and experiences in the salsa scene, but other factors are also at play.

First, the majority of Latino/a dancers in Los Angeles are not from Mexico, and the implicit assertion of Mexican salsa as "the authentic salsa" belies the historicity of salsa's Afro-Cuban and Afro-Caribbean roots, its unique (re)configuration everywhere it is danced, and the multiplicity of salsa styles that "undercut any kind of simplistic Latin/non-Latin dichotomy" (Bosse 2008: 48). Likewise, while the accusation of "dancing like a Mexican" may be made from a racist perspective, "Mexican" may also be used as a gloss for a type of family-socialized (versus instructor-trained) dancing style. What is being critiqued, then, is not ethnicity itself but rather a "movement dialect" (Bosse 2008: 48) that may signal cultural affiliation but not dance-specific dedication and that may not be compatible with the trained-style characteristic of the current L.A. scene.[21]

It follows that what seems most accurate is that authenticity often serves as "a form of symbolic capital, to be used in asserting power" (Lindholm 2008: 91),[22] gets deployed in considerations of salsa's origins and the legitimacy of different salsa dance styles, and always unfolds across multiple levels.[23] It is for exactly this reason that one Latino/a dancer can be dismissed as "Mexican" (per García's critique), while in another case the same ethnicity may be considered essential for true competence. Many, for instance, cast being Latino/a as "having [salsa] in your blood," and Bosse describes this very sentiment when she writes that, for members of a salsa dance team in central Illinois, "it was generally understood that lack of Latin American heritage was an essential barrier to gaining complete fluency in the dance" (2008: 40). Just as Judith Hamera asserts for concert and amateur dance practices in Los Angeles, salsa too (in all of its locations and forms) is perhaps best understood as a laboratory "for examining and revisioning the complex interrelationships between gender, sexuality, race, class, and culture in urban life" (2007: 1), allowing many dancers to "try on new identities . . . explore and push boundaries of the self" (Bosse 2008: 58).

Conclusion

Dancing, as Marta Savigliano notes, "starts out way before the actual dancing" (1998: 105). Thus, this chapter has examined the context and history undergirding L.A. salsa today, including its distinctive (and often distinguishing) norms and values. More than just a historical trajectory, however, this chapter describes the complex social and cultural contexts within which dancers cocreated L.A. salsa. Equally important is that salsa—like all dance forms—represents a deeply embodied system of practices, performances, techniques, and appraisals. The inherently physical nature of dance, as well as its participatory nature, has ramifications that are crucial for understanding L.A. salsa as it is experienced by the dancers in question.[24]

At the most basic level, leaders and followers depend on each other to learn and enact their respective parts, regularly cocreating the meanings and experiences of each dance anew. Perhaps even more important is the simple fact that salsa, like many participatory practices, involves interpersonal interaction. If larger dance-based codes construct something of a translocal "salsa world,"[25] this does not change the fact that most people's participation in this world is mostly local. One of the ways this plays out is in the forging of communal identity and identification, as in William McNeill's theory of muscular bonding (1995). Whether intended as such or not, the performative facet of dance is often about enhancement of the collective (Spencer 1985: 30; see, e.g., Turner 1987; Washabaugh 1998) and is always linked to social and ethical standards (Schechner 1987).

While the size and complexity of the salsa scene in Los Angeles make it impossible to suggest any definitive answers about L.A. salsa, this chapter has provided some explanations for how it has developed into its current form. First is a confluence of historical factors and unique dynamics. Second are the circumstances whereby L.A. salsa arrived on the world stage and the role it has played in the globalization of salsa dancing ever since. Embedded within and particularizing these larger frameworks, dancers' experiences demonstrate the always personal nature of the larger dynamics in question.

I opened this chapter using Redfield's concept of great and little religious traditions as a metaphor for salsa relative to its local L.A. iteration. In line with this religion-based metaphor, I then considered what might be called the "salsa syncretism" in Los Angeles (and California more generally), including the reconciliation between incoming music and dance trends with more local tendencies and dance practices. The materials presented here well demonstrate sociologist Roland Robertson's (1995) "glocalization," whereby global forces take shape in and through local forms. If the regionalization of larger practices in Los Angeles represents an important point of analysis, the other side of this coin is equally significant: the globalization of salsa—particularly through congresses and the Internet—built on the performance- and competition-based style and mentality of Los Angeles. A final and closely connected issue concerns how "people often do not experience their aesthetic beliefs as merely arbitrary and conventional; they feel that they are natural, proper and moral" (Becker (1974) 2001: 75). This point is an important one, as it helps explain the vehemence with which conflicting aesthetic standards often clash, such as between proponents and opponents of what is commonly recognized as L.A.-style salsa.[26] Like any other culture and community, the salsa scene in Los Angeles is constantly changing, and if its past cannot predict its future, whatever emerges will still be inexplicable save for what has come before.

NOTES

Acknowledgments: I owe special thanks to Enio Cordoba, Liz Lira, and Steve Vasco for their time, insights, and perspectives on L.A. salsa. Thanks too to those who went for "breakfast" from 5:00 to 7:00 A.M. Sunday morning after the 2009 L.A. Salsa Congress. Much of my own thinking started to crystallize around the discussions at the table, including the different perspectives of the L.A. regulars versus the out-of-town congress attendees. I am also indebted to Enio Cordoba for generously offering his time and assistance with the historical materials in the section "Becoming 'L.A. Style' Salsa"; to nine-time World Salsa Champion Liz Lira for her insights regarding the role and significance of the competitive circuit to the overall salsa scene in Los Angeles; and to Steve Vasco, winner of the first Salsa Championships at the Mayan with Natalie Mavor, for sharing his insights into the character of dancing and competition in Los Angeles over the past thirteen years.

1. This was the Second Annual West Coast Salsa Congress, at the time promoted by Albert Torres and Bacardi as part of the Congreso Mundial de la Salsa (World Salsa Congress) tour. Since 2001 Albert Torres has been the sole promoter for the annual Los Angeles Salsa Congress.

2. See Salazar 2002 for more on the early music, musicians, and venues in New York; also see Rondón 2008 and Chapter 2 herein.

3. See http://www.vidasalsera.com/salsaclubs.htm for current postings.

4. Exemplifying how labels and distinctions are not used in the same way everywhere salsa is danced is the term "New York style." Although it is commonly defined by breaking (changing direction) on count 2 in the United States, while in Denmark in 2003 I found that "New York style" was being used as a gloss for cross-body (versus circular) dancing.

5. This is in contrast with the original Palladium Mambo, ballroom mambo, and Eddie Torres's mambo (see Chapter 2).

6. For more on the popularity of cumbia dancing in Mexico, along the border area, and among Mexican Americans, see Hutchinson 2007.

7. Cross-body styles are in contrast to the circular Cuban, or *casino*, style, which also tends to be more physical and momentum based in its lead and follow connections and for many also tends to be associated with more machismo, especially in how the woman's wrists (versus hands) may be grasped (Lewis, n.d.; Chapter 6 herein).

8. I spell Vázquez, Martínez, and González with accent marks for consistency; however, on the web and in promotional materials, these dancers typically drop the accent marks from their names.

9. The first L.A. dancer to sell videotapes, Neglia was also the first vendor to advertise on the then newly established Salsaweb.com (Rose Knows 2002) and as of 2010 had sold over one million videos (Torres et al. 2010).

10. First held in 1989, Mambo Manias ran through 1998 (officially becoming an annual event in 1992) with seven of the nine held in Los Angeles, one in Miami, and one in San Francisco.

11. Importantly, and despite such one-upping, Edie Lewis—who has been to sixty-five countries—notes that Los Angeles is the "only city on earth [where] we [instructors] all get along" and that the early L.A. dancers never criticized each other's dancing, a practice that only "changed when [it] became a 'business'" (Torres et al. 2010).

12. Contrary to what one might expect on the basis of geographic proximity, most informants cited Colombian influence, not Mexican.

13. The theme and the slick performance of this routine were particularly noteworthy amid the rampant and often contentious debates between adherents of the on-1 and on-2 styles typical of the time.

14. The emerging L.A. and San Diego salsa scenes had surprisingly little overlap, although certainly some San Diego dancers regularly went to dance in Los Angeles, and a few San Diego instructors brought in top L.A. talent (such as the late Michael Snyder, who, before his untimely death on February 27, 2001, brought both Solomon Rivera and Josie Neglia to teach at his studio). The relative lack of overlap is best understood as the result of the large population in Los Angeles and its geographic proximity to San Diego. The population of Los Angeles sufficed to support all the city's instructors, whereas San Diego salsa teachers generally were not steering their own students to instructors based only a couple of hours away. Similarly, the initial trend of San Diego teams to dance on-2 style can largely be understood as a means of differentiating themselves from the well-known L.A. on-1 teams.

15. The largest prize money ($20,000) actually comes from World Salsa Championships, produced by the Salsa Seven for ESPN International, but it has yet to have a fixed annual location.

16. The argument I make here parallels that made by Juliet McMains: "Because, until recently, there was little precedent in Latin America for teaching social dance in formal classes, salsa professionals have relied heavily on models created by the ballroom dance industry for counting their rhythms, breaking down actions, and naming their steps"

(2009: 311). Likewise, the lack of precedent in salsa for formal competition and judging put ballroom's European-based criteria and standards (see Marion 2008: 39–52), such as "clean" dancing, at the fore.

17. The category of amateur salsa competitors itself is problematic, with many competitions defining professionals as those making a living in the dance industry and amateurs as all others. Some competitions offer a semipro division, for those whose primary occupation is not dance related but who earn some income through dance. Nonetheless, many dancers who train and perform on professional teams (even internationally) end up competing as amateurs.

18. This is not to say that stereotyped gender roles do not exist in L.A. salsa, which they certainly do, or to claim that sexist standards and practices are not part of the salsa scene, which they are.

19. While often overlapping, ghetto-style clothing and more acrobatic-style dancing are not coterminous elements in the L.A. salsa scene.

20. The Granada's dress code for "tastefully casual upscale evening wear" (Salsa Central, n.d.) reads:

> No T-shirts
> No sleeveless vests or tank tops for men
> No ripped or oversize jeans
> No baseball caps
> No wallet chains or ghetto gear
> Jeans, collarless shirts, hats and tennis shoes at our discretion. Typically if you
> are wearing any two of these discretionary items you will not be allowed
> in. (i.e., Jeans and Tennis Shoes = No) This dress code applies at all times.

21. Alma Latina dance company's Tijuana-based teams and dancers (which predate its San Diego– and Los Angeles–based teams), for instance, are never described as "dancing like Mexicans."

22. See Lindholm 2008: 88–97 for further discussions of dance authenticity and national identity.

23. Norman Urquía (2004) makes a parallel point in describing and differentiating ideas about ownership between non-Latin dancers and salsa teachers in London's salsa scene.

24. The people discussed in this chapter are the dancers who define the community through their ongoing patronage of clubs, studios, instructors, DJs, and bands—not the many people who only occasionally frequent salsa clubs or take a few lessons.

25. Following sociologist Howard Becker's (1984) notion of "art worlds," one might conceive of a "salsa world" given ever-expanding

> Line-ups of salsa congresses and festivals around the world
> Dissemination of salsa content online
> Traffic to and participation in salsa-related discussion forums (such as www
> .SalsaForums.com—where I am the primary site administrator—which
> has active site moderators in Germany, Sweden, Tokyo, and the United
> States and former moderators from Australia, Romania, and the United
> Kingdom)

26. This same dynamic also helps explain recurrent arguments regarding on-2 style being better than on-1, or cross-body-style salsa as better than circular-style salsa. One fortunate effect of salsa's globalization seems to be a growing familiarity with, and hence greater acceptance of, multiple salsa styles.

REFERENCES

Barnes, Ruth, and Joanne B. Eicher, eds. (1992) 1997. *Dress and Gender: Making and Meaning*. Oxford: Berg.

Becker, H. S. (1974) 2001. "Art as Collective Action." In *Popular Culture: Production and Consumption*, ed. C. Lee Harington and Denise D. Bielby, 67–79. Oxford: Blackwell.

———. 1984. *Art Worlds*. Berkeley: University of California Press.

Bosse, Joanna. 2008. "Salsa Dance and the Transformation of Style: An Ethnographic Study of Movement and Meaning in a Cross-Cultural Context." *Dance Research Journal* 40 (1): 45–64.

"Brownskin818." 2009. Post in "True to Your School" discussion. *SalsaForums*, July 10. Available at http://www.salsaforums.com/showthread.php?t=11193.

García, Cindy. 2007. "Un/Sequined Corporealities and the Politics of Immigration in Salsa Clubs." Paper presented at the Congress on Research in Dance 40th Anniversary Conference, New York City, November 10.

———. 2008. "'Don't Leave Me, Celia!' Salsera Homosociality and Pan-Latina Corporealities." *Women and Performance* 18 (3): 199–213.

Gómez, Raquel. 2011. Personal communication. May 29.

Hamera, Judith. 2007. *Dancing Communities: Performance, Difference, and Connection in the Global City*. New York: Palgrave Macmillan.

Hutchinson, Sydney. 2007. *From Quebradita to Duranguense: Dance in Mexican American Youth Culture*. Tucson: University of Arizona Press.

Jones, Terryl. n.d. "Controversial Moves, Controversial Contests." *Dance Forums*. Available at http://www.dance-forums.com/threads/controversial-moves-controversial-contests.463.

Lewis, Edie. n.d. "What Is the Difference between Puerto Rican Style, Cuban Style, L.A. Style, Israeli Style, Colombian Style, and the New York Style?" *Edie the Salsa Freak*. Previously available at http://www.salsafreak.com/stories/dance_styles.htm (accessed March 17, 2003).

Lindholm, Charles. 2008. *Culture and Authenticity*. Malden, MA: Blackwell.

Marion, Jonathan S. 2006. "Beyond Ballroom: Activity as Performance, Embodiment, and Identity." *Human Mosaic* 36 (2): 7–16.

———. 2008. *Ballroom: Culture and Costume in Competitive Dance*. Oxford: Berg.

———. 2012. "Circulation as Destination: Considerations from the Translocal Culture of Competitive Ballroom Dance." *Journal for the Anthropological Study of Human Movement* 17 (2).

McMains, Juliet. 2009. "Dancing Latin/Latin Dancing." In *Ballroom, Boogie, Shimmy Sham, Shake: A Social and Popular Dance Reader*, ed. Julie Malnig, 302–322. Champaign: University of Illinois Press.

McNeill, William H. 1995. *Keeping Together in Time: Dance and Drill in Human History*. Cambridge, MA: Harvard University Press.

Neglia, Josie. 2002. "The Different Styles of Salsa and Mambo." *LatinDance.com*, June 14. Available at http://www.latindance.com/life_as_a_professional_dancer.htm#Different%20Styles%20of%20Salsa%20and%20Mambo.

Pratt, Timothy. 2007. "Dancing for Gold." *Hispanic*, March, p. 46.

Redfield, Robert. 1956. *Peasant Society and Culture*. Chicago: University of Chicago Press.

Robertson, Roland. 1995. "Glocalization: Time-Space and Homogeneity-Heterogeneity." In *Global Modernities*, ed. Mike Featherstone, Scott Lash, and Roland Robertson, 25–44. London: Sage.

Rondón, César Miguel. 2008. *The Book of Salsa: A Chronicle of Urban Music from the Caribbean to New York City*, trans. Frances R. Aparicio and Jackie White. Chapel Hill: University of North Carolina Press.

Rose Knows. 2002. "Up Close and Personal with . . . Josie Neglia, the Princess of Salsa." *ToSalsa.com*, January. Available at http://www.tosalsa.com/goto.asp?http://www.to salsa.com/forum/interviews/interview020118roseknows_josieneglia.html.

Salazar, Max. 2002. *Mambo Kingdom: Latin Music in New York*. New York: Schirmer.

Salsa Central. n.d. "Salsa Central Dress Code." Previously available at http://www.lets dancela.com/salsacentral/ (accessed February 25, 2011).

Savigliano, Marta. 1998. "From Wallflowers to Femmes Fatales: Tango and the Performance of Passionate Femininity." In *The Passion of Music and Dance*, ed. William Washabaugh, 103–110. Oxford: Berg.

Schechner, Richard. 1987. "Victor Turner's Last Adventure." In *The Anthropology of Performance*, by Victor Turner, 7–20. New York: PAJ.

Spencer, Paul. 1985. *Society and the Dance: The Social Anthropology of Process and Performance*. Cambridge: Cambridge University Press.

Torres, Albert, Francisco Vázquez, Rogelio Moreno, Laura Canellias, Josie Neglia, Janette Valenzuela, and Edie Lewis. 2010. "History of Los Angeles Salsa Scene." Lecture given at Los Angeles Salsa Congress, May 28, Los Angeles, California.

Turner, Victor W. 1987. *The Anthropology of Performance*. New York: PAJ.

Urquia, Norman. 2004. "'Doin' It Right': Contested Authenticity in London's Salsa Scene." In *Music Scenes: Local, Translocal, and Virtual*, ed. Andy Bennet and Richard A. Peterson, 96–113. Nashville, TN: Vanderbilt University Press.

U.S. Census Bureau. 2010. "2010 Demographic Profile." *2010 Population Finder*. Available at https://www.census.gov/popfinder/?fl=06:06037:06059:06073:06065:06071.

Valenzuela, Janette. 2009. "Competitions in the Eyes of a Judge." Available at http://www .salsaforums.com/threads/judging-at-mayan-and-competitions.10834/.

Wade, Peter. 2000. *Music, Race and Nation: Música Tropical in Colombia*. Chicago: University of Chicago Press.

Washabaugh, William. 1998. *The Passion of Music and Dance: Body, Gender and Sexuality*. New York: Berg.

Waxer, Lise. 2002a. *The City of Musical Memory: Salsa, Record Grooves, and Popular Culture in Cali, Colombia*. Middletown, CT: Wesleyan University Press.

———, ed. 2002b. *Situating Salsa: Global Markets and Local Meanings in Latin Popular Music*. New York: Routledge.

5

Small-Town Cosmopolitans

Salsa Dance in Rural America

Joanna Bosse

RICK

It's close to 4:00 A.M., and we're halfway home from a night of salsa dancing at Inta's in Chicago, riding along southbound I-57. Everyone is sacked out in the back, except Rick,[1] who keeps me company while I drive. My willingness to serve as designated driver is one of the ways I have ingratiated myself with this group of dancers. Rick is talking of his family, his Cuban father and white American mother, growing up in a well-to-do northern Chicago suburb, and his newfound love of salsa. He says, "My father and his brothers, when they get together they tap out rhythms on the table, they dance with the women, and speak a little Spanish. And all growing up, I didn't want to have anything to do with that. It seemed old-fashioned. I was playing baseball and hanging out with my friends." It was only in graduate school, after being introduced to salsa by his Surinamese girlfriend Maria (who learned about it the year before from her Colombian friend Angel), that he became interested in anything "Latin." He then began dancing and collecting salsa recordings, learning Spanish, and taking conga lessons. In two years' time, he became one of the most popular salsa deejays in town and started a salsa band, Adelante, with two non-Latino ethnomusicology doctoral students. His aunt told me that his family is surprised at the transformation, and so is Rick to some degree. "I barely even noticed that I was Latin before, but now it means something to me, and I'm . . . well, protective of it. I'm wary of outsiders trying to figure it out," he says pointedly to me, an outsider trying to figure it out. We talk on about "Latinness" and outsiders, and I ask him about his favorite musicians and dancers. "Take, for example, Enrique," he continued. Enrique had just won yet another local dance competition earlier in the week, and he was also trying to break into the dance deejay business. "Don't get me wrong, I like Enrique and I think he is a good dancer," he says. "But he's not really dancing salsa. It's cumbia. *But no one around here knows that."*

ENRIQUE

Enrique eyes me on the periphery of the dance floor, sidles up beside me, slips his hand into mine, and we head to the dance floor for a popular song by Marc Anthony. A twenty-something Mexican immigrant, Enrique wears dress slacks and a dress shirt, unbuttoned enough to show the edge of an indecipherable tattoo and three large gold chains. Both ears shine with multiple piercings, and he wears several rings and bracelets. His short sleeves reveal several other tattoos; one, a small firefly, is for his father, an electrician in Mexico City.

It is clear that he misses his home and his family, a feeling magnified by the salsa music pumping through the sound system here in a club in rural Illinois. "I love salsa. It is my life, my heritage, you know? From the time I was this tall [he gestures to his waist], there was salsa in my house and we danced." For Enrique, dancing salsa was a way to connect to his homeland and his family far away. He was aware of salsa's Cuban roots, but this in no way hindered the music's ability to signify his own heritage, his homeland, and his family. He is one of the best salsa dancers in town, and we light into what will be the best salsa of my night.

Enrique works as a kitchen manager at a local T.G.I. Fridays, alongside two of his brothers. In a few years he will earn his American citizenship and request a transfer to an Indianapolis restaurant in the hopes of achieving his goal of promotion to house manager. "They don't usually want to put us [Mexicans] up in the front of the house," explains Enrique, "but I'm working on my English and my . . . you know, my presentation [with the word, he taps his chest with his hands and stands up taller, broadening his shoulders]. I think I can do it." Several years after this conversation I visited Enrique on my way through Indianapolis to visit family, and though he was still working as a kitchen manager in a new T.G.I. Fridays, he remained hopeful that a promotion would soon follow.

Overview

Implicit in the preceding case studies is the conflict that arose in the local salsa scene of Champaign-Urbana, Illinois, in the late 1990s. There, as in just about every local salsa context, competing notions of ownership and authenticity permeated the scene, but in Champaign-Urbana they took on a cast specific to the locale. This chapter explores the particularities of this local salsa scene, mooring it less to the discourse of ethnic identity and more to the context of class and commerce. While the ownership of cultural practices is commonly understood in the academy as an issue of identity politics, true here as well, it is also the case that ownership involves the tangible and material concerns of cash and access. This chapter considers salsa performance, and the discourse of authenticity that often surrounds it, in light of economic realities specific to the local entertainment industries in small-town America.

A great deal of literature on salsa music and dance highlights its potential in the expression of pan-Latino solidarity and, more recently, as a global phenomenon found across the Americas, Europe, and Asia.[2] Many of these studies of local and translocal salsa scenes focus on urban, usually coastal, contexts. This chapter "situate[s] salsa" performance (Waxer 2002b) in a different setting, focusing on the salsa scene in the small, midwestern university town of Champaign-Urbana, Illinois. I thus want to shift the discussion from an understanding of salsa performance as a site for the articulation of ethnic identity (whether regional or pan-Latino in nature) to an examination of how the particular configuration of economic and social conditions in central Illinois led to a different type of local salsa scene and an emerging cosmopolitan formation.

As Patria Román-Velázquez notes, despite salsa's stylistic variation and "semi-nomadic" character, "academic writers and commentators have sought to categorise salsa as primarily Puerto Rican, Cuban, Latin-Caribbean or more broadly 'Latin'. Trying to label salsa in such a way can be viewed as an attempt to claim it for a singular identity, to fix its rather fluid character and to limit its capability to be transformed as it travels" (2002: 212). This case study presents one way salsa can be transformed by its travels into the heartland of the American Midwest. Competing social factions within the social space of Champaign-Urbana deployed different discursive strategies that linked salsa performance variably to regionally specific Latino identities, pan-Latino identity, and a universal (nonethnic) cosmopolitan identity at different times in a struggle to compete in the local entertainment marketplace. In other words, this case study highlights how identity politics were deployed strategically by certain individuals for specific *economic* goals. The particular cosmopolitan social alliances that were forged through participation in salsa dancing were engineered by a particular set of economic interests: building and maintaining a market— a consumer demographic—for salsa, which, in the end, worked to minimize salsa's well-documented potential to articulate pan-Latino identity.[3]

In this case, shared class-based cosmopolitan interests bound middle- and upper-class salsa dancers, regardless of their racial identity, and placed them in opposition to the Mexican laborers who served as the initial economic engine that fueled salsa performance. Thus, this chapter demonstrates how class and cosmopolitanism trumped ethnic affiliation and salsa's role as a generator of pan-Latino solidarity and that this set of social alignments was the result of the structural configuration of the Champaign-Urbana entertainment industry. Within this particular salsa scene, cosmopolitan values and aesthetic dispositions were articulated and valorized through discourses surrounding musical taste, dance style, and physiosocial comportment. After first introducing the region and the particulars of the local entertainment industry, I then discuss the conventions of salsa performance within this context and how salsa served to signify and constitute a different set of strategic affiliations that bolstered and preserved cosmopolitan sensibilities.

This work is based on ethnographic fieldwork in the dance clubs of central Illinois that took place in the middle to late 1990s with a follow-up trip in 2005. Champaign-Urbana served as the central hub for my research, with spokes radiating out to Indianapolis, Saint Louis, and Chicago.

Seated in the heart of the midwestern agricultural beltway, the twin-city region of Champaign-Urbana, Illinois, is the most densely populated area in the county, with a combined population of 100,000 (county population 176,094).[4] Graduate or professional degrees are held by 19.4 percent of the population, which is more than double the U.S. average of 8.9 percent. The region is predominantly white (78.8 percent) with an estimated 4 percent Latino population (2.9 percent, according to the U.S. Census Bureau). The region witnessed a rapid increase in the Latino population between 1990 and 2000, with the 2000 U.S. census reporting a 79 percent increase for the period. These figures do not document the migrant agricultural workers who have traveled to the region every summer for decades to help with harvest. Among resident Latinos are two distinct groups of concern for this argument: (1) working-class Latinos, most of whom are from Mexico, constituting 57 percent of local Latino population, and (2) students associated with the University of Illinois, both domestic and international, who identify as Latin American (very few that I worked with identified as Mexican).

A triangulation of interests here merits attention: (1) a highly educated, upper-class population, predominantly white but comprising a significant minority of internationals, (2) a working-class resident Mexican population, and (3) a substantive group of college students who identified as Latin American. All of these groups were living and working—and dancing, deejaying, and performing salsa—in an otherwise white, rural, agricultural region. Studies of cosmopolitans and cosmopolitanism have provided a helpful rubric for understanding how a shared set of class-based values joined two of these groups, the local resident elites (predominantly white but with international membership) and the Latin American college students, in opposition to the local working-class Mexicans who (it was believed) were poised to dominate local salsa performance.[5] For the remainder of the chapter, I call members of this new alliance "local cosmopolitans" or "salsero cosmopolitans."

In contemporary contexts, most cosmopolitans hail from the economic or educated elite of their society and affirm translocal ideologies and practices that have been cultivated in and distributed from urban centers, such as "the political validity of the nation-state, the use of money, and industrial production" (Turino 2000: 10). In terms of the arts, I add to this general list a preference for complexity, virtuosity, and restraint within linear, goal-oriented forms, as well as aesthetic distance, control, and discipline, all couched in the discourse of sophistication. Genres that make their way into particular cosmopolitan formations are generally predisposed to this set of stylistic features or are soon modified to be consistent with them.

It might be best to consider cosmopolitan formations on a type of continuum. Most of the dancers I worked with in Illinois were cosmopolitan, and they were aligned aesthetically and socially in this regard. The major exception to this was the community of working-class Mexican dancers, who varied in terms of the degree to which they subscribed to cosmopolitan values. A minority of Mexican dancers, like Enrique, were interested in and ultimately able to assimilate to a limited degree with local cosmopolitan elites through strategic and purposeful relationship building. Most Mexicans dancers, however, embraced multiple signifiers of their lower-class status, displayed no outward interest in assimilating with local elites, and did not even suggest an awareness of the campaign being waged against them. Generally, the Mexicans I worked with in central Illinois, whether aspiring or not, were actively excluded from leadership positions in local cosmopolitan formations, as this case study documents.

The translocal and syncretic nature of salsa lent itself to absorption into a particular cosmopolitan formation, one that speaks to the lay usage of the term "cosmopolitan" as worldly and well traveled and serves as a positive musical signifier of this cosmopolitan formation. So while it continued to connote Latino identity and shifting notions of home, especially for local Latinos, it also became a powerful signifier of a particular type of hip cosmopolitanism for a core group of ethnically diverse local elites. To this latter constituency, fluency in salsa music and dance communicated a fluency in foreign lands and urban centers—substantial currency among cosmopolitans living in a quiet, bucolic college town in central Illinois.[6]

Salsa in Champaign-Urbana, Illinois

Salsa performance emerged in the area in the mid-1990s. Its rise to popularity was commonly credited to Maria, a Surinamese (of mixed European descent) graduate student in business who was said to have single-handedly started the local salsa craze. It was while living in Illinois that she was introduced to the genre by her boyfriend at the time, Angel, a Colombian graduate student. The two generated a significant amount of tax-free revenue (hundreds of dollars per week) by teaching salsa classes and persuading local clubs to include a salsa night, or "*salsa-teca*," in their weekly rotation of events. Maria was charming, gregarious, and generous. She was also savvy when it came to negotiating with club owners, and she convinced them of the marketability of salsa-tecas by putting it in terms they could understand.

Through teaching dance classes and networking, she was also instrumental in bringing newcomers from the local university population, Latinos and non-Latinos, into the dance scene. The small cadre of salsa aficionados that Maria represented could best be described as cosmopolitan. They were racially and culturally diverse—Latinos from throughout the Americas; U.S. whites and minorities; and internationals from Asia, Eastern Europe, the Middle East, and elsewhere. All were middle or upper class, holding or working toward advanced college degrees, and all subscribed, in varying degrees, to a particular educated, liberal, elite cosmopolitan sensibility in terms of social values and artistic practice.

Given the small Latino population, the region could not sustain a Little Havana or any kind of business district that catered specifically to Latinos or Latin American music and dance. Thus, this group lobbied various venues: some of the popular clubs, the local ballroom dance venue, and restaurants across town, including a Chinese restaurant in downtown Urbana (see Figure 5.1).

The local scene relied almost exclusively on recorded music (see Waxer 2002a; Aparicio 1998; Román-Velázquez 2002). One popular, semiprofessional salsa band, Adelante, eventually emerged from the local scene, although it was short lived. The group comprised graduate students (including salsa scholar Lise Waxer) who were busy with coursework, assistantships, and dissertation writing, and its membership rotated as individuals graduated and relocated to other parts of the world. Other dancers talked of starting their own bands, but few ever got off the ground and none rivaled the success, albeit limited and brief, that Adelante enjoyed. Maria and other dancers lobbied bar owners to book live

Figure 5.1. A 1990s flyer showing the week's events at the Blind Pig, a popular dance club in downtown Champaign, Illinois. *(Photograph by Joanna Bosse.)*

salsa bands from Chicago, but this was an expensive proposition and one most entrepreneurs were reluctant to undertake. When they did so, the bands played to sellout crowds and the dance floors were packed beyond danceability.

Other than in major urban areas, live music performance, especially by large professional groups of the sort salsa requires, is economically unfeasible for small-business owners. There are some exceptions, but by and large, deejays or jukeboxes are the most common form of music performance in bars and clubs in central Illinois. For every night of live salsa performance there were at least twenty (and often upward of fifty) deejayed events.

As is the case with other local salsa scenes, salsa performance centered on live dance rather than live music performance. That this salsa scene is largely a dance context employing recorded music is not unusual (see Aparicio 1998; Hosokawa 2002; Román-Velázquez 2002; Waxer 2002b). The international popularity of salsa music (recorded and live) is largely attributable to its intimate ties to the dance style, which has attracted fans from around the world (see Román-Velázquez 2002: 219). Given the diversity of participants in this midwestern case study, dance classes became fundamental to the project of salsa performance in the region (see also Aparicio 1998; Waxer 2002b).

Very few knew how to dance salsa before they arrived in central Illinois, and so dance instructors essentially created this music and dance scene by offering a dance class before the deejay started the music. These quickie classes held at the clubs functioned as a sampler for the more in-depth classes offered elsewhere, usually on university grounds. Through this process, and the regular blanketing of public spaces with advertisements, amateur dance instructors built studios that were a lucrative supplement to their graduate assistantships (see Figure 5.2).

The popular bars and live music and dance venues in Champaign-Urbana were generally locally owned and operated. The industry was small, competitive, and somewhat unstable. Almost all the establishments I visited opened, closed, changed hands, or changed operational formats during my research. Furthermore, clubs dedicated to one particular genre were seldom successful (unlike the salsa clubs in Chicago that dancers traveled to when times were lean nearby). Even the most stable of clubs had to diversify their offerings on a day-to-day basis to widen their audience base. For example, one local club, Bradleys (which closed and reopened under different management by the end of my fieldwork), hosted country dancing on Wednesday; rhythm and blues on Thursday; hip-hop on Friday; a live band on Saturday, although the genre or format of these live performances changed radically from week to week; and sometimes country and other times an open mic or an entirely different program on Sunday. At a whim, this schedule was changed to accommodate traveling musical acts, deejays who were ill or out of town, and so forth. This was common practice. No one constituency proved to be profitable for a dance club every night of the week, so management worked to attract all of them throughout the week.[7]

Figure 5.2. Salsa class in Champaign, Illinois, 2005. *(Photograph by Joanna Bosse.)*

Club owners generally measured success in terms of liquor sales.[8] Salsa dee-jays and live bands generally received the take at the door. Bar owners thus placed the burden of advertising and drawing large numbers on the deejays and live bands, who were then also placed in competition with one another and with other styles. In lobbying for salsa performance, Maria and her successors had to essentially promise bar owners that they would make more money (in alcohol sales) with salsa than they would with any other format. Owners of restaurants and the local ballroom were easier to persuade because they hosted salsa events after hours, times when they would otherwise be closed or taking in little anyway. So they were more likely to increase their profits with salsa than not. Because of these circumstances, salsa-tecas at these establishments were more successful in some ways than those at more customary dance clubs.

Given that the salsa crowd at this point was small (dozens of people), salsa promoters needed to broaden their base to succeed. They targeted an audience they believed would increase sales revenue from alcohol purchases: working-class Mexicans (predominantly male). And the influx of working-class Mexi-can men generally did boost the alcohol sales enough to keep bar owners happy, allowing the dances to continue for another week. A secondary benefit was that most of these men were accomplished dancers; they told me they grew up danc-ing salsa in Mexico. For the disproportionate number of female cosmopolitans hoping to learn salsa, having a large group of accomplished male dancers to

partner with helped improve the quality of their dance experiences. This arrangement resulted in two conditions: first, that salsa performance depended
on the coordinated and cooperative participation of local cosmopolitan elites
and working-class Mexicans, and second, that both salsa and the working-class
Mexicans gained entry into public spaces they might otherwise never have entered, permeating the community and increasing their exposure and direct
contact with local dominant culture.

Herein lies the crux of what became termed "the Mexican problem" by individuals in this community. Salsa performance within this small-town entertainment industry mandated cooperation between subgroups, each with their
own set of values and cultural practices, connected to salsa in different ways
and for different reasons: for one group, salsa served as an expression of their
educated, liberal, elite cosmopolitanism; for Mexican laborers, the genre served
as an index of their home and cultural heritage in a very specific and localized way. Furthermore, the two prevailing ways that salsa came to signify were
somewhat mutually exclusive. Mexicans connected to salsa as an index of their
specific hometowns in Mexico and of family celebrations. Cosmopolitans were
invested in salsa's universality, repeatedly connecting it to and generally understanding it to be stylistically tied to a general type of sophisticated urbanity.

By sheer numbers and their dance skills, Mexicans came to dominate local performance, even while they remained marginalized from leadership roles
in the salsa community and the local entertainment venues: they were denied
deejay jobs and were unable to arrange salsa dances themselves. Local cosmopolitan salseros became resentful of their influence in both social and stylistic
terms, a sentiment Rick expressed in the comments that open this chapter.

Eventually, salsa-tecas became so popular, attracting a wide range of students and local cosmopolitans, that the Mexican presence became unnecessary
to secure their success. In fact, in light of such widespread popularity, a concern that the Mexican presence might jeopardize the now vibrant salsa scene
emerged. When I asked cosmopolitan salsa dancers and club owners to explain
this response, they suggested that Mexicans drink too much, which might lead
to fighting. I attended well over a hundred such events and never once saw a
physical altercation break out. The worry over violence and property damage
was often extended to one of diminishing returns. Local cosmopolitans feared
that the number of Mexican men (and the supposed threat of violence they
presented) would scare away the middle- and upper-class newcomers who were
finding their way to the genre—cosmopolitans with expendable income and in
need of lessons.

One club owner expressed frustration for having to call the police to stop a
scuffle that broke out late into one salsa event, saying, "I will not have my place
broken up. I don't need this, and I'll just shut it down." He attributed the fight
to Mexicans and used this event as justification for promoting practices directed toward reducing the number of Mexican men who came out. Placing the
burden for self-policing on the local cosmopolitans who petitioned him to host

salsa events, he threatened to shut down his regular (and very popular) salsa dance events if they did not eliminate the potential for violence and property damage—code for keeping the Mexicans in check.

Local cosmopolitans, Latinos and non-Latinos alike, began a dialogue about how best to address the "Mexican problem." The goal was not to eliminate all Mexicans, just those who did not acquiesce to the cultural capital of the educated cosmopolitan elite: those who did not speak English, who dressed in "gangsta" clothing, who drank too much, who were not educated, and who did not aspire to a higher class status.

Attempts to disenfranchise Mexican dancers took several forms. One club agreed to institute a dress code for salsa nights in the hopes of diminishing the working-class Mexicans by targeting their clothing style. Their announcements read, "[We have] a non-smoking environment and a strict dress code: No hats, No jeans or baggie pants, No boots or tennis shoes. Shirts tucked in please." Salsero cosmopolitans warned club owners that Mexican deejays played a different kind of salsa that would not appeal to the "respectable" audiences they desired. They also tried to contain the ability of Mexican dancers to win local salsa dance competitions and complained bitterly when Mexicans did win in an effort to educate the outsiders as to what was "good" and "bad" salsa dancing. This conflict explains Rick's comment to me about Enrique dancing cumbia, made shortly after Enrique won a local dance competition.

Style, Commerce, and Control

Local cosmopolitans couched their marginalization of Mexicans in terms of aesthetics—the music, dance, and social style of Mexicans were not good or authentic—obscuring the class-based politics that were foundational to the enterprise. While it is true that Mexicans were not dancing in a Cuban, Puerto Rican, or even Nuyorican style, few people were. In this region, no singular style of salsa prevailed, unless it would be that of white, middle-class newcomers (see Bosse 2004, 2008). The sparse representation of any particular geographic region and the fact that most of the local dancers learned to dance as adults while living in central Illinois—for example, the Chilean who learned from a Korean-Australian who learned from a white American who learned from her Surinamese friend who learned from her Colombian boyfriend—make any claims to stylistic authenticity on the grounds of salsa's Caribbean or New York City origins logistically problematic. This cross-pollination was influenced by not only a variety of regional salsa styles but also entirely different genres popular in the region, including ballroom, swing, and the hustle.[9]

The Cuban style was lauded as the most authentic and ideal style of salsa and was the benchmark for every performance. However, very few local dancers performed this style.[10] Second to Cuban salsa style was New York, which most people assumed was Cuban style's closest relative.[11] Thus, the defining style of local performance was identified as existing outside local purview.

Local elites—situating themselves as being more traveled, more pedigreed, more worldly, or more discerning—became the representatives and arbiters of this style and critiqued local performances accordingly.

This community produced a variety of salsa styles that were largely identified by region. My informants recognized Cuban, Colombian, and Mexican styles as well as those of New York, Miami, and Chicago. Such knowledge was largely derived from the influence of relatively few representatives. For example, Rick, the dancer and deejay whose comments open this chapter, is of Cuban descent. He learned to dance salsa from his Surinamese girlfriend, though he had certainly absorbed some stylistic influence from having watched his elders dance during his childhood. He was the only regular dancer in attendance to dance in what was locally presumed to be "Cuban style." Compact and internal, Rick held his arms close to his body, with elbows always tucked in tight and his hands on his chest when not holding his partner. He took very small steps and performed very slight, almost imperceptible accents by shimmying or twitching forward one or another shoulder. He performed very little hip action, keeping his torso locked and active, and led his partner in very few turns or spins. While his style was admired for being "Cuban," he was not necessarily considered a good dancer; nor was he coveted as a dance partner by local female dancers.

Conversely to Rick, other dancers were considered very good dancers while being derided for performing a style that was considered compromised because it was not Cuban in origin. For example, the style of one Colombian dancer, Angel, became the representative for a general type of salsa style presumed to have originated in Colombia. His style included rapid, improvisatory footwork; arms high and out to the side; and an active waist, causing a lateral ripple effect from the hips to the shoulders with each step. Holding his partner's hand in his own, well above his head with his left elbow almost parallel to his ear, he pulled his partner so close that she too performed the lateral wave rising from hips to shoulders as if the two were one body. It was well known that Angel was also a fan of merengue. He played more merengues during a night of salsa dancing than any other local deejay and danced with great zeal to every merengue song played in a set. Angel's enthusiasm led to a commonly held belief that merengue was a Colombian genre. Early in my fieldwork in the mid-1990s, there were no Dominicans (or other Colombians) present to refute the claim. Local dancers celebrated Angel's virtuosity while claiming that his salsa style was too influenced by merengue to be authentic salsa.

Enrique, the Mexican dancer described in the opening paragraphs, was also recognized as a good dancer, one of the best in the region. His style, which was larger and took up more floor space than the styles of some other dancers, included side-to-side basic steps of longer than six inches; large, flowing arm circles; and plentiful displays of virtuosity, including spins, wraps, and sections of solo improvisatory footwork. Enrique threaded one spin into another of a different type so organically and with such innovation that it led to him and his partner traveling around the floor more than most others. Enrique was a popular dancer and in demand by partners representing all corners of the globe.

Most salsero cosmopolitans willingly confessed that Enrique was a fabulous dancer, but they were usually quick to add, as Rick does at the beginning of the chapter, that Enrique was just not dancing salsa. I heard this rhetorical strategy employed time and again as a means for qualifying the styles of salsa dancers, especially male dancers. In this case, denying the authenticity of various styles of salsa denied the very actuality of salsa performance for many of the dancers implicated by this powerful rhetorical stance.

Although not the only group affected, Mexicans (mostly males) were the most consistently maligned group in this regard, and they responded in myriad ways. The largest group of men remained on the periphery, saying little when sent away for violating the dress code and returning the next week with appropriate attire. They sat together in remote corners of the dance floor and often went entire nights without dancing because they had no inroad to the social network of female dancers.

Other dancers, like Enrique, worked toward the goal of inclusion with local cosmopolitan elites, and Enrique eventually served as a kind of local power broker for the other male Mexicans who were laborers. As mentioned, he was interested in upward mobility and had begun to work on the behavior necessary for promotion at work. Learning the English language and styles of self-presentation consistent with white American middle-class practice—including wardrobe, posture, pronunciation, and eventually American citizenship—were changes he was incorporating to fully assimilate with a particular American middle class. He invested a great deal of time building relationships with local cosmopolitans, including not only salsa dancers but other dance instructors as well. Enrique approached David Lin, the owner and operator of the most successful ballroom dance studio and the most reputable dance instructor in the region, about the possibility of taking lessons. Privy to the conversation, I followed up with Enrique later that evening, asking what he hoped he could learn. "I just want to, you know, add some class to my style, make it more sophisticated." Enrique was not the only Latin American salsa dancer to consider ballroom dance lessons as a way to "class up" his or her individual style.

Enrique's campaign for acceptance gained ground and he eventually found himself dancing among the local cosmopolitan elite, attending private dance parties, and joining them on road trips to Chicago. He used his position, betwixt and between local Mexican laborers and local elites, as a way to create new social networks. For instance, once his position was established, he incorporated a new technique: about halfway through a song, he would send me, or another of his partners, into a free spin. When I came out of the spin, I would find myself in the arms of one of his friends, someone I did not know and had never danced with before. Eventually, I was sent into a second free spin and Enrique returned. He used this strategy quite often to introduce new friends to local female salsa dancers.

Another technique employed by Mexican laborers attempting to operate within a context of marginalization was one of attracting outsiders. These dancers stood close to the door (which was also near the bar), looking awkward and unsure, and watched for newcomers—in particular, non-Latinas who were attending their first salsa dance or did not know how to dance. Unfamiliar with local conventions and anxious to try their hand at dancing, they often happily accepted the invitations to dance by the Mexican laborers who were rejected by salsero cosmopolitan elites. These women were often criticized by more established dancers because, by virtue of their whiteness or class status, they lent credibility to lower-class Mexican dancers and encouraged their style of performance.

It was only after it became clear that the local salsa scene could thrive on the revenue generated by a constituency of mainly non-Latino university students and community members that attempts were made to marginalize or divest Mexican laborers of their claim to space on the dance floor. The attempts to do so were not entirely successful in that salsa dances continued to attract dozens of Mexican men, but they remained largely on the periphery of performance, drinking more than dancing and feeling frustrated that they seldom got to dance. In a sense, the "Mexican problem" was never solved, but it continued to exist as a boundary in need of attention and maintenance to prevent incursion.[12]

Conclusion

That salsa has always been translocal, that it has cut across national and ethnic lines, is central to its success overall and is also one reason for its easy entrance into the global entertainment industry. While salsa's roots in a Latin American urban experience have been a key part of its global appeal, the genre also gained momentum in the global marketplace as an expression of a universal urbanity—an urban hipness that is presumed to translate across geography. As Shuhei Hosokawa notes, even in Japan, a region far removed from salsa's homeland, "what matters for Japanese salsa musicians and audiences is the 'hipness,' the groove, or the feeling of 'globality': that is, the experience of listening or dancing to a faraway cultural product" (2002: 294). The same is true for the salsero cosmopolitans featured in this study. Regardless of whether they identified as Latin American, they chose to dance and listen to salsa because they thought it was cooler than other kinds of traditions available to them. Salsero cosmopolitans connected salsa to a universal sophistication that emerged in part because it was born of racial strife and class struggle but also because the quality and complexity of the music is understood to have transcended this particular sociopolitical situation.

While the performance of salsa among Mexicans is yet another expression of both its pan-Latin and global appeal, the dance style of these working-class Mexicans also testified that their understanding of salsa is rooted in a Mexican context, influenced by cumbia and other regionally popular styles. In one historical moment salsero cosmopolitans defended the rights of Mexicans to perform salsa to bar and club owners, and in another, they worked to dissuade participation on the part of those very same individuals to maintain the successful scene they had created.

To better understand the shifting notions of affinity and difference in this particular dance scene, I followed the lead of Felix Padilla, who suggests:

> The manifestation of Latino ethnic-conscious identity is operative within specific situational contexts and not all of the time. The situational dimension of Latino identity implies that particular contexts determine whether the individual national/cultural identity of Puerto Ricans, Mexican Americans, Cubans, and Central and South Americans or the all-embracing Latino identification is most appropriate or salient for social action at a point in time. (1986: 154–155)

The particular economic realities of this small-town entertainment industry help us understand the strategies, rhetorical and otherwise, that were employed by salsero cosmopolitans to craft a sustainable salsa dance scene in this rural context. These strategies required drawing on pan-*latinidad* at some times and not at other times.

Presenting salsa as a small-town phenomenon in the midwestern United States rather than the more urban and coastal phenomenon we typically understand it to be, I suggest that salsa also exists within a slightly different structural configuration characteristic of smaller, localized entertainment industries and that its performance often requires different social practices that build on but also extend from salsa's original role as an expression of Latino identities and urban realities. In this case, salsa served as a nexus for shifting affinities that moved within and between ethnic and racial lines, cutting across those of socioeconomic class. Situating salsa within the sphere of commerce rather than identity politics leads to a different understanding of how the genre serves other kinds of identity formations and different or larger social goals.

Of course, it is not a rare occurrence for class tensions to masquerade as ethnic or racial conflict, especially in the United States. We might be tempted to think that salsa is immune to such mutability—that one of the most powerful expressions of the Latino immigrant experience and generators of pan-Latino solidarity might be precluded from the kind of semantic layering that would transform it into a vehicle for discriminating against working-class Latino immigrants. Or perhaps it is because of this power that it became the object of cosmopolitan aspirations in the first place. When couched entirely within the discourse of identity it is hard to say. However, when framed by a desire to better understand the commercial industries that mediate music and dance, different issues are brought into focus. While most, if not all, commercial spaces foster cooperation, coordination, and occasionally competition between disparate constituencies, in small-town entertainment venues it appears that this is a necessity for survival.

Employing pan-Latino rhetoric, salsero cosmopolitans first looked to coordinate efforts with Mexican laborers, bringing several different groups together to create a local salsa dance scene. As Padilla explains, "Latino ethnic-conscious behavior . . . represents a multi-group-generated behavior that transcends the boundaries of the individual national and cultural identities of the different Spanish-speaking populations and emerges as a distinct group identification and affiliation" (1986: 155). Cosmopolitans became concerned that this alliance presented a liability to the continued economic success of local salsa performance, and they enacted several strategies to reduce the effect of Mexicans on the overall scene.

While I have suggested that small-town entertainment industries present different kinds of challenges to local performance than those of their metropolitan counterparts, I must confess that a nagging but crucial question remains unanswered for me: To what degree is this kind of social and economic structural configuration unique and substantially different from urban settings? It is difficult to know. Much of the literature on salsa is somewhat silent on how much the economic infrastructure of *local*, urban entertainment industries promotes or obfuscates particular discourses of class and ethnic based social identity.[13] And as scholars, it is also sometimes difficult to know how our collective investment in music and dance as "authentic" expressions and generators of cultural affinity has caused us to overlook its reliance on the mundane and seemingly small details of cover charges, dance class admission, and the cost of a beer. Clearly, there is much work to do. What I do know is that as it travels, from the inner-city barrios to the upscale ballrooms, across the United States and around the world, salsa continually reveals to us the remarkable power of dance to communicate deeply held and sometimes conflicting notions of cultural identity while accruing new meanings along the way.

NOTES

1. All names have been changed.

2. See Aparicio 1998; Delgado and Muñoz 1997; Derno and Washburne 2002; Duany 1984; Hosokawa 2002; Loza 1993; Manuel 1991a, 1991b, 1994; Padilla 1990; Román-Velázquez 2002; Singer 1983; Steward 1989; Urquía 2005; Washburne 2008; and Waxer 1994, 2000, 2002a, 2002b.

3. Locating salsa performance in this specific and unlikely locale also documents how Latino ethnic consciousness and perceptions of pan-Latino solidarity can shift depending on the specific situational frame. In one instance, someone from Latin America might recognize affinity with another from a different Latin American country, at another she may distance herself on the grounds of regional or class-based differences, depending on, among other things, the perception of the availability of resources (Padilla 1986).

4. Population data taken from Executive Summary of the Latino Project of Champaign County (2003) and the U.S. Census Bureau, Census 2000.

5. While several scholars have developed this concept, I draw most heavily from the writing of ethnomusicologist Thomas Turino, who in turn built on that of writers such as Pierre Bourdieu (1984), Timothy Brennan (1997), James Clifford (1992), Jean Comaroff and John Comaroff (1993), and Bruce Robbins (1992). Turino describes cosmopolitanism as "a specific type of cultural formation and constitution of habitus that is translocal in purview" (2000: 7). Cosmopolitan formations are "like other cultural complexes in that they comprise aggregates of tendencies and resources for living and conceptualizing the world which are used variably by people engaged with that formation" (7). They are different from other kinds of social formations, say diasporas, in that they are generally unmoored from any particular geographic region or site of origin. For this reason, cosmopolitan formations are often described as "global" in common parlance. Nevertheless, they have to be "realized in specific locations and in the lives of actual people. . . . Cosmopolitan cultural formations are therefore always simultaneously local and translocal" (7). Multiple cosmopolitan formations exist at any one time. The dominant one these days is modernist-capitalism, but others such as modernist-socialist or fundamentalist-Islamic are also prevalent.

6. During the first decades of the twentieth century, cabaret clubs and open-admission dances replaced private parties as the dominant context for socializing. These new contexts afforded an opportunity for interaction among and between a greater diversity of participants than invitation-only events. As Lewis Erenberg (1986) and Linda Tomko (1999) both note, the diversity was generally restricted to groups within a particular economic class. Thus, like the contemporary case I provide in this chapter, clubs simultaneously encourage diversity in one dimension while reinforcing hegemonies according to others, most often that of economic class. Salsa dancing in central Illinois attracted a wide range of racial, ethnic, and regional affiliations that tacitly reinforced the class-based valuation of salsa music and dance.

7. Two establishments provide a challenge to this statement, and their exception proves the rule. The first was C-Street, a gay bar in downtown Champaign. The second was the Rose Bowl, a working-class country bar that hosted a house band, the Western Wheels, two nights a week in Urbana. In both of these, the venues appealed to a particular clientele, were purposely built to suit their clientele every night of the week, and had no rivals competing for their business. The respective, predominant clienteles—gay men and white, middle-age, working-class men—had enough numbers and finances to sustain their chosen venues.

8. See Tomko 1999: 21 for more on the historical precedents for the ongoing relationship between alcohol sales, public dance halls, and the commerce of dance.

9. Elsewhere (Bosse 2008) I have explored in detail the stylistic development of a regional salsa style by ballroom dancers for a salsa "formation team." This study also includes some discussion of local regional styles, as does my dissertation (Bosse 2004).

10. The dominance of Cuban-style salsa in the rhetoric surrounding salsa performance is an interesting phenomenon and deserving of scholarly attention. In every salsa context I have encountered—on the small-town midwestern scene, in Chicago clubs, in Tokyo, at ballroom and salsa congresses, and at mass-mediated and online forums—the Cuban style is considered the most prestigious. While in Tokyo conducting preliminary research on the local salsa scene in the Rippongi district, I encountered a Colombian who advertised his dance classes as in "authentic Cuban style" because he knew that would attract a larger clientele (of Japanese and white ex-pats from North America, Europe, and Australia). As one of the only Latinos working in this area, he enjoyed a great deal of latitude in how he presented salsa to this audience.

11. The common debate over ownership between Cubans and Puerto Ricans was not at all common in this region where there were so few Cubans and Puerto Ricans.

12. Paradoxically, it was this exclusion from full participation and equity that led to greater alcohol consumption and the potential for violence, and thus it could be said that salsa organizers created the very problem they supposedly wanted to correct.

13. A notable exception is Chris Washburne (2008), who provides a detailed ethnographic study of the salsa music business and the local New York City entertainment industry from the inside. Other than this important work, there has been very little attention paid to the commerce of local salsa dance contexts. Some attention has been paid to the commerce of the salsa recording industry, including Boggs 1992.

REFERENCES

Aparicio, Frances. 1998. *Listening to Salsa: Gender, Latin Popular Music, and Puerto Rican Cultures*. Middletown, CT: Wesleyan University Press.

Boggs, Vernon. 1992. *Salsiology: Afro-Cuban Music and the Evolution of Salsa in New York City*. Westport, CT: Greenwood.

Bosse, Joanna. 2004. "Exotica, Ethnicity, and Embodiment: An Ethnography of Latin Dance in US Popular Culture." Ph.D. diss., University of Illinois at Urbana-Champaign.

———. 2008. "Salsa Dance and the Transformation of Style: An Ethnographic Study of Movement and Meaning in a Cross-Cultural Context." *Dance Research Journal* 40 (1): 45–64.

Bourdieu, Pierre. 1984. *Distinction: A Social Critique of the Judgement of Taste*, trans. Richard Nice. Cambridge, MA: Harvard University Press.

Brennan, Timothy. 1997. *At Home in the World: Cosmopolitanism Now*. Cambridge, MA: Harvard University Press.

Clifford, James. 1992. "Traveling Cultures." In *Cultural Studies*, ed. Lawrence Grossberg, Cary Nelson, and Paula Treichler, 96–116. New York: Routledge.

Comaroff, Jean, and John Comaroff, eds. 1993. *Modernity and Its Malcontents: Ritual and Power in Postcolonial Africa*. Chicago: University of Chicago Press.

Delgado, Celeste Frasier, and José Esteban Muñoz, eds. 1997. *Everynight Life: Culture and Dance in Latin/o America*. Durham, NC: Duke University Press.

Derno, Maiken, and Christopher Washburne. 2002. "Masquerading Machismo: La India and the Staging of Chusmería on the Salsa Scene." *Women and Performance: A Journal of Feminist Theory* 12 (24): 140–156.

Duany, Jorge. 1984. "Popular Music in Puerto Rico: Toward an Anthropology of *Salsa*." *Latin American Music Review* 5 (2): 186–215.

Erenberg, Lewis A. 1986. "From New York to Middletown: Repeal and the Legitimization of Nightlife in the Great Depression." *American Quarterly* 38 (5): 761–778.

Hosokawa, Shuhei. 2002. "Salsa No Tiene Fronteras: Orquesta de la Luz and the Globalization of Popular Music." In *Situating Salsa: Global Markets and Local Meanings in Latin Popular Music*, ed. Lise Waxer, 289–312. New York: Routledge.

Loza, Steven. 1993. *Barrio Rhythm: Mexican American Music in Los Angeles*. Urbana: University of Illinois Press.

Manuel, Peter. 1991a. "Latin Music in the United States: Salsa and the Mass Media." *Journal of Communication* 41 (1): 104–116.

———. 1991b. "Salsa and the Music Industry: Corporate Control or Grassroots Expression?" *Essays on Cuban Music: North American and Cuban Perspectives*, ed. Peter Manuel, 27–47. Lanham, MD: University Press of America.

———. 1994. "Puerto Rican Music and Cultural Identity: Creative Appropriation of Cuban Sources from Danza to Salsa." *Ethnomusicology* 38 (2): 249–280.

Padilla, Felix. 1986. "Latino Ethnicity in the City of Chicago." In *Competitive Ethnic Relations*, ed. S. Olzak and J. Nagel, 153–172. Orlando, FL: Academic Press.

———. 1990. "Salsa: Puerto Rican and Latino Music." *Journal of Popular Culture* 24 (1): 87–104.

Robbins, Bruce. 1992. "Comparative Cosmopolitanism." *Social Text* 31 (2): 169–186.

Román-Velázquez, Patria. 2002. "Locating Salsa." In *Popular Music Studies*, ed. D. Hesmondhalgh and K. Negus, 210–222. London: Oxford University Press.

Singer, Roberta. 1983. "Tradition and Innovation in Contemporary Latin Popular Music in New York City." *Latin American Music Review* 4 (2): 183–202.

Steward, Sue. 1989. "Cuba and the Roots of Salsa." In *Rhythms of the World*, ed. F. Hanley and T. May, 24–37. London: BBC Books.

Tomko, Linda. 1999. *Dancing Class: Gender, Ethnicity, and Social Divides in American Dance, 1890–1920.* Bloomington: Indiana University Press.

Turino, Thomas. 2000. *Nationalists, Cosmopolitans, and Popular Music in Zimbabwe.* Chicago: University of Chicago Press.

Urquia, Norman. 2005. "The Re-branding of Salsa in London's Dance Clubs: How an Ethnicised Form of Cultural Capital was Institutionalised." *Leisure Studies* 24 (4): 385–397.

Washburne, Chris. 2008. *Sounding Salsa: Performing Latin Music in New York City.* Philadelphia: Temple University Press.

Waxer, Lise. 1994. "Of Mambo Kings and Songs of Love: Dance Music in Havana and New York from the 1930s to the 1950s." *Latin American Music Review* 15 (2): 139–176.

———. 2000. "En Conga, Bongó y Campana: The Rise of Colombian Salsa." *Latin American Music Review* 21 (2): 118–168.

———. 2002a. *The City of Musical Memory: Salsa, Record Grooves, and Popular Culture in Cali, Colombia.* Middletown, CT: Wesleyan University Press.

———, ed. 2002b. *Situating Salsa: Global Markets and Local Meanings in Latin Popular Music.* New York: Routledge.

6

Dancing Salsa in Cuba

Another Look

Bárbara Balbuena Gutiérrez

(Translated by Sydney Hutchinson)

*C*asino, known internationally as the Cuban style of salsa, is a popular, traditional social or ballroom dance. It emerged in the late 1950s through the evolution and integration of Cuban and other nationalities' music-dance genres. I describe it as popular not only because it was created by the people for their own enjoyment but also because it has maintained its popularity over four generations of dancers. Because durability of cultural manifestations is one of the principal traits defining tradition, casino may be categorized as traditional, but we must not forget the peculiar dynamic of this dance's development through a continual process of assimilation, negation, renovation, and progressive change toward new creations as it is passed from one generation to the next.

International and Cuban Ballroom Dance

It is essential to explain my understandings of the concepts of *social* or *ballroom* dance, since, on the one hand, the Cuban dance universe is broad and diverse, and on the other hand, two types of ballroom dance are currently internationally recognized: the social and the sport, or competition. Although both come from the same historical roots, there are palpable differences from the technical, stylistic, motivational, or contextual points of view. In Europe and elsewhere, competition ballroom dance is considered an athletic endeavor with artistic results for which the dancers submit themselves to rigorous, long-term training. It was recognized as a sport by the International Olympic Committee in 1997. In turn, two subcategories exist under sport dance: standard, or international, dances (such as the Viennese or English waltz, the foxtrot, quickstep, and tango) and the Latin dances (which include *chachachá* [Anglicized as cha-cha], rumba-bolero, samba, jive, *pasodoble*, and salsa). Choreographies correspond to patterns preestablished by an expert jury that evaluates the performances, taking the program for the couple's level into account.

I believe these parameters diminish the spontaneity, freedom of expression, and creativity afforded by the improvisation of social dance or traditional ballroom dance. The stylization and standardization of the Latin genres make some practically unrecognizable when compared with their original homologues, and in others the transformations are so profound that they have provoked the disappearance of their cultural identity or essence. Competitive dance has influenced how most salsa styles are danced socially around the world today: as styles introduced fundamentally through teaching.

In Cuba, *ballroom dance* (*baile de salón*) refers to dances held in social centers in urban locations, such as recreation societies, social circles, clubs, cabarets, ballrooms in private homes, and public plazas. Ballroom dance is intimately linked to social events where dance is the main attraction, although other collateral activities take place. The popular *verbenas*, carnivals, *parrandas*, *charangas* (all words for kinds of parties with music and dance), and all types of public or private parties provide the proper circumstances for couple dancing, which permits not only the free, sensual union of couples but also collective solidarity with no distinctions between social class, age, sex, or race.

Nineteenth- and Twentieth-Century Precursors

Casino's predecessor is the *contradanza*, introduced to Cuba via Spain in the eighteenth century, which was transformed into a creole contradance at the turn of the nineteenth century. The contradance contributed its four-beat, forward-and-back basic step to Cuban ballroom dance. This basic form was maintained in *danza*, *danzón*, *son*, and casino, although it changed in terms of bodily and rhythmic accents and the execution of new figures.

The principal figures of the contradance include promenade, chain, hold, sieve, placing the dance, whiplash, lasso, allemande, throne, wings, turns, rounds, mills, and bridge.[1] Its spatial designs include two rows of couples, circles, quartets, trios, and duos. Traces of contradance figures appear in the turns and spatial patterns of casino, both in the circle, or *rueda*, and in independent couple dancing. However, the contradanza was executed in the open social dance position.

When the danza emerged in the early nineteenth century, it had a musical form similar to that of the contradance but modified its choreographic aspects. Its basic step was essentially the same as the contradance's, and it was performed by free couples in an embrace. This disposition of the pairs resulted from the worldwide influence of the waltz and was used in danzón, *danzonete*, chachachá, son, and finally casino. The continual turns of the embracing couple, characteristic of this genre, became part of the danza and, later, with certain adaptations, the danzón, danzonete, son, chachachá, and casino. Another danza figure that survives today is the *paseo*, or promenade, similar to the rueda figure *vamos arriba, vamos abajo* (we go up, we go down).

At the end of the nineteenth century, the danzón emerges with slower, graceful movements and greater creative freedom. A whole series of musical and danced configurations alluding to distinctive traits of our national culture converge in the danzón, so that today it is still considered the Cuban national dance. A novel characteristic for the time was the alternation of danced parts called *cedazos* with resting parts, making the musical form of a rondo (ABACAD).[2] The fundamental figures of danzón include promenade, the man's mark, the box, and the screw turn,[3] all of which can be in the casino dance.

The chachachá and the son also had a direct relationship to the birth of the casino in the 1950s. Throughout the island, different varieties of son music developed. However, from the choreographic point of view, there are two fundamental styles: the *son montuno*, or mountain son, and the *son urbano*, or urban son. The *son montuno* is characterized by accentuated movement of the torso from side to side, deep bending of the legs that provokes a constant up-and-down motion in the body, and frequent up-and-down movement of the arms, identified by dance specialists as "taking water from the well" (*sacar agua del pozo*). The *son urbano* is characterized by movements that are slower, smoother, and more elegant; a more upright social dance position; a less-pronounced bending of the legs; and omission of the arm movements. This latter son had the greater influence on the emergence of casino.

The urban son's basic step was performed either to the clave beat, with the melody, or in opposition (*contratiempo*, or offbeat) to the clave. Many specialists consider the latter mode of execution the most authentic form. The inseparable link between rhythmic pattern, melody, and the timing of the step transferred to casino.

The basic son step is similar to that of casino in its musical timing and bodily and spatial form. Both styles are executed in four beats, the first three corresponding to steps and the fourth a pause, and in a closed social dance position. Some turns, arm combinations, and the opening and closing of the dancers are also shared.

Chachachá emerged as a result of the need to create something different from the danzón, and it was popularized in 1951. Chachachá contributed its figures to casino, not its basic step. This dance is performed both in a closed social dance position and by separated dancers. This characteristic of executing the steps and variations freely, face to face and without holding one another, later acquired great importance in the development of casino. Several figures in chachachá coincide with those of casino, including the opening and closing of the couple (also found in son), known among dancers as *pa' ti, pa' mí* (for you, for me), turn combinations, and above all, the execution of the rueda (wheel or circle form).

The Emergence of *Rueda de Casino*

In the late 1950s, the rueda emerged as a new variety of chachachá. It was called rueda (wheel), because it consisted of couples executing the figures while forming a circle that moved clockwise or counterclockwise. It was directed by a man with demonstrated dancing ability who signaled to the dancers changes of partners, turn combinations, and other figures. However, the son was also performed in rueda form before the 1950s, and in the *montuno* simple figures and exchanges of partners were frequently executed.

Urban son and chachachá were thus the principal pillars in the creation of casino as a new style of Cuban ballroom dance. In the 1950s the former reached a great height and the latter emerged with considerable success. In this stage, important factors converged, including the proliferation of recreational societies, the popularity of certain Cuban musical groups, and the beginnings of television. In addition, U.S. cultural influence grew.

In approximately 1956 the chachachá's circle of independent couples began to be reproduced with the urban son's basic step to the musical accompaniment of *sones* or other popular music. This was called *rueda de casino*. It occurred at first exclusively in the Club Casino Deportivo, a white social club, today the Cristino Naranjo Workers' Social Circle (see Figure 6.1), but it caught on among young people and was imitated by dancers in other nautical beachside clubs and, later, in the capital city. People would say, "Let's do *rueda* like in the casino," and "Let's do the *rueda de casino*"; through reduction these phrases became "Let's do the casino."

In the 1950s, various foreign genres of music and dance, principally North American ones, were also popular. They became known in the early 1930s through the mass media and the foreign tours of Cuban artists, which noticeably influenced our dance-music culture and were one of the causes of the decline of genres like the danzón.

In the 1950s, Cuban youth very much enjoyed dancing to North American rock and roll; however, to counter its foreign influence and maintain their cultural values they often alternated it with chachachá. Rock also left its trace in casino in its spectacular style with acrobatic elements and couple turns. Other similar aspects include the figure *pa' tí, pa' mí*, the continuous turns with enlaced arms, and the beats on which the step is marked. North American influence is easily seen in figures in the final coda of the first chachachá, like the *cojito* (limp) and the *suiza* (Swiss). These figures did not last. In early casino, a small jump and a circular movement of the clasped arms (woman's right and man's left) were performed that no doubt came from rock and roll.

In its early days, casino was danced in an organized circle made up of friends, relatives, or impromptu members who rehearsed together; later it began to be performed as a dance of independent couples; and last it was performed in a double line, with the head couple inventing the figure or step. The necessity of employing choreographies for spectators caused new spatial designs to appear,

Figure 6.1. The building housing today's Círculo Social Obrero Cristino Naranjo (Cristino Naranjo Workers' Social Circle), which formerly housed the Club Casino Deportivo (Casino Sports Club), the birthplace of casino, or rueda. *(Photograph by Bárbara Balbuena Gutiérrez.)*

among them the double line (inherited from the contradance), quartets, duos, trios, and above all, circles, as in the chachachá. To understand the guide's commands and execute them in unison, it became essential to name each of the figures, turn combinations, gestures, and directions. This dance style spread throughout the capital and later the entire island.

The mass media, principally television, were important for the spread of Cuban popular music and dance. The most prestigious singers, musical groups, dancers, and artists of the era appeared on television, which was introduced and commercialized in Cuba in 1950. In addition, this medium made the conjunction of all kinds of artistic resources possible, such as costuming, gesture, oral expression, and above all, choreographic elements. The audience that did not attend ballrooms, clubs, or associations learned dance genres through the mediation of television.

Casino emerged, then, in an environment integrating genres of high prestige among the people, such as danzón, *guaracha*, son, and chachachá. In approximately 1956, "the casino style—a kind of dance—[was] introduced among youth" (Linares 1974: 200), although informants do not remember exactly when this dance was performed independently from the others already analyzed.

No specific musical genre is attached to casino, unlike the ballroom dances that preceded it. Through all its years of popularity, it has been performed to all the musical genres that were in style that, because of their rhythmic scheme or musical beat, allowed the basic step to be realized.

The people themselves designated the new dance phenomenon as "casino style" from the very first. A description of how the rueda might have emerged and of the basic casino step appears in the novel *Las iniciales de la tierra* (*The Beginnings of the Earth*), by Jesús Díaz, which takes place in the Casino Deportivo in 1956–1957. Díaz's precision of detail suggests that he took part in this important event:

> The Rueda was a brotherhood, a sect, a kind of danced religion. . . . Sunday after Sunday, a brotherhood of founders would gather that imitated, when dancing and walking, certain lascivious, elegant, and rhythmic gestures of the black Habaneros. Little by little they came up with a style that was . . . a bit spectacular, choreographic, coordinated, and in its own way beautiful, sensual, and flavorful like the son.
>
> When the four hours for tea were too little for them, they began to make appointments around the Victrola that was behind the pool hall. . . . They began a double step, maintaining the structure of the three beats of the danza but marking each one twice. . . . They produced a new central step, the square, which had comings and goings and allowed the couple to open to the ballroom, pursuing one another through the counterpoint of rhythm and harmony, like cats in heat. When someone asked what kind of dance this was, they would invariably answer: casino style. Sundays they had an audience; the first applause incited emulation and several groups of couples began to combine forces to produce figures. One night twelve got together and began to improvise; that night Benny [Moré, the great *sonero*] was singing. . . . That night the rueda was born. (Díaz 1987: 96–97)

During this first phase, casino borrowed practices from son and chachachá, such as the figure names for-you-for-me (*pa' tí, pa' mí*, also known as *abre y cierra*, or open-and-close) and shoulder turn (*vuelta al hombro*). But most figures were performed by imitation over the years without a specific name. In prior music-dance genres these figures had usually been danced by free, independent couples; however, in casino they were performed in the rueda, interspersed with other, newly created ones that made movement in a circle, and above all changes of partner, possible.

The basic step was essentially the same as in the Havana, or urban, son. The body was slightly leaning forward but straight. Hip movements were smooth and pronounced, those of the torso light and lateral, the two executed in opposition. This swaying of the hips and the torso gave sensuality to the dance, particularly to the woman. The man was the one who led: he decided which figures to execute, decided what musical timing to follow, and had the greatest possibility for improvising, playing with the basic step and the rhythm of the music. The turns or figures, those executed by independent couples and those performed in rueda, definitively identified the casino as a new ballroom dance and distinguished it from its precursors.

Ruedas during Revolutionary Times

With the Cuban revolution in 1959, sociocultural changes influenced the development and diffusion of Cuban popular music and dance. New projects for the recreation of youth and the general public emerged.

Law 890 of October 13, 1960, nationalized dance clubs, societies, and ballrooms. Some were abandoned by their owners, who left the country for political and economic reasons. Most clubs were turned over to workers' unions, and in 1961 workers' social circles were inaugurated. These became the principal recreation centers for youth throughout the country, holding matinee dances, or tea dances, serving no alcoholic beverages, only soft drinks or water. On Saturdays and Sundays, people danced, had fun, and made new friends from two in the afternoon until late.

Many young people got together in the workers' social circles in the outskirts of the old municipality of Marianao, in the capital, since most of the scholarship plans set up by the revolution were situated there. Thousands of students attended these social circles, which constituted a social phenomenon with a special connotation unique in Cuban cultural history. In these recreational centers a new generation of *casineros*, dancers of casino, was born. Couples came together, whether preexisting or meeting in that moment: "Dance in the 1970s was impelled by the human relationships and interests among the dancers; the bonds of friendship played an important role" (Aguilera 1998).

In the early years of the 1960s, casino reached great heights. Ruedas made up of acquaintances and friends developed and spread to barrios, schools, or workers' social circles. Some ruedas became famous thanks to dancers whose skill and rhythmic sense offered true spectacles. They were known by the name or alias of their director or the location in which they danced, as, for example, the Rueda de los Jimaguas de Regla (a Havana neighborhood), the Rueda del Patricio (the rueda of the Patrice Lumumba workers' social circle), or the Rueda del Oso (the bear's rueda, after the nickname of dancer Joaquín "El Oso" Roche).

The Rueda del Patricio was very famous and had a hundred couples (Sainz-Baranda 1998). To join, one had to demonstrate skill in the dance after being presented as the friend of another member. Errors would lead to expulsion. The rueda was led by Rosendo Eugenio González Doncel, who stood out for his virtuosity and the skill and creativity he showed in combining figures and guiding the rueda.

The Rueda del Oso emerged after the Patricio and had thirty-two couples: "It began with a group, mainly white, in Havana's park. Later they began to frequent the Patricio and added to their numbers, as well as incorporating blacks and mulattos, anyone, without regard to skin color" (Gómez 1992: 40). They were famous for rarely making a mistake, and when one did occur they expelled the one who committed the error, after making fun of him or her.

The peak of casino resulted from the unlimited access people had to culture and to recreation as a new means of development. On January 4, 1961, the National Cultural Council was founded. Its principal objectives were to recover our traditions, reform artistic education, and dignify artistic and literary work. It created organizations, institutions, and cultural groups such as the National School of Art, the Training Schools for Art Instructors, National Dance of Cuba (Danza Nacional de Cuba), and the National Folkloric Ensemble (Conjunto Folklórico Nacional).

The artistic groups recovered musical and danced expressions of a national character, including the Cuban ballroom dances. For example, the National Folkloric Ensemble included a cycle of popular dances in its repertoire, and National Dance of Cuba included a panorama of Cuban music and dance. In addition, study of modern and folkloric dance in the National School of Art incorporated Cuban ballroom dances, among them casino, into its program. But the fans of Cuban popular music themselves, rather than these institutions, were perhaps most responsible for its knowledge, performance, and diffusion because this movement enfolded workers, peasants, students, and the general public into artistic groups en masse.

Dance Music in Cuba

In the early 1960s, music declined following the socioeconomic changes in the country resulting from the 1959 revolution, which led to the birth of new cultural institutions and the transformation of the musical infrastructure. This infrastructure included performance sites, media outlets and their programming, and nightlife in general, as clubs shed their formerly elitist characters. Some musical groups and artists of great quality emigrated, and others died. Nonetheless, noteworthy singers, musicians, and composers stayed on the island, creating new music and dance styles such as the *mozambique*, created by Pedro Izquierdo (known as Pello el Afrocán); the *pilón*, from the composer Enrique Bonne; the *pacá* of Juanito Márquez; the *dengue*, created by Dámaso Pérez Prado; and the *guapaché, chiqui-chaca, mozan-chá*, and *guaguá*. These did not last, in part because music could not easily spread inside or outside the country. Outside, few people knew about or had access to the new developments in Cuban music, and so people heard only the music of the 1950s. Inside, the media did not disseminate Cuban rhythms sufficiently, and foreign music, such as the bossa nova, twist, beat, *beyé*, go-go, and rock, took their place. Cuban dance music was in crisis, while rock, for example, was so strong that young people, the principal dancing public, began to prefer foreign music.

These new foreign genres and Cuban ones influenced casino. The dancers added complexity to turns and figures, incorporating movements from other dance forms. In the late 1970s, a musical renewal began within the charanga-type *orquestas* (ensembles)[4] such as Elio Revé's group, founded in 1956, which featured innovative and hugely popular arrangements by composer and bass player Juan Formell, one of its members (Valdés 1988: 5). Formell also introduced new instruments that revolutionized the charanga, including electric bass and guitar and amplified cello and violins. Formell founded his own group in December 1969, Los Van Van, with which he created *songo*, a new type of son (Loyola 1997: 197). During this period, casino was danced to different types of music, including the *changüí-shake, changüí 68, songo, ranchera-son, conga-son, palo-son, guaracha*, and son. Among the most famous groups were Neno González, Chapotín, Rumba Habana, and Aragón, which, though founded in 1939, was still the queen of charangas in the 1970s.

In these years, ballrooms and other dance areas were scarce. The workers' social circles, contrary to their original objectives, were invaded by alcohol, knives, and fights, and the public began to avoid their dance parties, matinees, and other activities.

In the 1970s, as a consequence of the National Cultural Council's work to revitalize and recover popular dance music, new musical groups were formed, new albums recorded, compositions and choreographies created, and films made that spread Cuban music and dance. In addition, talks and roundtables were given at festivals of son, danzón, chachachá, and other styles.

In 1979, since "young people were only dancing to foreign music" (Rodríguez Riverón 1998), a television program, *Para Bailar*, for promoting Cuban popular dances was created. The idea for dancing couples to compete on air came from Cáceres "Cachito" Manso, a cameraman and later the program's director, and was supported by Cristi Domínguez, Félix Erbiti, and Caruca and Rosendo (Caridad "Caruca" Rodríguez Riverón and Rosendo Eugenio González Doncel), all dancers with the Cuban Television Ballet, where Caruca still teaches. For four years (1980–1983) Caruca and Rosendo won the Girasol de Opina, a prize given out by the eponymous magazine on the basis of popularity, demonstrating the people's respect and admiration for these dancers. Rosendo's role was particularly important, since he served as dance advisor to the program and chose the jury that selected the winning couples. The program aired until 1985. Rosendo died in 1986, a great loss for Cuban culture.

In the 1970s salsa music's effects were also felt. Promoted principally by Puerto Ricans residing in New York, Miami, and other U.S. cities, as well as Cubans who had emigrated in the late 1950s, salsa reflects a complex Caribbean cultural interaction that comes from the rich musical tradition of these peoples. However, a general conviction currently exists that Cuban dance music, principally son, is its fundamental trunk. Ángel Quintero Rivera defines salsa as "a heterogenous integration that manifests common and differentiable elements in each composition and in every territory in which it is produced. . . . It must be understood, above all, as a practice: 'a way of making music'" (1999: 119). In the 1970s, salsa was a huge business outside Cuba. In Cuba this genre was vehemently challenged, not only by musicians but also by specialists and the entire musical dissemination apparatus. Yet the works of Rubén Blades and

Willie Colón, founders of "political salsa" or "conscious salsa," were widely played and very much accepted by the public, above all by the casineros.

Casino dancing in this time, its age of splendor, was characterized by the quality, virtuosity, and style of the dancers. The fundamental parameters defining a virtuosic dancer included the following:

1. Dancing on the offbeats, or in syncopation (*contratiempo*), in relation to the clave. This was a symbol of elegance; done wrong it was considered "crossed" (*atravesao*) or "dancing like whites," without style or grace.[5] "The complexity of dancing in *contratiempo* produced pleasure; it was like a challenge" (Aguilera 1998).[6]
2. Executing rapid changes in timing; performing a continual fast turn and stopping momentarily on the exact musical count
3. Performing very fast turns as an embracing couple, on their axis, without losing the step and keeping a face-to-face position
4. Executing different turns, as many as possible, continually and without error. "The more turns you knew, the better you danced. Just doing the step was not dancing" (Aguilera 1998).
5. Knowing how to *dibujar* (literally, "to draw"). This term, much used in those years, referred to the improvisation performed mainly by the man, who played with the rhythm and combined the basic step with other leg movements, such as kicking in the air, standing on the toes, and making quick figures with the legs.
6. Covering a large space in the ballroom without losing track of the music or one's partner
7. Not erring in the rueda. Casino couples who could achieve this were virtuosos. Just belonging to a famous rueda showed that one possessed quality, ability, and skill.
8. "Singing" (*cantar*) the rueda. The task of directing and saying the figures was carried out by a noteworthy dancer.

Despite casino's widespread popularity, there were restrictions; the average dancer could not dance in some ballrooms and groups, and all dancers generally had to dress elegantly.

The man played a central role, since he determined the turns and figures. The woman demonstrated her ability by letting herself be led without losing the rhythm or the step, aspects important for allowing the man to improvise. Most of the time, casino was danced with the couples in an embrace; they rarely let go. When they did, it was *guarachar* or *dibujar* (to improvise), and they quickly reassumed the original position.

The term "*pasillo*" was widely used to designate the turn or figure combinations. To invent a new pasillo was a creative act, and dancers constantly sought new ones: casino was competitive. The style of dance depended on the social environment; the casino of Playa was not the same as that of Regla.

Some marginal people used dance to express their personality. The men were called *reparteros*, the women *reparteras*, and they incorporated gestures and manners of their milieu, not always accepted by others, into their choreography. They were called *ambientosos* or *guaposos*.[7] Some characteristics of this style were exaggerated movements, sticking out and biting the tongue, raising pant legs, and making pelvis movements. Their dress—for example, very baggy pants and shirts—also distinguished them. Nevertheless, many of their gestures were accepted and reproduced by the casineros, since in more than a few cases they corresponded to the movements of rumba. Their creations are discussed further below.

Casino reached its height of stylistic and choreographic development between 1960 and 1980. The rueda continued to have the same basic form as in its beginnings, but new figures emerged, others disappeared, and some names were changed. The rueda became more complicated as figures were combined in different orders—for example, in *al medio con dos y biquini* (to the center with two and bikini), the *prima y biquinea* (cousin and bikini), and *bótala y dame* (toss her out and give me one). My informants have forgotten how some classic figures were performed, although they do remember their names, such as the *aguja* (needle).

In the early 1980s, most instrumentalists in popular dance music groups were graduates of national and local schools of music, the conservatories, and the Higher Institute of Art (Instituto Superior de Arte; see Figure 6.2). This trend produced surprising developments in casino, resulting in the international phenomenon of salsa. At the same time, salsa in the United States experienced a profound crisis, in part because of excessive commercialization and abandonment of experimentation.

In 1983 *salsero* Oscar D'León traveled from Venezuela to visit Cuba. He was already known in our country from television broadcasts of his music and for his reception of Cuban musical groups that had toured in his country, such as Aragón, Son 14, and Barbarito Díez. His visit caused "certain canons to break down and a series of stagnant patterns to be submitted to revision" (García 1997: 7).

D'León's performance at the Varadero Festival resonated with the Cuban public, although he was also criticized for vulgar or tasteless elements in his performance. However, apart from his abilities as a musician, he was an agile dancer, playing bass at the same time. Casineros quickly copied his movements and gestures. Many still recall a choreographic phrase of D'León and his singers that consisted of marking the basic casino step with certain turns while moving to the side and, later, in coordination with rhythmic accents, adding several kicks. This phrase caught on among dancers so strongly that it today forms part of one of the casino figures, executed both by independent, face-to-face couples and in the rueda, now synthesized and combined with other elements.

After D'León's visit, a rejuvenation of Cuban musical life began. In 1988 NG La Banda was born under the direction of José Luis "El Tosco" Cortés,

Figure 6.2. Students at Havana's Instituto Superior de Arte (ISA [Institute for Higher Education in the Arts]) performing in the Villena Hall of the Unión Nacional de Escritores y Artistas de Cuba (UNEAC [National Union of Writers and Artists of Cuba]). *(Photograph by Bárbara Balbuena Gutiérrez.)*

one of the first generation of students of the National School of Art, who had belonged to groups like Los Van Van and Irakere. La Banda "opened the way for the boom of salsa" in Cuba (Lam 1997: 9) and created important experimental works like "Siglo 1" (García 1997: 7). After NG's founding, new dance music groups exploded onto the scene, including Issac Delgado, Dan Den, La Charanga Habanera, Manolín, and Paulito FG y Su Élite. Most of these new groups are characterized by a theatricality that includes attention-getting choreographic movements performed by the singers and sometimes by the director. The bodily and spatial designs oscillate between the basic casino step, with changing rhythmic accents of the clave, and its combination with steps from other Cuban dance genres like mambo, rumba, and conga.

Song lyrics relate the music to the dance. Almost all the successful groups' songs have meaningful lyrics. Composers use the genuine expressions of the people—their sayings, mottos, sentences, and praises, blended with double entendres; Cubans' ironic views; or analysis of the Cuban situation—as a humorous reflection of our conflicts and deficiencies. These expressions are mostly used in the refrain (*estribillo*), and their choice determines the tune's success.

The meanings in the lyrics are also expressed through social, emotional, functional, and ritual gestures, manifested in different body parts. Many of these movements and gestures are created by the musicians who, on occasion, are excellent dancers. The public imitates them or simply invents other pasillos.

If casino had earlier been characterized by the couple's maintaining their embrace as long as possible, now it is danced in free couples, ruedas, or lines of couples, one man with several women, individuals, and so forth. The main objective is plain fun, breaking down all types of social barriers as a demonstration of the spiritual satisfaction that many Cubans find in dance.

International tourism and musical groups' new openness toward the outside world sent the Cuban music explosion into other parts of the Americas, Europe, and Asia, contributing to the international rebirth of salsa and Afro-Cuban music.

Ballrooms are an extremely important connection between musicians and dancers. Since approximately 1985, several in Cuba have reopened, "recovering dance as one of the Cuban's favorite occupations in his free moments, empowering Cuban traditional and new music through live performances by groups from all parts of the country" (Bello 1992: 36). For example, the Salón Rosado at La Tropical is today the most important such venue in the capital, and visiting it is a must for both musicians and tourists.

Casino and Cuban Salsa Today

With the international rebirth of salsa, and especially of Cuban son-salsa, the dance began to be identified with the name of the musical style, and thus casino started to be called salsa dance.

At the same time, casino has incorporated movements, figures, and steps from other Cuban popular or folkloric genres. The basic casino step is today performed to different musical accents, whether in time with the clave or in opposition to it. The tempos are usually faster than in its earlier days, and the percussion has extensive polyrhythm, which allows addition of foot movements as ornaments without altering the traditional form. Graciela Chao Carbonero notes that the basic step may accent any beat of a measure: in Havana, the different accents may all be seen even during the same party, but young casino dancers tend to accentuate the third beat. While scholars endlessly debate which count is the more traditional one, Chao believes, "Reality imposes the analysis, so that there is no single way of marking the step in relation to the music" (1996: 8). Today, casino is danced by couples in the closed social dance position, in free pairs, in lines of couples, or in the rueda.

Unlike in earlier forms of casino, the couples separate to have greater freedom of movement and, above all, to improvise. Improvisation can come at any time but most often when the music's climax arrives: when there is great polyrhythm in the percussion, the tempo becomes faster, the singer improvises, and there is call-and-response singing. Cuban musicians call this part *bomba* or *timba*.

"*Timba*" has many meanings in Cuba, but it acquired a special musical connotation during the 1990s; musicians use it to identify not only the climactic moment of music but also their most recent artistic work. As occurred with salsa in the 1980s, critics, researchers, and musicologists now debate timba, trying to define this complex musical phenomenon. Among the most recent specialist views are those of Neris González Bello and Liliana Casanella. In a shrewd essay, they posit several musical meanings, one for all 1990s Cuban dance music, one for a particular style of it, and one used for marketing purposes to distinguish Cuban son-salsa productions from others. Early approaches to timba emphasized specific approaches to orchestration and musical style, while more recently Danilo Orozco has defined it as an "intergenre" (González and Casanella 2002: 3–4).

People dance casino to enjoy timba and Cuban salsa, confirming that this ballroom dance has no specific musical equivalent. The climax in the son-salsa compositions that Cuban musicians call bomba or timba has, in the dance, been baptized *despelote*,[8] which is performed by free couples in any position. For the new generation of casineros, despelote is a "hot" moment in the music, meaning to dance in a frenzy, to move the body without hindrance. This is also the moment in which the singer gestures and moves or sings the chorus.

Another term related to dance that has recently appeared in this context is *"tembleque,"* a vibratory movement of the whole body beginning with the pelvis. To do the tembleque requires total independence of each body part, but mainly the pelvis, giving the move an apparent sexual undercurrent. The tembleque is not a new dance or choreography, as some have stated, but another creative movement that forms part of the despelote.

Performers do other steps derived from Afro-Cuban expressions, such as Santería dances (those of Elegguá, Ogún, Ochosi, and other orishas), rumba figures (principally from *columbia* and *guaguancó*), and movements or steps from *makuta*, *yuca*, and other Afro-Cuban dances. Other movements correspond to steps from ballroom or other dances that preceded casino, including the mambo, chachachá, or conga. The integration of these dances began, first, with the opening up and new popularity of Cuban syncretic popular religious practices in the past two decades and, second, with the diffusion of the African-origin cultural expressions that constitute one of the principal sources of our folklore. To the dance are added ritual gestures, such as crossing oneself, the ritual greeting of *santeros*, or followers of Santería. The introduction of *batá* drums or other percussion instruments from these expressions into the musical groups provides further enrichment and merits a separate musicological analysis.

The rueda is today the preferred form of dancing casino. In the past two decades, it has developed on a large scale, principally because of the quantity of turns, figures, choreographic phrases, and step variations the people have invented by taking traditional ones as their starting point, imitating the singers and leaders of musical groups, combining aspects of the heterogenous Cuban dance culture, or incorporating mannerisms and expressions of characters from movies or *telenovelas* (television soap operas).

To achieve greater complexity, in the 1980s dancers began to execute double ruedas in two concentric circles that advanced in different directions, either with independent guides or with just one for both. This practice resulted in true dance mastery and creativity. At parties, improvised ruedas still form among friends or acquaintances; those made up of family members can have unique designs and characteristics.

The family has influenced the development of Cuban ballroom dance in all its eras and, above all, in the people's preference for this diversion. Parents, siblings, and cousins teach children and relatives to dance. Radamés Villegas Jaurequizar told me, "In my family, if you did not dance casino, the other members discriminated against you; you were a *'pasmao'* [party pooper]. One practiced marking steps against the wall and doing turns with a broom, because you can't mistreat the women" (Villegas 1998).

The excellence of male casineros has reached the point that just one dances with two women at once, one on each hand, realizing a series of turns. But the man's role in the casino dance is not as dominant as it was in the 1970s or 1980s, because the woman is important in either the despelote or improvisation. Similarly, women have learned to lead turns as the men do, and when men are scarce at parties, they dance among themselves. Nonetheless, it is still the men who direct the rueda and, almost always, the lines of couples and guide the women when dancing in couples.

In casino today, the dance style called *reparto* (literally "cast," as for a role in a movie or play) is much criticized but also frequently emulated. The so-called *reparteros* and *reparteras*—they are also called *elementos* (marginal people)—have become outstanding dancers. They come from marginal barrios, or poor areas, in Havana, and, as noted previously, their style is characterized by their vulgar or obscene movements, gestures, and steps. When they arrive at any place, they make way by pushing people and stepping on others' feet on purpose, and they start alcohol-fueled fights and disturbances. However, these men and women are recognized as excellent and creative dancers who compete to invent ever-more-complicated steps. Many of their bodily designs have been imitated, mainly in the despelote; the figures have caught on among casineros and are now some of the most performed. Among these are "making the train" (*hacer trencito*), the *santeros'* ritual greeting of crossing themselves, and wave-like movements of the body beginning from the pelvis.

The basic casino step is today performed in the same way as in earlier periods, but the younger dancers perform it only by stepping, or crossing, back. Yet it is impossible to follow the untiring and plentiful creativity of the dancers who create a new turn every day. Most of the current well-known figures performed among independent couples are also performed in the rueda. Some are already traditional, others have a changed name, still others have become more complicated, and many are new. Writing all the casino figures down would be an interminable task. Some of the most mentioned are "Coppelia" (a popular ice cream parlor in Havana), "curly," "two with two," "three with three," "croquette," "eighty-eight," "modern style," "the three graces," "the dark prince," "like the Charanga [Habanera]," "like the doctor" (Manolín, known as *el médico de la salsa*), "the line," "give her to me by [any body part]," "fly," "Echeverría" (whose etymology is unknown), *"mambea"* ("dance as in the mambo"), "vaccinate her" (a rumba reference), and *"tumba francesa"* (a traditional dance of eastern Cuba).[9]

In the rueda, some of the figures just mentioned are combined with others, but the so-called *enchufle* (plug-in) is almost always the one used for changing partner. When several figures are put in a continuous order, this is commonly called "making a chain" (*hacer una cadena*). If the guide says, "Lie!" (*¡Mentira!*), after having "sung" a figure, it is a counterorder, and the action should be undone. Many dancers get lost in the rueda when "*¡Mentira!*" is called, and it is an occasion for fun and disorder.

Casino's principal characteristics that differentiate it from other styles of salsa include the following:

1. It is fundamentally a dance of embracing couples whose figures are performed in a constant rotating motion, whether in place or moving freely through space, in contrast to the linear form that prevails in other styles, such as that of New York.

2. The basic step is generally executed while stepping on the whole foot in a natural way, not in relevé, or on the metatarsals, as women do in other styles.

3. Despite the man leading and deciding the figures, the couple is balanced in the turns, so that both dancers turn alternately. The woman does not turn on her own axis multiple times, as if she were a top, as in other salsa dance styles.

4. To execute the figures without losing the step in relation to the musical rhythm is a principal and valued ability in casino. The man never holds his step for several counts to turn the woman, later reconnecting depending on the rhythmic or turning ability of his partner. Neither does the woman.

5. Traditional, popular casino does not contain stereotyped, fixed gestures such as sharp movements of the head to the sides or the back or movements of the arms or hands touching the hair, clothing, or any body part.

6. Casino is not acrobatic. There is little in the way of lifts, sliding on the floor, spinning in the air, or poses at the conclusion of the dance, as is common in other salsa styles.

7. The couples improvise, using diverse steps or movements from folk dances or other ballroom dances, but these are not choreographed or practiced beforehand to be realized in unison. This occurs only in the genre's theatrical or artistic contexts.

Conclusion

Casino today strongly reflects the character of the Cuban people because it is a synthesis of all the components of our country. Its popularity here has endured for four decades, so that it now forms a part of our cultural patrimony.

Casino is the latest ballroom dance created by the Cuban people. In it, diverse elements contributed by their ancestors converge in an organic and evolving process. It emerged as an anonymous expression of urban people, and it does not correspond to any particular musical genre or style. It is a dance for individual and collective diversion, whose contemporary dynamic is reflected in the great creativity and liberty of its bodily and spatial movements.

Casino is the most popular and relevant ballroom dance in Cuba today; it is a sociocultural event that has directly influenced the development, creativity, and diversity of dance music in our country from the late 1950s to the present. This give and take between popular music and ballroom dance has been indispensable for satisfying the Cuban taste for dancing well and, above all, for maintaining popular music and ballroom dance as the preferred means of recreation and social relation between different social strata for several generations. Casino dance is performed with greater or lesser skill by children, teenagers, and adults and in the most diverse venues, big or small.

Most people who attend dance schools or academies at the international level do so for two reasons: (1) to dissipate the tensions of daily life and work and (2) to encourage and develop social relations. Others learn dance to open their own academies and teach professionally, for it is no secret that dance academies are a lucrative business.

In Cuba, unlike most of the world, no dance academies teach ballroom dance, and hence casino, to the population. Parents teach their children, or one learns among siblings, cousins, or friends. The same occurs between lovers, colleagues, and even people who meet that same day during parties or dance events. This popular style is taught in a professional way only as part of the curriculum in folkloric dance in art schools and in the Higher Institute of Art, as one way to preserve this cultural legacy.

The most important factor to have affected the rise of casino in Cuba and abroad is the dimension salsa music has taken in the international sphere. Identified as Cuban salsa dance, casino has become the vehicle for enjoying salsa as a way of making music, something not at all paradoxical when one recalls that both styles have the Cuban son as an origin.

Casino is disseminated internationally in diverse ways and forms, including the artistic shows offered to tourists, international courses in Cuban ballroom dances, international tours by professional or amateur folkloric groups, courses given by Cuban teachers through collaboration agreements with other countries, regular instruction by Cubans living in other parts of the world or by foreigners, and salsa festivals. This dissemination spreads the values of our national culture and Latin American culture in general. But unscrupulous people, "predators" of traditional popular culture and art hoping to make money, present "methodologies," "steps," or "figures" that have nothing to do with the reality of casino and other Cuban ballroom dances.

Drawing from my own experience giving international courses or workshops on Cuban social or ballroom dances, as well as my observation of world salsa events, I have noticed an incipient tendency toward learning, understanding, and interiorizing the movements, rhythm, steps, and figures of the Cuban style in some teachers and aficionados. This trend is now one of the principal generating sources of the diverse tendencies of salsa style around the world. Young people and adults from many parts of the world have demonstrated interest in learning to dance casino "just as the Cubans do," which is really the difficult part, since how Cubans dance is fundamentally a condition of our own gestures, attitudes, feelings, thoughts, and soul. I therefore believe that casino will continue to develop in its native social dynamic, in the inexhaustible wisdom of its country of origin, its traditions, and its ways of making human contact.

NOTES

1. Spanish names for the steps are *paseo, cadena, sostenido, cedazo, poner danza, latigazo, lazo, alemanda, trono, alas, vueltas, roderos, molinos,* and *puente.*

2. This modified rondo form lacks the final A of the classical rondo.

3. The Spanish translations are *paseo, marque del hombre, cajón,* and *vuelta tornillo.*

4. First called *charanga francesas* (French ensembles), these groups emerged in Cuba in the early years of the last century, deriving from the former *orquesta típica.* The original instrumental format consisted of "flute, violin, piano, contrabass, *timbal* or *paila criolla,* and a *güiro*; later the *tumbadora* [conga drum], two more violins and three singers [were added]" (Orovio 1981: 114). They first played danzones and later chachachá.

5. Even today, in Cuba the phrase "dancing like whites" means to be out of time, to be uncoordinated, or to dance without *sabor* (flavor), in an inorganic way that lacks richness in bodily movements. Although casino dancing was created by whites in a whites-only club that excluded blacks until 1959, casino was later enriched with moves and styles from Afro-Cuban music-dance genres like rumba, *abakuá,* and santería. In Cuban popular speech, it is said that blacks dance better than whites. Of course, there are whites who dance well, and they are told, "You dance like a black person," or "You were possessed by a *congo* [black spirit]." Generally, this is not a pejorative phrase but praise. In its negative aspect, it can mean to dance in a vulgar, exaggerated, or show-off way. Blacks who dance poorly or who do not have a musical ear are told, "The only thing black about you is your skin color, because you dance just like the whites."

6. In Cuba today, dancing in *contratiempo* refers to dancing on-2 by initiating the step on count 4 and pausing on count 1.

7. [Impossible to render exactly in English, these terms translate roughly as "live wires" and "pretty boys," respectively.—Trans.]

8. [*Despelote* is difficult to render in English but roughly means something disorderly or chaotic and, perhaps, a little risqué.—Trans.]

9. The Spanish translations are *coppelia, rizado, dos con dos, tres con tres, croqueta, ochenta y ocho, a lo moderno, las tres gracias, príncipe negro, como la charanga, como el médico, línea, dámela por* [any part of the body], *fly, Echeverría, mambea, vacúnala, tumba francesa.*

REFERENCES

Aguilera, Jorge Luis. 1998. Interview by Bárbara Balbuena Gutiérrez. May 4.

Bello, Roberto. 1992. "Música viva: Salón Rosado de La Tropical; El imperio de la salsa." *Musicalia Dos* (Havana) 1 (1): 36–38.

Chao Carbonero, Graciela. 1996. "De la contradanza al casino." *Toda la Danza—La Danza Toda*, no. 2: 8.

Díaz, Jesús. 1987. *Las iniciales de la tierra* [The beginnings of the earth]. Havana: Editorial Letras Cubanas.

García, Emir. 1997. "Música popular cubana: 1963–1990 ¿Qué tiene que sigue ahí?" *Musicalia Dos* (Havana) 1 (1): 7.

Gómez, María Elena. 1992. "El casino." Unpublished thesis. Instituto Superior de Arte, Havana.

González, Neris, and Liliana Casanella. 2002. "La timba cubana: Un intergénero contemporáneo." *Clave* 4 (1): 2–9.

Lam, Rafael. 1997. "NG, la banda que manda." *Musicalia Dos* (Havana) 1 (1): 9–21.

Linares, María Teresa. 1974. *La música y el pueblo.* Havana: Editorial Pueblo y Educación.

Loyola, José. 1997. *En ritmo de bolero en la música bailable cubana.* Havana: Ediciones Unión.

Orovio, Helio. 1981. *Diccionario de la música cubana.* Havana: Editorial Letras Cubanas.

Quintero Rivera, Ángel G. 1999. *¡Salsa, sabor y control! Sociología de la música "tropical."* 2nd ed. Mexico City: Siglo Veintiuno.

Rodríguez Riverón, Caridad. 1998. Interview by Bárbara Balbuena Gutiérrez. January 20.

Sainz-Baranda, Hilda Vila. 1998. Interview by Bárbara Balbuena Gutiérrez. February 26.

Valdés, Alicia. 1988. *Formell en tres tiempos (1965–1988).* Havana: CIDMUC.

Villegas, Radamés. 1998. Interview by Bárbara Balbuena Gutiérrez. September 16. Havana, Cuba.

7

The Global Commercialization
of Salsa Dancing and *Sabor*
(Puerto Rico)

Priscilla Renta

Western ideals of beauty, elegance, and grace influence competitive salsa dancing and ballroom dancing and have had significant impact on the globalization of salsa dancing and *sabor*, flavor, and the related concept of *sentimiento*, feeling. World salsa dance competition rules and regulations, for instance, often mirror globalization's centralization of power[1] and tendency toward homogenization, thus suppressing sabor, cultural creativity, improvisation, and individual expression.

Three world salsa championships serve as regulating bodies for competitive salsa dancing, performance, and instruction at the moment: (1) the World Salsa Federation (WSF) Championship, or Campeonato Mundial, in Miami, Florida, (2) El Congreso Mundial de la Salsa (World Salsa Congress; now known as the Puerto Rico Salsa Congress) and its World Salsa Open Championship in Puerto Rico, and (3) the World Salsa Championships in Las Vegas, Nevada, renamed the World Latin Dance Cup. The global commercialization of salsa dancing and sabor has a symbiotic relationship with these organizations and events, generating diverse global, transnational, and national perspectives among Latin American and Caribbean observers.

This chapter discusses the globalization of salsa dancing and its effects on the concept of sabor, beginning with my own localized experience. This project is native-ethnographic, given that I am both Puerto Rican and a salsa dancer. Thus, an aspect of my analysis is testimonial, particularly with regard to sabor as a spiritual principle. The first half of this chapter deals with the cultural capital of sabor on the basis of several phases of my own experience. It describes the Caribbean cosmology underpinning salsa music making, which centers on dancing with sabor and sentimiento. It also includes my performance experience with the Eddie Torres Dancers at the RMM (Ralph Mercado Management)

Twenty-Third Annual Salsa Music Festival at Madison Square Garden, which inspired my scholarship on salsa dancing. Thus, the first half chronicles the transformation of salsa dancing from a form of Caribbean everyday life experience to staged choreography, emphasizing its role in Puerto Rican cultural life.

The second half of the chapter examines competitive salsa dancing, the global commercialization of salsa, and sabor in three different scenarios. First, the WSF has created an instructional video called *Latin Body Rhythms*, which influences global concepts of and access to sabor by focusing on its corporeal aspects. Second is a YouTube clip of dancers from Spain performing the routine that won them the 2009 title at the Congreso Mundial de la Salsa. This performance generated a transnational Latin American and Caribbean online discussion regarding what constitutes salsa dancing, sabor, and the sentimiento it engenders and how competitive salsa dancing, influenced by Western concepts of grace and elegance, destabilizes national identification with salsa. Finally, I turn to my archival and ethnographic research on the Congreso Mundial de la Salsa.

My work demonstrates that dancing salsa with sabor serves as a symbolic form of cultural nationalism, which Jorge Duany describes as the "spiritual autonomy of a people" (2002: 5; see also Duany 2001: 15, on the Puerto Rican "nation" as a spiritual principle). Sabor is the heart and soul of salsa dancing, an aesthetic tradition involving improvisation, creativity, and a corporeal response to the polyrhythmic quality of salsa music that stems from its African heritage. While some Puerto Ricans believe salsa loses sabor as it moves away from its history as a street dance with working-class roots and into the context of the Congreso Mundial, which focuses on staged, choreographed salsa dance performance and competitive dancing, global legitimacy has nonetheless caused the island's middle and upper classes to embrace salsa dancing.[2]

This chapter voices the concerns of Puerto Ricans, particularly those on the island, about salsa and sabor and considers the impact of the global commercialization of salsa dancing on Puerto Rican nationhood. I draw from online discussions; formal and informal interviews I conducted in Puerto Rico (2006) and New York (2002–2003); and my attendance at the first Congreso Mundial in Puerto Rico in 1997, the third in 1999, and the 2006 tenth-anniversary celebration. I focus primarily on global commercialization and the reception of competitive salsa dancing while remaining conscious that the production side is equally significant and requires additional space and research.

What Is Sabor? Sabor in Salsa Music (the Meaning Is in the Feeling)

> It don't mean a thing if it ain't got that swing. —Duke Ellington

Salsa music's globalization and industrialization beginning in the sixties set the stage for the global commercialization of salsa dancing and sabor at the turn of the new millennium. The concept of sabor has been circulating for as long as the word "salsa," or sauce, has been used as a commercial term. Varying in degrees of complexity and geographically determined ingredients, sauce provides flavor to cuisines around the world. Izzy Sanabria, the man responsible for commercializing and using "salsa" as a marketing term during the seventies, writes that "salsa is what gives Latin food its flavor" (Sanabria, n.d.). There are, nonetheless, variations in how sauce and flavor are created in Latin-Caribbean cooking. In Puerto Rico, the foundation of the creole sauce added to seafood and rice dishes, beans, and soups is called *sofrito*. Sofrito, a creole method of cooking, combines cilantro, *recao* (culantro), sweet *ajíes* (red peppers), onions, and garlic, all sautéed in either olive oil or pork fat, and is the key to Puerto Rican culinary flavor. *Cocinando* (cooking), eating, and dancing are all sensual experiences that are often metaphorically intertwined in Caribbean music. Sanabria says that in Latin music, as in North American jazz, "when a band was really swinging, people would say, 'They're cooking' . . . in Spanish— '*¡Cocinando!*' And when all the ingredients were cookin' just right . . . Latinos would say, 'It had *Salsa y Sabor*' (sauce and taste). So what [salsa] really denotes is music with flavor and spice" (Sanabria, n.d.).

Resonating with this claim is a recent album by El Gran Combo de Puerto Rico called *Arroz con habichuela* (Rice and Beans), on which the band sings, "Cuatro décadas Gran Combo en la cocina, cocinando salsa para la gente latina" (Four decades [with] Gran Combo in the kitchen, cooking salsa for the Latin people). The lyrics are an example of how salsa continues to be conceptually connected with the sensual experience of cooking. Gran Combo's reference to a broad Latin American audience also reflects their transnational reach, which helped give rise to their fame in the late fifties and early sixties.

Winning a Latin Grammy award for Best Tropical Album in 2006, *Arroz con habichuela* comments on the globalization and Americanization of salsa in a characteristically playful, tongue-in-cheek manner. Promoting a discourse of salsa and sabor that involves the senses, Latin food, music and dance, the lyrics affirm that the music is neither a "light salad" nor rock 'n' roll; it "takes some years to be played as it should." The lyrics enumerate the ingredients of their creole "recipe": Cuban *son*, New York swing, rumba, *plena*, Spanish poetry, and African drumming with a hint of *melao* (molasses or sweetness). "Arroz con habichuela" thus delivers its critique by juxtaposing the substance of Puerto Rican food with light American fare. Rice, beans, and root vegetables are a substantial meal that provides sustenance and nourishment, a culinary metaphor for the substance and complexity of Latin music. "Arroz con habichuela" warns the novice to stand back, watch, listen, and learn. "Don't dare jump in," the band advises, because the clave will knock down an outsider with a flippant attitude. A light, presumably North American, salad has neither the flavor nor the substance necessary for learning salsa.

The song's lyrics continue by defining salsa in a variety of ways, including through the concepts of *cadencia* (cadence) and *elegancia* (elegance), referencing the Cuban son that preceded and influenced the development of salsa dancing as well as the New York way of playing salsa with swing. Both swing and cadencia can be synonymous with sabor, while cadencia is particularly associated with musical structure (measure and count), flow, rhythm, and the interaction of the voice and the clave in the music. The association Gran Combo makes between Afro-Caribbean cadencia, the European aesthetic of elegance, and a diasporic approach to creating Latin music with swing also symbolizes the creolization inherent in salsa music and dance. Cadencia relates to dance in that it can also be defined as "the correspondence of the motion of the body with the music" (*SpanishDict*, n.d.) In the same way as with music, dancing salsa with cadencia and sabor develops over time. Sabor is in the dancing of elders as it is in the old-school, Afro-Caribbean rumba from Cuba and the plena from Puerto Rico, both of which also influenced salsa.

"Arroz con habichuela" comments on the institutionalization of Latin music and salsa, asserting that the genre is not contained in books or schools. Rather, its substance is learned through practice on the street and requires full immersion. The *sancocho*, or stew of root vegetables, red meat, and sofrito with ingredients that make it *sabroso*, or full of flavor, is slow-cooked over a fire, usually in the open air of the tropics, rather than in the microwave that cooks instant, North American–style meals. In other words, tradition and the investment it requires help Gran Combo prepare a musical banquet for their global, transnational Latin American and Caribbean audience, one with a uniquely Puerto Rican flavor.

The Cultural Capital and Habitus of Sabor: A Native-Ethnographic Perspective

> Salsa is living, breathing, and experiencing the power of the moment.

The substance of sabor is important not only for Puerto Rican salsa bands like Gran Combo but also for salsa dancing, both professional and everyday. The Latin-Caribbean cosmology on which salsa dancing is founded fuels the corporeal processes of listening to, translating, and interpreting music. My first perceptions of sabor as a spiritual, emotional, and corporeal form of musical interpretation and appreciation involved witnessing my mother dancing and singing along to old records by El Gran Combo, Celia Cruz, and Johnny Pacheco, cofounder of Fania Records, as well as many merengue tunes popular in the eighties and late seventies. As a result, my younger sister and I grew up listening and moving to Latin-Caribbean rhythms—including salsa, which would come to play a significant role in my life.

Although merengue, through which my sister and I learned to move polycentrically and polyrhythmically, became my mother's music of choice in the eighties—reflecting the decline of salsa during that time (see Pietrobruno 2006: 65)—my aunts and uncles taught me the Latin hustle, a combination of salsa and disco resulting from Puerto Rican circular migration (see Duany 2001) during the seventies (Conrad 2006). This early familiarity, coupled with my ethnographic experiences in Puerto Rico and New York, contributed to my understanding of sabor's connection to Latino public and personal histories and music.

I, as do many Latinos, credit my mother as my first teacher in my early formation as a dancer. With roots in Puerto Rico's capital city of San Juan and the mountains of Jayuya, she has danced for most of her life, from her childhood on the island to her adult days in the United States. My mother prefers Gran Combo's first phase, after the band's founding by Rafael Cortijo, featuring Ismael Rivera as the band's lead vocalist. This was the era when Cortijo combined the Cuban son and *guaracha* with the Afro–Puerto Rican rhythms of *bomba* and plena, a practice that set the stage for the emergence of New York–Puerto Rican salsa later in the seventies.

Mami also enjoys the earlier music of Celia Cruz, who came to be known as the Queen of Salsa in the United States. One of my mother's favorite pieces continues to be "Burundanga," performed and recorded originally by the renowned Cuban band La Sonora Matancera and featuring Cruz, later remade by New York–Puerto Rican *salsero* Willie Colón. During a performance of "Burundanga" recorded for television in the sixties or seventies, Celia shouts *"¡Sabor!"* and *"¡Azúcar!"* (sweetness or sugar)—her signature phrases—while briefly dancing with the show's host, who seems challenged by her polycentric movement.[3] Celia's moves—small, tight, and mostly in place, grounded through knee flexion and downward energy, allowing the hips, torso, and shoulders to move polycentrically—remind me of my mom's strong connection to Caribbean music and how she used to dance to "Burundanga" at home.

Mami captured the song's feel and Celia's vocal sabor, as she did with other Caribbean music, during her performances in our living room, at family gatherings, or while she was cleaning the house with Caribbean music playing in the background. The music we played at home growing up reflected that of the community of Cubans, Puerto Ricans, and Dominicans living in our neighborhood, groups that all contributed to the birth of salsa.

Celia y Johnny, for example, is another of my mom's favorite albums. César Miguel Rondón describes the album as "full of old *sones*" but with a "Nuyorican salsa. . . . [P]erhaps the best cut of the entire album [is] 'Quimbara,'" which Celia interpreted with "intelligence and *sabor*" (2008: 87). Johnny Pacheco created a path for Cruz, a self-exiled Cuban, to make her way into the contemporary world of salsa music, which drew primarily from the Afro-Cuban son in its initial phase. The son has a strong history in the Dominican Republic, and Rondón describes Dominican-born Pacheco as a "complete musician who possessed one of the most important talents in this trade: a sense of *sabor* . . . [which enabled him] to move easily among all styles and popular tastes. . . . [I]t was precisely his *sabor* that contributed to his success" (70). These assertions demonstrate the belief, shared by performers from around the Caribbean, that sabor is a feature of excellent musicianship in salsa music.

Musical sabor involves the feeling produced by the combination of musical arrangement and instrumentation, vocal and lyrical composition, and exposition. It is expressed in the mambo, *montuno*, and *descarga* (jam) sections in salsa, all of which feature improvisation and motivate dancers to move. The songs that inspire dancers to connect with the music's sabor and express their own unique flavor through corporeal translation, interpretation, and expression are a matter of personal choice. Furthermore, Rondón writes, "in the context of Latino popular music [sabor] is an untranslatable term that refers to an undefinable quality in a musical performance, a unique sense of style and rhythm, an edge and passion that allows listeners to identify with the music" (2008: 4). Suggesting a form of *je ne sais quoi*, or *yo no sé qué*, Rondón's definition stresses sabor's grounding in the performer's sense of personal expression and uniqueness, leading to an intangible quality that escapes verbalization. This kind of sabor also manifests in dance, through which the connection and identification with the music is catalyzed.

The connection my mom has with Caribbean music is the foundation of her sabor and unique personal flavor. When asked, for instance, how she learned to dance, my mom responds, "A mí nadie me enseñó. . . . Yo siempre bailo al ritmo de la música, a lo que me inspira la música; así es como yo me muevo, de acuerdo a lo que oigo. . . . La música me hizo aprender; la música me decía como mover mi cuerpo" (No one taught me. . . . I always dance to the rhythm of the music, to what the music inspires in me; that is how I move, based on what I hear. . . . Music made me learn; the music would tell me how to move my body). The music's recognizable and unique qualities, as described by Rondón, move social dancers to connect with the music and translate its sabor into corporeal expression on the basis of a common Caribbean experience rooted in everyday life.

Sabor also involves the spiritual and emotional aspects of music making, listening, dancing, and performing that escape verbalization, as Rondón suggests. For instance, I can recall my mother dancing with eyes closed, one hand on the center of her solar plexus and the other facing up, palm open, as if to connect with divine energy. To dance with sabor in this way is to experience one's higher self, transcending material experience by surrendering to what the music enables dancers to feel in the present moment. As Juan Carlos Quintero Herencia writes referring to a 1975 performance by Celia Cruz, "Salsa associates itself with divinities" (1997: 190).

Combining the sacred and secular is common in Latino culture. These days, my mother, my sister, and I still dance to old son records by Celina and Reutilio, who incorporate songs and rhythms of Santería into their tunes. Grooving to favorites such as "Santa Bárbara/Que viva Changó," which refers to Santería's father of music and the drum, and "San Lázaro," which pays homage to Babaluayé, father of healing, my mom uses a red handkerchief to cleanse her aura and body of negative energy, despite being profoundly Catholic. A kind of *despojo*, or spiritual cleansing, her dance does not adhere to specific steps but serves as a profound form of expression through improvisation that involves a level of surrender. My sister and I also learned how to feel music this way, through witnessing and moving.

Powerful states of consciousness that include present-moment awareness are central to the salsa listening and production experience as well as to dance. Enrique Romero, quoting Raphy Leavit of Orquesta la Selecta, describes salsa as "vivir el presente a pleno pulmón y con la máxima intensidad. . . . [La salsa] aconseja: 'Vive la vida, mira que se va y no vuelve'" (to live the present full on and with maximum intensity. . . . [Salsa] advises: "Live life, because before you know it, it's gone") (Romero 2000: 41). Romero refers to the breath of life, filling the lungs—*pulmones*—to capacity. Puerto Ricans on the island describe salsa dancing as *una forma de curarse* (a form of healing oneself). Present-moment awareness, which encompasses the healing capacity of breath, is one of the reasons some consider salsa dancing therapeutic. Romero reminds me of a popular *refrán*, or saying, I often hear from my mother: "*La vida es un soplo; hay que saber vivirla, hay que saber gozarla*" (Life is just a breath; one has to know how to live it and enjoy it). She describes dancing to Caribbean music as something that filled her with life and brought her joy in the context of *la vida cotidiana*, everyday life, entertainment she preferred to watching U.S. television.

The Caribbean cosmology Romero discusses underpins salsa music's poetic universe, which is founded on the power of language and everyday experience (2000: 42). My mother, for instance, recalls how the Gran Combo's humorous lyrics motivated her to laugh, dance, and have fun at home. Romero describes this process of identification with Caribbean music and lyrics as an aesthetic endeavor produced "thanks to that powerful bond between life and music, pleasure . . . which is called *sabor* and *sentimiento*" (42). Romero's explanation of sabor and sentimiento centers on the validation of everyday life expressed in Caribbean music. Rondón's aforementioned definition of sabor focuses on musicians' identification with musical sonority and their unique personal expression. Romero's focus is lyrical composition and rhythm, whereas Rondón references musical arrangement, style, sonority, and instrumentation. These concepts are equally important factors in the processes of corporeal translation and interpretation.

Salsa's poetic universe musicalizes *la lógica de la clase obrera or de la calle*, the logic of the working class or of the street, through *el caló caribeño*, Caribbean vernacular (Romero 2000: 42–43), a way of validating Caribbean experiences of everyday life and fueling corporeal expression. This Caribbean *caló* is complex, moving beyond the repetition of the joyful experience of dance and music alone. Caribbean musical production, recording, performance, listening, and dancing unfold within a context of oppressive socioeconomic conditions that can generate experiences of suffering, struggle, separation, trauma, racism, pain, and loss—all of which inform musical arrangement, lyrical composition, corporeal expression, and sabor. Salsa, in particular, creates powerful states of consciousness, including the harmonization and coexistence of emotions ranging from pleasure, happiness, humor, playfulness, joy, excitement, and intensity to sadness, pain, longing, nostalgia, melancholy, competition, rancor, *despecho* (spite, bitterness), indignation, and *burla* (mocking). The broad gamut of emotions experienced through salsa culminates in a form of polycentric, polyrhythmic catharsis.

Romero elegantly describes this type of multilayered corporeal-sonorous experience from the perspective of the listener when he writes that salsa's joyful music is only half the story:

> La otra mitad la compone la historia que cuenta en medio de su alegre sonoridad. Los textos de la salsa (la crónica del Caribe) narran historias tristes. . . . Y aunque hay también textos gozosos, son los otros los que priman con su melancolía, su dolor u su tristeza. Esto se da en los textos, pero se refleja también en los arreglos instrumentales que, incitando a bailar, dan alegría al cuerpo y cierta tristeza al alma, pero una tristeza que se vive con felicidad. A este binomio, aparentemente contradictorio, se le llama sabor y sentimiento. (2000: 40–41)

> (The other half comprises the story it tells in the midst of its happy sonority. Salsa's texts (chronicles of the Caribbean) narrate sad stories. . . . And although there are also joyful texts, it's the others that predominate with their melancholy, pain and sadness. This happens with the texts, but is also reflected in the musical arrangements which, inciting one to dance, bring joy to the body and a certain sadness to the soul, but a sadness that is lived with happiness. This binary, apparently contradictory, is called *sabor* and *sentimiento*.)

Romero's words describe the more complex layers of the concept of sabor as a Caribbean aesthetic practice that engages a binomial he calls *el dolor que se baila*, pain that is danced (40).

Sabor, as Romero suggests, is pleasure, pain, sorrow, and sadness as well as happiness and joy. The dialectical tension that arises from the Caribbean aesthetic technique of juxtaposition (see Gottschild 1996: 17), stemming from cultural philosophy and cosmology, manifests lyrically as well as in the dialogue between music and text). This corporeal-sonorous experience involves surrendering to what one feels in the present moment as a source of resilience within what Romero calls the Caribbean habitat (2000: 44).

The Caribbean habitat and the resilience of its people also involve salsa compositions whose sabor and sentimiento come from contesting cultural imperialism, rebellion, intense indignation, and a sense of social justice. There are many salsa music compositions whose musical arrangements and lyrics symbolically mirror one another. For example, Eddie Palmieri's "La libertad, lógico" (Freedom, of course) musicalizes revolution and rebellion against imperialism, combining a symbolic confrontation between the brass and percussion sections with simple yet profound lyrics that describe the logic of freedom.[4] Yet within the context of salsa dancing's globalization, the complex meaning of music that is danceable and joyful but whose lyrics deal with disturbing, troubling, or sad matters can be misinterpreted or lost to the corporeal experience. While the global commercialization of salsa dancing has its benefits, there are internal aesthetic norms that are vital and integral to the genre. Romero, for instance, writes that if a band or singer does not have musical sabor, "*no están en nada*" (they have nothing going on) (2000: 137). The same is true for salsa dancing in both its social contexts and its staged, choreographed versions that emerged in the late nineties.

The RMM Salsa Music Concert: Performance, Sabor, and Choreography

The Congreso Mundial disseminated salsa dancing techniques and distinct regional styles throughout the world in an unprecedented and unparalleled manner. New York–Puerto Rican choreographer Eddie Torres was also particularly pivotal to the globalization of salsa dancing before the congress. For instance, during the late nineties salsa dance aficionados from across the globe, particularly Asia and Europe, would come to study with Torres, sometimes relocating to New York to learn from him for extended periods. Torres is both an originator of stylized, choreographed salsa dancing (see Chapter 2) and an example of the role Puerto Ricans have played in its globalization. In this section, I use my perspective as a performer with the Eddie Torres Latin Dance Company in New York to show how staged choreography can be created and performed with sabor, but not without challenges. I also demonstrate how the move toward choreographed rather than improvised movement transformed the Latin-Caribbean dancing I learned with my mother and sister in our living room.

Although I have danced to Latin-Caribbean music throughout my life, my particular interest in salsa did not begin to grow until my adolescence in the eighties, when I first witnessed my cousin and his wife dancing at a family party. I was mesmerized by their smooth, flowing synchronicity and their relaxed, seemingly effortless movements. In college, salsa dancing became a way to ground myself as one among only a handful of Puerto Rican women at the liberal arts college I attended on scholarship. The mostly wealthy, upper- and upper-middle-class student body contrasted dramatically with my family's blue-collar background. Having grown up in a working-class neighborhood where we were the only Puerto Rican family, I found something both familiar and foreign in the social aspect of my college experience, where I discovered that I lacked the upper-class cultural capital in circulation.

Once I graduated college, I entered the financial industry and worked in communications for close to ten years during the nineties. Within that world, it was similarly necessary to remain connected to the culture in which I had grown up. Going to Latin nightclubs and restaurants offering Latin music and dance reignited my interest in salsa dancing. Stylized, staged salsa dancing was emerging during this time, and salsa dance classes in New York, where I worked, and New Jersey, where I lived, were beginning to proliferate. My cultural background and personal interests motivated me to become involved. I was also attracted to the dance's beauty.

I began performing and training with the Eddie Torres Latin Dance Company in the late nineties, after taking lessons with Torres for a few months and New Jersey–based salsa instructor Ismael Otero, director of Caribbean Soul Dancers, for close to two years. My informal training at home had prepared me to move in ways I was not consciously aware I could, serving as an empowering experience that demonstrated the cultural capital of growing up surrounded by Latin-Caribbean music, dance, and the complex, multilayered life-world of sabor.

My work with Torres culminated in a 1998 performance at Madison Square Garden as part of the twenty-third-annual Salsa Music Festival concert, organized by Ralph Mercado, founder and owner of the biggest salsa label at that time (RMM). The salsa musicians we performed with that evening included La India, Tito Rojas, Elvis Crespo, El Gran Combo, and Eddie Palmieri.

Salsa musicians tend to create and improvise on the spot when playing live, expressing their own sabor and transmitting it to the audience. Knowing this, Torres choreographed short sequences and left room for the dancers to improvise, thus helping us become more proficient in improvisation—a vital aspect of sabor that is often suppressed in competitive salsa dancing influenced by ballroom dance aesthetics. Staged choreography nonetheless affects improvisation for both musicians and dancers, just as "recording imposes control over improvisatory elements" in salsa music (Quintero Herencia 1997: 177). Performing to live music at the concert was also challenging given that rehearsals were conducted to recordings.

"Vamonos pa'l monte" (Let's go to the mountains), a powerful piece by Eddie Palmieri, was the opening number. Rondón fittingly describes how this salsa classic has "a mysterious force, full of power and *sabor*, with all its feeling intact" even today, despite having been recorded so long ago (Rondón 2008: 283). Successfully and safely completing eight spins within one clave cycle (eight beats) in three-inch heels on a precariously narrow platform above and behind the band was one of the most challenging aspects of the partnered choreography, but it was met with a loud roar from the crowd at Madison Square Garden, some of whom could see the performers only from projections on large screens. The dancers felt the excitement the audience transmitted; it was an energy that was unlike anything I had experienced before, despite previous performance experience with live bands.

The opening line of the song says, "Vamonos pa'l monte, pa'l monte pa' guarachar"—Let's go to the mountains, to the mountains to party and dance (*guarachar*). Going to the mountains can be viewed as a form of *cimarronaje*, or maroonage—in this case, freedom or escape from industrialized urban society to connect with tradition and nature while experiencing the joy of movement and music.[5] Ángel Quintero Rivera discusses the song's improvisatory *descarga* (jam), *montuno*, and *soneo* sections as further expressions of freedom in salsa (1999: 336). For me, performing to this song represented freedom from corporate American culture. There was also a collective power in performing synchronized choreography.

For the RMM salsa music concert that year, Torres created a visual and corporeal expression of the music's audible flavor by choreographing aggressive, intricate, and fast-paced open footwork. While Torres is a forerunner of stylized, choreographed salsa dancing, his choreography demonstrates his strong connection with salsa music's flavor, perhaps stemming from his experience as a musician. Furthermore, while choreography can seem mechanical, when salsa dancers possess confidence in their technical ability based on formal and/ or informal training, practice, and repetition, they are able to bring the flavor of their connection with the music to life on stage, much as experienced musicians do.

The Global Circulation of Sabor and Salsa Dancing through the World Salsa Federation

Performing inspired me to pursue an academic career in performance studies. *Salsa, sabor y control* by Quintero Rivera (1999) motivated my ethnographic research on the role of sabor in salsa dancing in New York (2000–2003) and Puerto Rico (2006), and Frances Aparicio's "Salsa, maracas and baile" (1989–1990) inspired me to explore the spiritual dimensions of sabor.

The global commercialization of sabor has emerged through the WSF's efforts to centralize salsa dancing performance standards and instruction, but the Puerto Rico Salsa Congress has had the most significant globalizing power. Both organizations include competitive salsa dancing and often mirror the ballroom dance industry's suppression of improvisation (see McMains 2009). However, transnational Latin American and Caribbean contestation of competitive salsa dancing, which demonstrates class consciousness with regard to sabor and sentimiento, persists. Furthermore, as mentioned previously, my native-ethnographic research indicated that dancing salsa with sabor can serve as a symbolic form of cultural nationalism, which is also transnational. A shared class consciousness and concern for Africanist tradition also exists among Puerto Ricans. This section explores these topics.

The WSF, founded by ballroom dancers Isaac and Laura Castro Altman, is a corporation with headquarters in Miami, Florida. The organization describes itself as the "recognized world governing body for salsa competition" (World Salsa Federation, n.d.). In 2012 the WSF website also emphasized that the organization was recognized by the International Olympic Committee. The WSF has been at the forefront of bringing Latin ballroom standards to competitive salsa dancing since 2001. Its mission includes setting official rules, securing international recognition of rules, and creating a salsa dance instruction syllabus to promote the dance as both sport and art (World Salsa Federation, n.d.).

While competition has its virtues, the use of Latin ballroom standards for salsa dancing can be troubling, particularly with regard to sabor as a form of creativity. Furthermore, the WSF's emphasis on Latin ballroom standards, official rules, and uniformity reflect the cultural imperialism of the ballroom dance industry while mirroring globalization's movement toward "transforming the world into a single social and cultural setting" (Roland Robertson, quoted in Pietrobruno 2006: 23), which can lead to homogenization. Nonetheless, the WSF promotes its DVD *Latin Body Rhythms* as "a must if you want to dance Salsa with the maximum body action and SABOR!" (United States Dance Foundation, n.d.). Given the WSF's investment in combining competitive salsa dancing with Euro-American-derived Latin ballroom standards (see Pietrobruno 2006: 132) and the misappropriation of Caribbean and Latin American dances of African lineage, it is commendable that the organization has recognized the aesthetic concept of sabor and its corporeal expression in this production; however, I focus here on the production's use of ballroom dance vocabulary and its relationship to the Latin-Caribbean aspects of sabor.

Starring Castro Altman, the DVD presents a holistic corporeal approach to what I have elsewhere described as "Latin motion" (Renta 2004), a polycentrism (see Gottschild 1996) and polyrhythm evident in most Afro-Latin dances, which the ballroom industry describes as "Cuban motion" (likely because the Latin-Caribbean dances imported in the early twentieth century were primarily Cuban and because of Cuba's role as a tropical playground for Americans before the Revolution). Elsewhere, I have explained how this is the most challenging aspect of salsa for aspiring dancers, since it requires a kind of immersion that resists commodification (Renta 2004: 148; see also Pietrobruno 2006: 140). Nonetheless, the WSF has created a way to package and sell Latin motion. The ballroom version of Latin motion seems to include a large, somewhat exaggerated hip motion that concludes with a rolling and twisting action designed to emphasize the movement visually. This action differs from the more contained Afro-Latin-Caribbean movement, which is powerful yet flexible and relaxed. It emphasizes the kinesthetic feeling produced through the dancer's body, which in turn creates a kinesthetic effect on those watching. The difference between these two aesthetics is likely based on the difference between stylized dance for competition and performance versus social, leisure-time dance in everyday life. Nonetheless, one cannot ignore the hegemonic tropicalization (Aparicio and Chávez-Silverman 1997) at the foundation of ballroom interpretations of Latin social dances, which tend to either distort Latin motion's body isolations and polycentric, polyrhythmic quality—creating a tropicalized representation of the movement aesthetic—or suppress it altogether.

The *Latin Body Rhythms* "cool body movements" section also demonstrates Latin ballroom's historical relationship with Latin motion. For instance, Castro Altman teaches the aforementioned ballroom version, describing it as "adding spice"—or perhaps flavor—for show or social dance. Castro Altman also teaches an "Afro-Caribbean side movement" involving what the ballroom industry calls the "cucaracha," a lateral movement in the rib cage with the shoulders rolling back in unison. The WSF does make an effort to create consciousness surrounding salsa's body isolations, but Castro Altman's interpretation misses the fluid aspect of polycentrism, as well as the comfortable, relaxed feeling that it engenders through its grounded, rooted stance and deep knee flexion. The DVD attempts to capture the complexity of sabor as a corporeal technique, but misses the opportunity to validate the concept of feeling, which salsa dancers can produce and experience through creativity, improvisation, and connection with the music. The WSF's Latin ballroom-inspired interpretation of sabor thus reflects the view that the dance is primarily a corporeal technique rather than a holistic practice that involves spiritual and emotional consciousness. The following section focuses on the significance of sabor as, in contrast, a form of sentimiento, or feeling, within the context of the Congreso Mundial's World Salsa Open Championship, developed in the new millennium.

Global, Transnational, Latin American, and Caribbean Concepts of Sabor and Salsa

A 2010 performance by three-time World Salsa Open champions Anita Santos and Adrián Rodríguez posted on YouTube generated passionate commentary that revealed how the polemics of sentimiento and sabor in salsa dancing are connected to concepts of nationhood, class, and race.[6] The winning couple's original performance at the annual World Salsa Open Championship took place in 2009. Although the couple was representing Spain, which is where they currently live and operate their dance business, Santos is from Brazil, and Rodríguez is from Uruguay. After viewing the YouTube clip of their repeat performance at the Latin Festival in Ludwigsburg in 2010, one user from Venezuela commented, "Que fastidio con la manía de convertir en 'balet' todos los estilo [*sic*]" (What a nuisance, the obsession of converting every style into ballet). The comment serves as an archival ethnographic example of Latino sentiment regarding the influence of Europeanist aesthetic values. To be able to enter the market of dance, with its legacy of cultural imperialism, Latinos have to stylize salsa dancing to serve Europeanist aesthetic values, subsumed here under the canon of ballet that influenced ballroom dance (see Pietrobruno 2006: 120–122). Meanwhile, the repeat performance in Ludwigsburg demonstrates the global circulation of competitive salsa dancing, which destabilizes Latin American and Caribbean national identification with the genre.

While numerous competitive salsa dancing forms from many parts of the world circulate on the Internet, functioning as a global theater for a virtual audience, this video generated more heated commentary than any other I have seen, particularly with regard to questions of sabor, sentimiento, and the definition of salsa dancing. The responses came from an audience representing different countries, all chiming in on what it means to dance salsa with feeling. They include the following (all with original spelling, accentuation, and capitalization; the country of the commenters or city, if known, has also been included to demonstrate the global cross-section):

Bonita pareja, pero carecen del sabor a salsa.

(Beautiful couple, but they are missing the flavor of salsa.) —United States

Que espectacular se vio pero prefiero una buena salsa de un viernes en la noche de gente con ritmo y sabor.

(Spectacular, but I prefer some good salsa on a Friday night with people who have rhythm and flavor.) —Mexico

La salsa callejera tiene mas sabor esta es mas formal.

(Street salsa has more flavor[;] this one is more formal.) —United States

Lots o enegies:) [sic] but no grace, no sabor. —Canada

No flavor, cuban dance is not some kind of sport, is not about speed and weird moves, its all about feeling. —Miami, Spanish surname

Me parece "lo mismo de siempre", mùsica a 300km x hora y ellos que le caen atràs como locos sin saborear lo que estàn tratando de hacer. Seràn personas excelentes, pero esa mùsica y ese estilo no me transmite sensaciones, ni me recuerda nada que tenga que ver con el origen del baile de la mùsica cubana (de donde nace todo). Algunas de esas cosas se podìan apreciar, pero solo a nivel de cabaret (Tropicana) y no como baile popular.

(It seems to me that it is "the same old thing," music at 300km/hour and they chase after it without savoring what they are trying to do. They may be excellent people, but that music and that style do not give me any sensations, and it does not remind me at all of anything that has to do with the origin of Cuban dance music (from which everything comes). Some of those things can be appreciated, but only at the level of cabaret (Tropicana) and not as a dance of the people.) —Italy, Cuban respondent

On the surface these comments reflect a preference for salsa as a social dance, as opposed to competitive, professionalized performance dance. The responses also associate sabor with the concept of street dance, emphasizing its ritual value over its exhibition value (see Schechner 2003) and the value of process over product. Nonetheless, the comments also communicate something deeper.

The respondent from Canada, for instance, equates sabor with grace, which is a challenging concept to quantify, qualify, and define in a competitive and cross-cultural context. Grace is a form of elegance and beauty, and Brenda Dixon Gottschild defines elegance with regard to Europeanist dance as "dominating the dancing body" with a centered, vertical, and straight spine, which functions as a "monarch" from which all other movement emanates (1996: 8). For Gottschild, the ballet canon on which the concept of elegance symbiotically centers and organizes itself is a "structural principle" whereby "Europe posited itself as the center of the world, with everything else controlled and defined by it" (8). This element is visible in the world of competitive salsa dancing, dominated by Europeanist aesthetic values of grace, elegance, beauty, and form despite recent advances in the global appeal of Afro-Latin, Afro-Caribbean aesthetic concepts and practices such as sabor. It is possible that the cultural capital of sabor has transformed it into a status symbol on the global, professional social dance floor over the last several years but not in competition. How well the cultural capital of sabor can generate monetary compensation for competitive salsa dancers remains to be seen.

Some online comments suggest that competitive salsa dancing can be spectacular and beautiful from a visual standpoint, perhaps employing Latin ballroom's concept of grace based on "extended legs and straight joints" (Pietrobruno 2006: 131) yet completely devoid of sentimiento and sabor. Thus, salsa as a Latin-Caribbean dance with a vibrant African lineage contains its own form of grace with the power to change dominant cultural values in competitive salsa dancing toward valuing percussion and its correspondent African "get-down" stance (Gottschild 1996: 8). This posture can seem profane by Europeanist standards but is indispensable to polycentric and polyrhythmic forms of corporeal expression.

Sanabria (n.d.) associates the soul of salsa with percussion and rhythm, also related to sentimiento and sabor, and Jorge Duany likewise writes, "The very term salsa—roughly equivalent to 'soul' among North American blacks—hints that percussion and especially drumming is central to this type of music" (1984: 199). Thus, it is reasonable to connect salsa dancing and sabor's soul and life-force to corporeal interpretation of the music's percussive and rhythmic elements. This aesthetic philosophy and corporeal practice, which engages a discourse on race, also involves the cathartic experience related to salsa music's mambo, *descarga*, and *soneo* sections, which feature percussion and necessitate the get-down stance.

While I have focused on the more critical online comments, the dancers nonetheless inspired respect for their commitment to excellence, technical expertise, capacity to create beauty, and ability to dance with sabor to the extent possible within competition. *Sentimiento* and sabor seem most palpable, however, when the percussive aspects of the music are expressed visually through the body to a greater extent.

Cultural habitus has indeed shaped my interpretation and aesthetic sensibility. Yet, as Pierre Bourdieu writes, "a work of art has meaning and interest only for someone who possesses cultural competence" (1984: 2). The Europeanist concepts of grace and elegance are related to class and race, therefore it is likewise feasible that the grace of sabor in salsa dancing may be found in and based on the sensibilities of the working, lower, and under classes, and that it has been valuable enough to endure oppression.

Reception theory based on Stuart Hall's decoding model (2006), which distinguishes between preferred dominant readings and negotiated or oppositional readings of performance, is useful here. Competitive salsa dancing, for instance, functions within the sphere of dominant readings based on Europeanist aesthetic values, whereas the online commentaries are oppositional ones. Bourdieu's concept of the "legitimate" culture's "hierarchy of taste" (Allen and Anderson 1994: 70–74) can also be applied to salsa dancing's transformation into a concert-style art form and competitive ballroom dance in the context of its global commercialization.

Sabor (flavor) and sentimiento (feeling) function within the concept and practice of "legitimate" taste (Bourdieu 1984: 16) rooted in Western ideals. These include elegance, associated with Europeanist "good" taste, which itself is influenced by socioeconomic class, according to Bourdieu (1984: 75). Sabor's association with street salsa is thus powerful from a sociocultural standpoint in that it challenges the dominant culture's hierarchy of taste. However, the class positions of the online respondents are not evident, and so the connection between taste and social class becomes destabilized in the age of globalization and the equalizing Internet (Friedman 2005). And while YouTube clips may share key ontological features with live performance (Blades 2011: 49), they document without necessarily capturing feeling. Thus, watching salsa dancing on YouTube can affect the perception and reception of sentimiento and sabor. In light of this, the section that follows discusses my live native-ethnographic experience on the island, focusing on the Congreso Mundial de la Salsa/Puerto Rico Salsa Congress, including how the World Salsa Open Championship in 2006 destabilized the connection between Puerto Rican nationhood, salsa dancing, and sabor. My research also indicated that some Puerto Ricans on the island associate specific styles and dance techniques with sabor (see Renta

2008), leading to contentious discussions about the Congreso Mundial, global commercialization, and competitive salsa dancing.

El Congreso Mundial de la Salsa and the Globalization of Salsa Dancing

While salsa dance congresses now happen around the world year-round, it was nonetheless the transnational collaboration between Puerto Ricans Elí Irizarry from the island and Quetzy Olmos from New York that gave birth to the first Congreso Mundial de la Salsa (World Salsa Congress) in Puerto Rico in 1997, now called the Puerto Rico Salsa Congress. With the aid of the Internet, the congress has had tremendous globalizing power. The event centers on staged performances and workshops taught by salsa dancers from around the globe, including Puerto Ricans from both the island and the U.S. diaspora. The transnational aspect of the salsa dancing industry, combined with the significance sabor holds for Puerto Ricans in the United States, challenges official, insular, classist, and racist concepts of nationhood on the island that exclude Diasporicans (see Mariposa, n.d.), Puerto Rico's African heritage, and the working-class sectors of society that felt it necessary to migrate. This has been a postmodern ideological shift also tied to salsa's transformation from a social dance to a globalized genre of stylized techniques, choreographed concert dance performances, competition, and dancesport.

Salsa dancing has gone from a maligned street dance with African roots to a showcase for the tourism industry as a result of the congress. Hosted annually in the Grand Ballroom of the prestigious San Juan Hotel (located in the popular tourist area of Isla Verde), the congress has also transformed salsa dancing into an official symbol or display of Puerto Rican nationhood. Thus, the global commercialization of salsa dancing, the tourism industry in Puerto Rico, and Puerto Rican nationalism have a symbiotic relationship.

The promotional alliance between the congress and the Puerto Rico Tourism Company endorses salsa music and dance as a global, transnational Latin American, Caribbean, and Puerto Rican national genre.[7] Salsa music concerts performed by the most renowned, nationally symbolic Puerto Rican salsa bands and musicians, including the island's *bandera musical* (musical flag), El Gran Combo, are an integral part of the congress, highlighting the close relationship between salsa music, dance, and nationhood. The globalization of salsa music has set the stage for the globalization of salsa dancing through the congress; thus, salsa dancing now joins music in its ambassadorship of Puerto Rican culture around the world.

The global, transnational salsa music styles that have developed throughout the last several decades include Cuban, New York, Puerto Rican, Venezuelan, Colombian, Japanese, African, and European salsa (see Waxer 2002: 10–11, 13); national salsa dancing styles have also developed across the globe. Irizarry identified six styles of dancing salsa in 2006, including Cuban *rueda*, New York mambo, Puerto Rican, Colombian, Venezuelan, Los Angeles, and Dutch ("Arranca" 2005). One could argue that these national styles and their local varieties of sabor challenge homogenization, despite the success of the congress in globalizing salsa dancing.

Professional salsa dance instructor Miguel Pérez differentiated Puerto Rican from other styles in 2006, stating, "Con el congreso se creó una nueva manera de bailar: Los Angeles, acrobacia; New York, vueltas; Puerto Rico, sabor" (The congress created a new way of dancing: Los Angeles, acrobatics; New York, turns; Puerto Rico, flavor) (2006). Yet rather than a new way of dancing, the congress brought a new way of classifying and categorizing what was already happening. Pérez highlighted the relationship between Puerto Rican nationhood, salsa dancing, and sabor within the context of global commercialization. He also noted that at one point in Puerto Rico salsa dancing was "*paso libre na' ma'*" (free-style steps only), which he believed allowed for greater creativity, and affirmed that the renowned dancer Papito Jalajala from Puerto Rico "*bailaba más que nada pasos libres, no en pareja*" (danced free-style steps more than anything, not partner work). Papito Jalajala was recognized globally, especially in Italy, for his sabor, which may also make a case for the possibility that some New York approaches to salsa dancing can limit the expression of sabor. For example, while New York dancers were known for excelling in Palladium-style open footwork in the late nineties, they developed an emphasis on spinning and turn patterns over the last ten years that can inhibit improvisation and expression, particularly for the follower (typically women). One could say that, in limiting expression in this way, sabor is suppressed; however, that does not diminish the aesthetic value of sabor for Diasporicans. Sabor is transnational in scope.

The 2006 World Salsa Open Championship in Puerto Rico

The predominance of turn patterns relates to the ballroom dance industry's influence, which has made way for competitive salsa dancing. Competitive salsa dancing also disrupts the dance's perceived connection to Puerto Rican nationhood, as demonstrated by comments regarding the World Salsa Open Championship's 2006 winners, Australian dance duo Luda Kroiter and Oliver Pineda. Puerto Rican Ángel Rodríguez and Venezuelan Sheila de Jesús won the championship in 2005, and Rodríguez competed once again in 2006. During intermission a mechanical engineer who dances professional salsa said, "Angelito always gains points on improvisation; those focused on lifts and choreography don't do well in this area" (Santos 2006). Yet the 2006 title went to the Australians.

Kroiter is a *Dancing with the Stars* celebrity in Australia, and Pineda, of Chilean descent, danced in the opening ceremony of the Sydney 2000 Olympics. A well-known instructor who often challenges congress practices seemed vexed when he heard the announcement the following day. It appeared that the connection between Puerto Rican nationhood and salsa dancing was becoming unstable as a result of the new dance practices congress organizers brought to the island. This viewpoint is reminiscent of Agustín Laó-Montes's concern over how "'world historical identities' . . . in Western modernity have been decentered, fragmented, and eroded in the current phase of globalization of capital and culture" (2001: 12). And just as Aparicio and Cándida Jáquez voice concern about the effects of globalization on Latin popular music, especially "how local meanings are transformed and lost" (2003: 1–2), the mechanical engineer worried, "Se puede globalizar [la salsa] pero no [debemos] desatender la raíz, por ejemplo, el sabor. . . . Tenemos que responsabilizarnos de esto, los que tienen el poder, como el congreso no lo está haciendo" (Salsa can be globalized, but we should not neglect our roots, such as sabor. . . . We have to take responsibility for this, those who are in power, since the congress is not doing it) (Santos 2006). These concerns suggest the sense of belonging salsa provides for Puerto Ricans, while pointing to the congress's role in salsa dancing's perceived loss of national and local flavor in the context of globalization.

Sabor in Puerto Rico: Style and Technique

The competitive salsa dancing the congress brought to Puerto Rico was influenced by what many describe as *salsa de salón*, ballroom salsa, which emphasizes Europeanist aesthetic values over Afro-Caribbean sensibilities. Some also critique the congress for what they call classist and elitist practices. For instance, Arthur Murray Caribbean Dance Academy owner Tato Conrad recalls that, partly as a result of the first Puerto Rico Salsa Congress, promotion for salsa classes on the island began to read, "Aprenda a bailar salsa con estilo, con clase, con cachet" (Learn to dance salsa with style, with class, with cachet), demonstrating the connection between stylization and notions of class within the space of the dance academy. According to Conrad (2006), who is also a musician, percussionist, and founder of the Museo Taller Africano de Puerto Rico (African Museum Workshop of Puerto Rico), housed within the Arthur Murray Dance Academy, these dance classes were part of a movement that solidified the practice of dancing on-2, or beginning on the second count of an eight-beat bar, in Puerto Rico (see Chapters 2 and 4).

Puerto Rican–style salsa dancing is associated with sabor, improvisation, and polycentrism but also with technique.[8] According to Tito Ortos, one of the island's most sought-after professional salsa performers, televised dancing was the island's first exposure to dancing on-2 (*bailar en dos*). Before that, Puerto Ricans from the island danced primarily on-1, or to "*el tiempo natural de la música*" (the natural time of the music). While the worldwide cultural imperialism of the Arthur Murray studios, which teach salsa dancing on-1, raises concerns, Puerto Rico's Arthur Murray Caribbean Dance Academy continues to teach salsa dancing on-1 in a style Conrad calls *estilo cocolo*, rooted in the practice of salsa as a social dance with working-class, Afro–Puerto Rican roots. He describes dancing *salsa cocola* as follows: "*Se baila doblao, se marca el paso; es circular*" (It is danced bent forward, you mark the steps; it is circular). This approach to dancing salsa contrasts with the *salsa de salón* promoted by the congress, a more linear form that focuses on lengthening the body. The grounding and flexion Conrad mentions are the foundation of the polycentric aspect of sabor. In contrast, professional salsa dance instructor Miguel Rodríguez affirms that for him "dancing on clave," which is how Puerto Ricans on the island refer to dancing on-2, has more sabor (Rodríguez 2006).

Clave underpins salsa music's polyrhythm. As an African element in Latin music, it is intimately tied to the concept of tradition. Ortos explains that the reasoning behind the preference for the technique is that the second beat in a bar of salsa music arranged in 2-3 coincides with the first strike of the clave (Ortos 2006).[9] Some performers, instructors, and dancers in Puerto Rico also consider dancing on clave the more correct and "authentic" approach to dancing salsa. In contrast, to Conrad, "el 'uno' es cocolo . . . y es también clave" (the "one" is cocolo . . . and is also clave), indicating that perceptions of authenticity are not necessarily tied to a particular technique. Such contradictions suggest that the embodiment of sabor and its connection to Afro–Puerto Rican tradition can manifest through different approaches. Conrad further states, "Bailar no es un conteo, es una expresión" (Dancing is not counting, it is expression). In my view, what is "authentic" is the "spirit" of the dance, despite dancers' wanting to concretize it in terms of the material experiences of race and class. Furthermore, a salsa dancing champion from Latin America said, regarding authenticity, *competencia, y deporte* (competition and dancesport), "No nos permite ser auténticos porque todos sentimos [la música] diferente" (It does not allow us to be authentic because everyone feels [the music] differently) (Santos 2006).

Material experiences of this kind necessitate discussion, despite the risk that they will be perceived as essentialist from a postmodern academic perspective. Salsa dancers can express who they are and connect with the most authentic part of themselves when embodying the aesthetic concept of sabor. As an authentic expression of creativity—for example, through improvisation—sabor may be among the losses involved in the global commercialization of salsa dancing. Salsa's nomenclature is based on the concept of flavor. Eliminating sabor obliterates salsa's purpose in the world of global movement and sound.

Conclusion

Salsa dancing and sabor are forms of performance, aesthetic expressions of consciousness involving the spiritual, mental, emotional, and corporeal in relation to the global, transnational, national, and sociopolitical. Different performance contexts may, however, focus on only one aspect of salsa, thus moving it away from its holistic practice.

This chapter has been a journey through the global commercialization of salsa dancing and sabor in the context of the Puerto Rico Salsa Congress and competitive salsa dancing, as well as the private, everyday practices of salsa dancing and sabor in my own family. Through these very different lenses, I have explored the rise of professional, staged, choreographed salsa dancing and instruction and the polemics surrounding sabor and technique, including issues of class and race. A key aspect of the conversation has been the contrast between the soul force and life force of salsa and sabor involving Africanist aesthetic values, including the emphasis on percussion and rhythm, and Latin ballroom and Europeanist values.

Through my discussion of the WSF, I have elaborated on the relationship between the globalization of salsa dancing, the centralization of power, and the homogenization often inherent in ballroom dance practices, which national salsa dancing styles challenge. Focusing on the Puerto Rican style of performing and dancing salsa on the island, I have demonstrated that its relationship to sabor reveals it to be associated with embodying Puerto Rican nationhood. The WSF is generating a globalized and commercialized concept of sabor influenced by the ballroom industry, Europeanist aesthetics, and tropicalization. While the Puerto Rico Salsa Congress is also influenced by these features, it has produced a concept of Puerto Rican nationhood connected to salsa and sabor, based on national or local philosophies, values, ideals, and practices. These philosophies are still taking shape and may sometimes be in conflict but nonetheless reveal a shared concern for honoring tradition, African consciousness, and aesthetics. Globalized, commercialized, staged representations of salsa dance may indeed lead to a loss of sabor in salsa dancing. Nonetheless, sabor, in its embodiment of working-class taste and its increased use as cultural capital in the global salsa scene, may have the power to alter Europeanist concepts of beauty, elegance, and grace.

NOTES

Acknowledgments: This work was made possible by a Center for Puerto Rican Studies Diaspora Research Grant and a Northwestern University Graduate Research Grant in 2006.

1. See Schechner 2003: 227.

2. Regarding salsa music and global legitimacy, see Aparicio 1998: 73–74.

3. See http://www.youtube.com/watch?v=yFPzVMnryCY.

4. See http://www.youtube.com/watch?v=WzVdwZlrxwo.

5. According to Quintero Herencia, salsa of this kind camouflages and conceals contestation. Thus, to "thematize this camouflage . . . is a strategy in the war over the sabor (flavor) of the nation" (1997: 195), which is transnational.

6. See http://www.youtube.com/watch?v=01f-oLGZvls.

7. The congress emerged during a prostatehood context that promoted entrepreneurship, competition, privatization, and the governor's New Economic Model. The February–March 2006 issue of *¡Qué Pasa!* magazine reported that "Puerto Rico receives approximately 3.7 million tourists annually which represent a $3,209 million injection into

the local economy" ("Que Pasa TV!" 2006: 115). Puerto Rico Tourism Company strategist Mario González de la Fuente, who collaborated with the tourist cultural initiative for eight years, affirmed that the congress is "the summer event that generates the most nights/ rooms in the hotel industry," representing "an economic injection of 1.8 million dollars" in the area of tourism alone (quoted in "Arranca" 2005; my translation). Diasporicans are part of this phenomenon. González adds, "Producers of the event also contribute to the local economy . . . while promoting the cultural element: music." Thus, it makes sense that the congress holds such significance for Puerto Rico.

8. The influence of dancing on-2 on the island is the result of the circular migration of Puerto Rican salsa dancers and instructors between the island and New York. This transnational movement, which dates back decades, was pivotal to the development of the transnational salsa dancing industry and the context in which the congress emerged. Professional New York mambo dancers Aníbal Vásquez and Mike Ramos return-migrated to the island in the fifties, bringing the practice of dancing on-2 back with them, which led to the development of this dance practice in the following decades. Ramos was the choreographer for Gran Combo, which began to be featured on Puerto Rican television in the early sixties.

9. Chris Washburne writes that sabor is also synonymous with the clave, which "provides rhythmic momentum," "drive," and "swing" (2008: 178–179) in the world of professional salsa musicians, salsa music production, performance, and recording in New York.

REFERENCES

Allen, Douglas E., and Paul F. Anderson. 1994. "Consumption and Social Stratification: Bourdieu's Distinction." In *Advances in Consumer Research*, vol. 21, ed. Chris T. Allen and Deborah Roedder, 70–74. Duluth, MN: Association for Consumer Research.

Aparicio, Frances. 1989–1990. "Salsa, Maracas and Baile: Latin Popular Music in the Poetry of Victor Hernandez Cruz." *Melus* 16 (1): 43–58.

———. 1998. *Listening to Salsa: Gender, Latin Popular Music, and Puerto Rican Cultures.* Middletown, CT: Wesleyan University Press.

Aparicio, Frances R., and Susana Chávez-Silverman. 1997. *Tropicalizations: Transcultural Representations of 'Latinidad.'* Hanover, NH: Dartmouth College.

Aparicio, Frances, and Cándida Jáquez, with María Elena Cepeda. 2003. *Musical Migrations: Transnationalism and Cultural Hybridity in Latin/o America.* New York: Palgrave.

"Arranca el Puerto Rico Salsa Congress." 2005. Fundación Nacional para la Cultura Popular, July 23. Available at http://www.prpop.org/noticias/jul05/congresosalsa_jul23 .shtml.

Blades, Hetty. 2011. "Dance on the Internet: An Ontological Investigation." *Postgraduate Journal of Aesthetics* 8 (1): 40–52. Available at http://pjaesthetics.org/index.php/pjaes thetics/article/download/64/61.

Bourdieu, Pierre. 1984. *Distinction: A Social Critique of the Judgement of Taste*, trans. Richard Nice. Cambridge, MA: Harvard University Press.

Conrad, Tato. 2006. Personal communication. July 30. Puerto Rico.

Duany, Jorge. 1984. "Popular Music in Puerto Rico: Toward an Anthropology of *Salsa*." *Latin American Music Review* 5 (2): 186–215.

———. 2001. *The Puerto Rican Nation on the Move: Identities on the Island and in the United States.* Chapel Hill: University of North Carolina Press.

Friedman, Thomas L. 2005. *The World Is Flat: A Brief History of the Twenty-First Century.* New York: Farrar, Straus, and Giroux.

Gottschild, Brenda Dixon. 1996. *Digging the Africanist Presence in American Performance: Dance and Other Contexts.* Westport, CT: Praeger.

Hall, Stuart. 2006. *Culture, Media, Language: Working Papers in Cultural Studies, 1972–79.* Abingdon, UK: Routledge.

Laó-Montes, Agustín. 2001. "Introduction." In *Mambo Montage: The Latinization of New York*, ed. Agustín Laó-Montes and Arlene M. Dávila, 1–54. New York: Columbia University Press.

Mariposa (María Teresa Fernández). n.d. "Ode to the Diasporican." *Boricua Poetry.* Available at http://www.virtualboricua.org/Docs/poem_mtf.htm (accessed December 27, 2012).

McMains, Juliet. 2009. "Dancing Latin/Latin Dancing." In *Ballroom, Boogie, Shimmy Sham, Shake: A Social and Popular Dance Reader*, ed. Julie Malnig, 302–323. Urbana: University of Illinois Press.

Ortos, Tito. 2006. Interview by Priscilla Renta. June 7. San Juan, Puerto Rico.

Pérez, Miguel. 2006. Personal communication. July 21. Puerto Rico.

Pietrobruno, Sheenagh. 2006. *Salsa and Its Transnational Moves.* Lanham, MD: Lexington Books.

"*Que Pasa* TV! A New Medium for the Promotion of Tourism Is Born!" 2006. *¡Qué Pasa!* February–March, p. 115.

Quintero Herencia, Juan Carlos. 1997. "Notes toward a Reading of Salsa," trans. Celeste Fraser Delgado. In *Everynight Life: Culture and Dance in Latin/o America*, ed. Celeste Fraser Delgado and José Esteban Muñoz, 189–222. Durham, NC: Duke University Press.

Quintero Rivera, Ángel G. 1999. *¡Salsa, sabor y control! Sociología de la música "tropical."* 2nd ed. Mexico City: Siglo Veintiuno.

Renta, Priscilla. 2004. "Salsa Dance: Latino/a History in Motion." *Centro: Journal of the Center for Puerto Rican Studies* 16 (2): 138–157.

———. 2008. "Migración de retorno y decisiones estéticas: Bailando salsa entre Nueva York y Puerto Rico." In *El son y la salsa en la identidad del Caribe*, ed. Darío Tejeda and Rafael Emilio Yunén, 155–165. Proceedings of the I Congreso de Música, Identidad, y Cultura en el Caribe. Santiago: Centro León and INEC.

Rodríguez, Miguel. 2006. Interview by Priscilla Renta. July 22. San Juan, Puerto Rico.

Romero, Enrique. 2000. *Salsa: El orgullo del barrio.* Madrid: Celeste Ediciones.

Rondón, César Miguel. 2008. *The Book of Salsa: A Chronicle of Urban Music from the Caribbean to New York City*, trans. Frances R. Aparicio and Jackie White. Chapel Hill: University of North Carolina Press.

Sanabria, Izzy. n.d. "What Is Salsa." *IzzySanabria.com.* Available at http://www.izzy sanabria.com/WhatisSalsa.php (accessed December 26, 2012.

Santos, Manuel (pseudonym). 2006. Personal communication. July 24.

Schechner, Richard. 2003. *Performance Studies: An Introduction.* London: Routledge.

SpanishDict, s.v. "cadencia." Available at http://www.spanishdict.com/translate/cadencia (accessed January 1, 2013).

United States Dance Foundation. n.d. "Latin Body Rhythms." Available at http://wsf.cc/latin_body_rhythms.html (accessed September 17, 2012).

Washburne, Chris. 2008. *Sounding Salsa: Performing Latin Music in New York City.* Philadelphia: Temple University Press.

Waxer, Lise, ed. 2002. *Situating Salsa: Global Markets and Local Meanings in Latin Popular Music.* New York: Routledge.

World Salsa Federation. n.d. "About Page." Available at http://www.worldsalsafederation.com/about.html (accessed July 8, 2013).

8

Identity Is Also Danced (Cali, Colombia)

Alejandro Ulloa Sanmiguel

(Translated by Sydney Hutchinson)

Bailar es	Dancing is
escribir con el cuerpo en el espacio	writing with the body in space
representar el tiempo sin nombrarlo	representing time without naming it
marcar con el gesto un sólo instante	marking a single instant with a gesture
soñar que uno no es uno sino el ritmo	dreaming that one is not oneself, but rhythm
sentir que es la vida la que baila	feeling that it is life itself that is dancing

Identity as Story: A Constructed Discourse

I consider identity to be a story constructed by a social actor about that actor to differentiate him- or herself from others. Participants in a construction may include "different historical actors, like schools, governments, intellectuals, [and] cultural researchers," or mass media (Melo 2006: 87). Once the story is defined, community members latch onto it to identify themselves inside and outside the community as having particular characteristics and as being linked to a group, a territory, a tradition.

The narrative about identity that is constructed presents certain arbitrary features, since some characteristics are discarded and others are selected as those that the subjects must accept to represent themselves and to be represented. The identity constructed in this way attributes the selected properties to an entire community, as if everyone were equal, homogenous, and culturally uniform. The homogenizing discourse of identity denies tensions and differences that may exist within the group at the same time that it ignores other, equally constructed identity stories. Social agents identify with some stories more than others insofar as those stories have common referents within the group that adopts them. This identification is a form of recognition that is generally interpreted as identity.

In recent decades, the identity story of Santiago de Cali has unavoidably intersected with the image created around salsa and its dance, as expressed in the slogan, "Cali, world capital of salsa." In my book *Salsa in Cali* (1992),

I discuss this and speak of the social process through which this music gains meaning for the "popular" sectors of the city.[1] Here I discuss the dance to argue that identity is also danced. This means that through salsa dancing, identity is constructed and expressed from the performativity of the body and not from a rational or political discourse. Dance, as a kinesic and proxemic configuration, makes the body a site for the enunciation of identity. It is not through verbal language but through movement and body language that this new identity attached to the city of Cali and its sectors is defined.

Dances and Dancers

If we define dance as a system of nonverbal communication and as an act through which social relations are projected, we may now establish a distinction between studio dancers and social dancers. I use the term *"bailadores"*[2] for those who enjoy dance as a recreational practice—"social dance"—linked to leisure and spare time, undertaken for the pleasure it provokes, for desire, or for other motivating factors. Bailadores have no pretensions to professionalism or participation in the spectacle of show business, although they do have an underlying interest in transcending the functional routines of daily life.

I use the term *"bailarines"*[3] for the type of dancer who takes up dance not only for pleasure but also as a profession, engaging in formalized exercises of teaching or apprenticeship such as rehearsals and workshops. Bailarines perform in public or private shows, either as soloists or as members of a school, group, or artistic company, and they obtain economic and symbolic capital from their profession. Bailarines thus insert themselves into the show business market and into a field of practices where they share the opportunities and tensions of that environment with peers (companions and rivals) and also compete for available resources within small or large cultural industries.

A bailarín begins as a bailador, becoming a bailarín if he or she has the intention and the necessary conditions to do so. On the other hand, a bailarín is a bailarín insofar as he or she achieves competence—creative capacity, not only technical ability—and exhibits it to peers and audiences who endorse and recognize it. In addition, however, the bailarín becomes more of a bailador when participating in a festivity (*rumba*), detached from his or her mercantile or corporate function. Another difference between the two is that bailarines dance for an audience for whom they exhibit their qualities and virtues, while bailadores do this principally for themselves and their partners, although they also expose themselves to the gaze of others.

One can conceive of a third category to designate the bailadores who submit themselves to formal pedagogy, not necessarily to participate in show business or become part of the market for spectacle but only to qualify their abilities and perform better in social dancing. In any case, transitioning from bailador to bailarín requires advancing through stages, such as belonging to a school or academy, participating in festivals and competitions (Figure 8.1), abiding by

Figure 8.1. A 1990s salsa competition held in Cali. *(Photograph by Orlando Narváez. From the collection of Alejandro Ulloa Sanmiguel.)*

rules and procedures, and achieving standards of measurement and qualification, besides the routes of practice and training.

The distinction between bailarines and bailadores as social roles is universal, whether they dance, for example, salsa, tango, or Brazilian samba. At the same time, the relationship between the two is normally more complex, given that bailarines arise from bailadores who, as part of a dance tradition (like salsa dancing in Cali), not only become professionalized but also contribute to the development of the dance, to its aesthetic re-creation as a highly elaborated artistic language, different from more conventional dance.

Cali is located in southwest Colombia, on a plateau in the Andes mountains but close to the port of Buenaventura on the Pacific coast. However, it is musically tied to the Caribbean, above all to Cuba and Puerto Rico, influenced by recordings and live performances by the most important groups from those islands as well as by Mexican cinema. The population of Cali, or Caleños, is the product of the a mixture of three ethnic groups: the white, Spanish minority; the indigenous, who survive to this day; and the black African descendants. Mestizos, blacks, and mulattos form the majority of the current population of 2.8 million. Cali's economy was linked to gold mining between the seventeenth and nineteenth centuries, which explains the presence of slaves. In the twentieth century, manufacturing and the sugar industry were most important in the city's economy. In the twenty-first, Cali is developing into a city of services thanks to growth in the service industry. A black population and sugar industry are further similarities to Cuba and Puerto Rico.

The historical conjunction between bailadores, bailarines, and the dance tradition in a city like Cali gave rise to different bodily modes of salsa genres—different ways of dancing salsa—in Cali's recent history. Among these, the one I call the classic Caleño style, developed by bailadores in the 1940s and 1950s, stands out. Bailarines have presented this style on the international stage in contests, congresses, films, and festivals since the 1970s.

This style, continued today by salsa's old guard in dances and at *viejotecas*,[4] has influences from *son*, swing, and foxtrot in the 1930s; the *guaracha* and mambo that Caleños danced in the 1940s and 1950s, influenced by the Mexican *pachucos* (youths belonging to a subculture characterized by its distinctive dress, speech, and dancing) in the movies; and bolero, *pasodoble*, and *chachachá*, all danced in cabarets and brothels in Cali's red-light district in the 1950s. After the 1960s and with the popularity of *pachangas* (parties), it was updated with the jumps of boogaloo, the improvisations of *guaguancó*, the softness of the *guajira*, and the feeling of the *son montuno*, all grouped under the generic term of "salsa." During the last five years in bailarines' shows, classic Caleño style has been fortified with movements originating in classical dance and ballet, such as standing on the toes or extending the arms and turning the hands.

From the 1950s to the 1970s, this language spread throughout the lower-class barrios of Cali, embedding itself in the generations that developed it and passed it on to their descendants and to the city that gave them life. The gestation and consolidation of this dance language was a marginal construction of the streets, far from formal institutions, foreign to official support, and in opposition to dominant morality. It was a language created initially outside schools and academies, although today these institutions have catalyzed the existing repertoires to re-create and empower them within a new context. This language has lived on in the feet and the memories of the current world champions in the cabaret salsa category as a style with agility in leg movement, audacity in the lifts and aerials, speed in the feet, and sophistication in improvisation.

The language re-created and transformed by contemporary Caleño dancers from some fifty schools and academies as cabaret salsa encompasses the heritage contributed by several generations. This rigorous and demanding language is the synthesis of a long-term process whose most remote antecedents take us back to the colonial period, the seventeenth to nineteenth centuries, when slavery existed in our region.

The Body in History

The presence of the bailarines and the classic Caleño style on the contemporary global scene since 2000 is a conquest of great value for them and for Cali. But it is not because of luck or happenstance. It is the result of a long historical and social process throughout the twentieth century in which the popular sectors

Figure 8.2. *Verbena callejera* (salsa street party) at the Cali Feria in the 1970s or 1980s. *(From the collection of Alejandro Ulloa Sanmiguel.)*

have participated with their musical and dance practices. In the second half of the century, the style multiplied in street parties, or *verbenas* (see Figure 8.2), during Cali's Feria, a festival celebrated since 1957 between December 25 and January 1, which includes bullfights, musical performances, and dances. It was also reproduced in kiosks and discos and in the terraces and shelters (with dance floor included) constructed whenever the city expanded and a new barrio was founded. It was a style without a name, promoted by these *griles* (dancing spots) in the city center through informal competitions in which couples competed on the dance floor to win applause. Thus emerged the first famous dancers of the 1960s and 1970s, who traveled from floor to floor throughout the city, earning applause and free drinks on the dance's tab.

It was in those spaces and in these practices, and others described below, that the classic Caleño style was consolidated as a matrix that accepts variations and improvisations in accordance with the salsa music played.

From Yesterday's Slave to Today's Dancer

The dancing body is a historically determined body, one that is modeled and molded according to values, cognitive schemes, and social practices that we can locate with relative precision in time and space. Dancing salsa in Cali is associated historically and anthropologically with the black body, the slave body submitted to an economic system of merciless exploitation from the seventeenth to the nineteenth centuries in this city. Literary works like *María* by Jorge Isaacs, *El alférez real* by Eustaquio Palacios, and chronicles of the nineteenth century allude to dances and parties, at haciendas or in villages, where blacks and mulattos were the principal actors.

Because of slavery and the sociocultural legacy of the slave hacienda, Cali became a mulatto city, ethnically speaking, with a wide plebian social base that generated fundamental values including personal autonomy and a more flexible morality regarding the body and sexuality, less rigid than that imposed by the white, Catholic, patriarchal elite of colonial society and the slave system. A body repressed by Christian morality and control over sexuality could undertake many activities but could freely deploy itself in dance only with difficulty. Flexible morality meant that the body and eroticism were less constrained by the Catholic religion, which imposes a strong censure on instincts and rigid control over posture and bodily expression, both conscious and unconscious. A less constrained body is freer to feel and to make itself felt, is a body less repressed in communicating gesturally, without words, a body less inhibited in its relations to others. Blacks developed those two values, flexible morality about the body and sexuality and personal autonomy, as forms of cultural resistance in the context of unequal interactions with slaveholders but relative equality in relation to other plebian sectors.

The survival and cultural reproduction of these values, together with the availability of time in subaltern sectors, would be the anthropological basis that made possible the development of dance as a language particular to the plebian social base of Cali. Subaltern sectors, united by similar socioeconomic conditions, had greater racial tolerance than did the elites and a democratization of social relations. The town council therefore forbade "the plebians to celebrate dances in the day or at night, or at any time, because of the evils they brought: drunkenness, incest, concubinage, and other scandals and public crimes" (Rodríguez 1996: 76).

In this complex cultural heritage of values, body, and social practices, one can find the "cement" of the modern popular dance that develops in Cali in the mid-twentieth century in the new subaltern social sectors.[5]

Although this corporeal language has been elevated to its maximal expression in recent decades, one must recognize these historical and anthropological antecedents. It is no accident that the majority of the world champions of cabaret-style salsa are young blacks and mulattos from poor families and barrios, descendants of former slaves and of the popular social strata I have described. The dancers of salsa and Antillean music in the 1950s–1970s in Cali were also mainly blacks or mulattos: Benigno Holguín, "El Negro Domingo," "Telembi King," "Catacolí," "El Negro Manchura," "Yimy Bugalú," Evelio Carabalí, "Watusi," and many others who came from the outskirts and the margins, young people who made use of the street and free time to make dance their raison d'être.[6] Black and mulatto women have also distinguished themselves as great dancers. Mulatta-mestiza "Amparo Arrebato" and, later, the black women Liliana Salinas and Venicia Cárdenas, inheritors of the 1980s–1990s Cali Rumba dance company, contributed to the consolidation of this danced language.

Salinas was the first to participate in an international congress in Puerto Rico, where she danced with Luis Eduardo "El Mulato" Hernández in the mid-1990s. As in a relay race, El Mulato then took over the task of continuing to promote classic Caleño style and to develop it with new steps, figures, and choreographies. Throughout this process, the black body has been indispensable. And although not only black dancers excel at this artistic activity, many of the best dancers are black or mulatto youth.

This proficiency is not a result of any essentialist reason or the lack of other talents but rather of the absence of opportunities in most other, perhaps more lucrative, areas of artistic or economic production. Thanks to these dancers, however, a new identity story has been constructed with respect to the black population and its aptitudes for music and dance. This story is directly tied to the similar imaginaries that emerged from Latin music and salsa to circulate throughout the world, vindicating Africa, its music, and its descendants. But it is also an identity story involving black and nonblack dancers and favoring Santiago de Cali, a tale globalized through the television and print media that highlight these dancers' achievements. Without doubt, strategies of professionalization were necessary to allow them to get to the summit where they are today, but without historical antecedents and the popular acceptance that sustain them, these strategies would have borne fruit only with difficulty.

Through salsa and its dance, black Caleños have been vindicated as musicians and dancers. In both roles they have gained centrality and visibility and thus some social inclusion, although only in small groups. As John Genner Vásquez, one of the dancers I interviewed for this chapter, commented, "Thanks to salsa dancing, I have been able to 'change my closet' [i.e., upgrade my wardrobe and appearance], I have helped my mother, and my life has changed, as it has changed for other dancers" (2007). But this is not a vindication achieved through an explicit political discourse or through a social movement that fights for the rights of ethnic minorities. It is a vindication achieved in a completely different arena, that of the salsa event in Santiago de Cali, where many of these young dancers are also gay.

This perspective reveals a changed pattern of action and a broken stereotype about salsa dancing, assumed generally to fall within a *machista* (male-dominant) context, in which the man shows off his body and his dance and seduces and conquers women, affirming his role as a macho. The gay dancer, when he and his (female) partner compete with other couples, must assume a masculine role like any other macho, denying or hiding his gay identity. This role is imposed on him—or established—as one of the conditions of the entertainment market. But when going out informally as a bailador in a disco, the same bailarín exhibits his gay identity and assumes both masculine and feminine roles when dancing with other men, whether gay or not, or when dancing with women. In both cases, this irruption of the bailarín and the gay bailador— or of the gay as a bailarín and as a bailador—is a very important achievement for gays and for society in general, although it is still a small-scale phenomenon.

Even so, some gay discos in Cali have modified their usual pop, rock, techno, or electronica musical programming to include more salsa, so that gay bailarines, who attend as bailadores, will display their dance abilities and creativity.

The growth in number and visibility of gay male dancers is a result of factors such as greater acceptance of homosexuality in contemporary society; the political work of lesbian, gay, bisexual, and transgender groups; and new social dynamics like the expansion of civil rights, recognition of diversity, and acceptance of minorities. While some mestizo and white gay dancers have also become dance stars, the many black and mulatto members of the salsa schools have found double vindication in the dance: vindication of their racialized ethnicity and of their homosexuality, both stigmatized and discriminated against through racist and religious ideologies. Their visible, central presence contrasts with the image of the macho, womanizing dancer that predominated among the professional dancers of Cali until twenty years ago, and although this type of male dancer still exists, it is no longer the only valid model for male Caleño dancers.

Caleño Dance: From the Antillean Old Guard to Salsa

In Cali, different ways of dancing salsa come together. First is the classic Caleño style, characterized by the agility and speed of the feet, with movement concentrated in the lower part of the body. This style is associated with the acceleration by young barrio dancers of 33 rpm records to 45 rpm during the 1960s, which distorted the voice, sound, rhythm, and indeed the entire piece and as a consequence affected the dance, causing more rapid foot movements. It was done with only some songs, especially salsas and boogaloos, which seemed very slow to the young Caleños, including "Palo de mango," written by Eddie Palmieri and Cheo Feliciano, sung by Ismael Quintana; "At the Party," written by Héctor Rivera; "Cinturita," written by Eddie Palmieri and Ismael Quintana; and the boogaloos "Micaela" and "I Like It like That," written by Pete Rodríguez. Some of these pieces continue to be accelerated today, often in the *viejotecas* and sometimes when played on radio stations.

Another style is the *cobao*, originating with the blacks of Buenaventura in the 1960s or slightly earlier and arriving in Cali with migrants from that city. It consists of dancing extremely close to one's partner, nearly still, with a light back-and-forth motion of the hips, while staying in almost the same place. In contrast to the classic Caleño style, the *cobao* is almost imperceptible, appropriate for erotic encounters and face-to-face caresses.

A third is the *pasito cañandonga*, created between Cali, New York, and Miami in the 1980s, during the height of drug trafficking. In these cities, Colombians and capital circulated intensely with different purposes. Its name comes from a Cuban song written by José Antonio Pinares and popularized by Cervando Díaz. It gave its name to a salsa club in Cali in the mid-1980s, the same time the romantic salsa style emerged.[7] The change in music style generated a change in the dance, which took its name from a prestigious club that closed in 2002 after a bloody shoot-out. It has less agility and speed than the classic style but emphasizes other parts of the body, like the arms and the torso, which rocks back and forth. The couple does not separate.

A fourth style is *casino*, or *rueda de casino*, defined principally by the turns and movements of the couple in different directions. Finally, we have the many possible combinations of these styles or their fragments, given the multiplicity of interactions that occur in salsa spaces of the Cali scene, such as barrio open-air dances; bars and discos; *salsotecas*, or parks, where salsa fans and music collectors meet; or the Feria, during the last week of the year.

Popular Festivities: From *Champú* Dances to Fee Dances

While some of these early contexts for Caleño-style Antillean dance no longer exist, having been replaced by others, I have been able to find testimonies from around 1930 in primary sources about the origin of the *champú* dances in the barrios of San Nicolás, El Hoyo, Vilachí (next to San Antonio), Sucre, and Obrero.[8] The champú dances were evening get-togethers in family homes with ample patios, where youths and adolescents would go to dance on Sundays, from the afternoon until early evening. They were called "champú" dances because the eponymous nonalcoholic beverage typical of the Cauca valley, prepared from corn, pieces of *lulo* fruit and pineapple, and leaves of bitter orange, was served at them, along with empanadas and fried snacks. Afterward beer and hard liquor would appear, which adult men would drink while the youth filled up on champús.[9] Champú dances were permanent fixtures in those barrios for several decades until the *aguaelulo* dances appeared during the 1960s, in which the champú drinks were replaced with soft drinks and only the word "*lulo*" remained as a verbal reminder of what the popular festivity once had been.[10]

In the champú dances of the 1930s, one danced the *rumbas criollas* by Emilio Sierra, the *porros* of Guillermo Buitrago, and the foxtrot, bolero, *pasodoble*, conga, son, *bote*, rumba, and guaracha popular at the time. I believe that it was in those champú dances that many of the future dancers of 1940s–1950s Cali learned to dance, including the mulatto Benigno Holguín, who created the first dance academy (La Cumparsita) in 1949 and in whose family home in the Vilachí barrio champús took place.

In the 1940s, according to my inquiries, "fee" dances (*bailes de cuota*) appeared in the house of Doña Trinidad Martínez on Fifteenth Street between Thirteenth and Fourteenth Avenues (Barrio Fray Damián). Her son, Héctor "La Sombra" Martínez, a dark-skinned mulatto who was a professional soccer player in Cali's Boca Jrs. and a maraca player and singer for the Cali Boys in the 1940s, spoke to me of these parties.[11]

The fee dances emerged as a different kind of party from champús. They charged five pesos as a cover that included drinks, tamales, or roast pig and continued through the 1950s and 1960s. Attendees wore long jackets that hung past the knees and wide, Mexican *pachuco*-style pants with a chain hanging between the pocket and waistband, much like Tin Tán at the height of his career. The dance would begin at nine o'clock and last until the next day, having migrated to Lucho Lenis's El Avispero, a shop in Barrio Obrero that became an after-hours club (*amanecedero*) after 1948. Sometimes an *orquesta* (ensemble) would play at the party, led by the Ospino brothers, Tito Cortés, or other local musicians. Men and women, adults and young people of the nearby barrios, would all attend—the same people who had formerly participated in the champú dances and who now continued with the obligatory party every week, when Cali was still more a large town than a modern city.

Both the champú dances and the fee dances that began in the older lower-class barrios of Cali (San Nicolás and Obrero) would reappear with different characteristics and a different name in the 1960s in other, more recently founded barrios, like El Jardín or Santa Elena. The dances for minors were now known as *aguaelulos*, and the fee dances for adults raised their prices, customers brought their own drinks, the roast pig and tamales disappeared, and cold dishes with potato salad were served in their place. The parties were no longer so calm, and one could no longer drink without fear of robbery. Times had definitely changed in the intervening decades. The city had grown, and violence had taken hold.

The "Big Mamas" of the Cali Scene

According to testimonies I gathered, reception practices, or ways for listening to and consuming music, for popular and Antillean music[12] arose in houses with ample patios, where the rhythms and their dances brought together adolescents and adults, despite their different schedules, different attire, and different drink preferences, as part of a ritual of enjoyment and the pleasure of dancing. This ritual was made possible in its early days by the "big mamas of the scene" ("*mamás grandes de la rumba*"), like Doña Gregoria Echeverri of Barrio El Hoyo, Trinidad Martínez of Fray Damián, Doña Ernestina and Doña Encarnación of Barrios Obrero and San Nicolás, and "Misiá" Leonor of El Avispero, who lent their houses for the parties. This barrio matriarchy was decisive in initiating the earliest manifestations of the working-class dance in the poor areas of Cali from the 1930s onward.

I believe that both the champú dances and the fee dances corresponded to new forms of sociability in a city undergoing a slow and late process of modernization. In the music's case, the new forms were influenced by the novel and fascinating impetus of the culture industry through radio, recordings, and cinema.

Families' access to many of the epicenters of the scene, such as kiosks, *casetas*, *terrazas*, and clubs, made these a necessary part of life. Here, women were exposed from early adolescence to parties and dances. Dance was a fundamental means of socialization, since through it women had direct interaction with men. This early interaction, shown by the fact that children learned to dance before they could read or write, had repercussions in future social relations, in behavior, and in the woman's role as conceived in terms of both her own performance of self and the man's understanding of it. Given the high symbolic value placed on dancing well, parties became a school for molding the body and an attitude toward it, as well as for seduction and courtship. This attitude toward the body was fundamental for turning dance into a nonverbal language that communicated sentiments, emotions, and sensibilities (see Ulloa 2005).

The attitude was transmitted, reproduced, and culturally inherited by later generations, and today it materializes in the upsurge of dance schools in Cali. There, perhaps, are keys for understanding the hedonistic image of the city and of the Caleña, the woman from Cali, projected in the Colombian imaginary and reflected in the poem "Cali mío" by Gonzalo Arango (see Ulloa Sanmiguel 1992: 392), founder of nadaism in Colombia, from about 1960. Arango uses natural imagery to express his perception of Cali as a sensual, hedonistic, and joyful city, full of beautiful women and made from "one of Eve's breasts," and as an open city, receptive and informal, that he represents in a vision that matches Colombians' imaginings of Cali, an imaginary that grows ever stronger. The participation of women in different settings and with different roles contributed decisively to the configuration of the classic Caleño style of salsa dancing as an elaborated, complex language, which today is recognized worldwide and has been included in international competitions under the category of cabaret salsa.

With respect to this style, my in situ observations reveal a pattern of dance systematically differentiated from the international canon, or the one that begins on the second beat of the rhythmic phrase, following the Cuban clave timeline. In classic Caleño, one begins not on count 2 but on the first beat of the rhythmic cycle, where the accent falls in salsa music. The fourth beat is a rest marked not by silence but by a *pique* (tap) of one foot in place or else by moving forward or to the sides, or it is simultaneously indicated with another body part (the arms, the head, or the hips).

This pattern does not coincide with the clave canon, for which reason Caleño bailarines have been considered rather unorthodox salsa dancers in the international sphere, although their great ability as improvisers is widely recognized, and the diversity of steps and choreographies they perform, different from those that characterize dancers from elsewhere in Latin America, the Caribbean, or North America, is appreciated.[13] Also noteworthy is their facility in subdividing the musical beat with their feet, in which they ornament and embellish their stylistic repertoire, whether following the percussionists' breaks or inventing figures that accompany the melodic instruments like piano or the brass section. This characteristic is not common among dancers of other nationalities, who are more expressive in the use of their upper body, particularly in moving the torso, arms, head, hair (for women), and shoulders.

In other words, in salsa music the strong beats are the first and third, and this rhythmic pattern is kept in the classic Caleño style of dance, which also begins on the first beat. Preliminary observations suggest that in some cases the first and third beats are exchanged, without interrupting the flow of the dance.

In conjunction, these properties of classic Caleño style constitute the dance as language, or rather as bodily knowledge that is simultaneously known and unknown to the conscious mind, since it is learned in a spontaneous, intuitive way, having been taught by a sociocultural environment before any formal schooling, such as through a later apprenticeship to a teacher or an academy. Now, the conscious technical intervention experienced in an academy, as one of the strategies of professionalization mentioned at the beginning of this chapter, has allowed a qualitative transformation of the dance and those bailadores who become bailarines. This cognitive transformation and its routinization is one of the conditions that have allowed the latter to become world champions of cabaret style. The strategies implemented for this transformation not only have widened the gap between bailadores and bailarines but also have irrupted into the conventional modes of dancing salsa in Cali. In other words, there is a dialectical movement that begins with the bailador who becomes a bailarín, moves on to the transformations that this change produces in relation to shows and international competitions, and ends with the impact that bailarines with their shows have on the everyday dancer. This impact is expressed in not only the ways of appreciating and evaluating techniques or styles but also the steps or figures that gradually begin to be adopted, which enrich the dance from start to finish.

I believe that classic Caleño style, with all its variations, is as legitimate as any other style, even though it is not ruled by the clave beat. It represents a different mode of embodying rhythm and music, or rather another way of feeling, another sensibility expressed through dance. If this is true, we are looking at a characteristic that sustains the identity story constructed through dance in Santiago de Cali. This characteristic emerges through relation and contrast with the pattern governed by clave, which predominates in Cuba and Puerto Rico, for example.

One must inquire after the historical and cultural reasons for the origination of this dance pattern, this distinctive feature that characterizes Caleño dancers, which until a few years ago was not recognized as a part of the international salsa dance canon. Preliminary reflections lead me to think that in Cali the learning of dance, principally guaracha and mambo, arrived already with the marking of the downbeat. Older generations learned these dances as medialized through the Mexican cinema of the 1940s and 1950s, and in some of those films in which mambos and guarachas were danced, I have observed that the downbeat is marked, and the clave is not followed as a rhythmic basis. In other words, Mexicans had already transformed the dance from the way Cubans danced it. And this dance matrix was the one that was assimilated in Cali, despite the music being indeed originally Cuban or Puerto Rican. This matrix was transmitted to the following generations at the family party, the barrio celebration, and the discotheque or when dancing at the kiosks, *terrazas*, and *casetas* where salsa culture developed in Cali from the 1960s.

Another reason that may explain the adoption and establishment of this dance pattern is the physical and symbolic absence of clave (the instrument), congas, and bongos from Caleño popular dance, which creates a situation similar to that found in the Mexican case. In contrast, these instruments and many others with which Cuban and Puerto Rican polyrhythms are produced have been present in those islands and other parts of the Caribbean for two hundred or three hundred years, or since the time of slavery, initially as a part of black and mulatto daily life during colonial periods and, later, during the republican periods, broadening into other segments of society in a process that has lasted from the dawn of modernity up to the present time. Historically, percussion instruments were integrated in a natural and decisive manner into family, work, and neighborhood spheres, fulfilling multiple functions in magical or religious rituals and secular festivities, transcending different spaces throughout the Caribbean but particularly those in which slavery had existed. Thus, they are an integral part of a culture lived through rhythm, song, and dance, re-created by generation after generation, as can well be seen in the social and cultural histories of Cuban and Puerto Rican music, especially in the lower social strata.

This has not been the case in a city like Cali, where after the 1930s music from recordings, radio, and cinema predominated over live musical production, such that contact with musical instruments—their uses, functions, timbres, and polyrhythms—was mediated by the communication technologies born with the twentieth century. Reception through communication media rather than live performance, and industrialized, technical reproduction rather than collective and popular creation, are the watermarks that define our musical culture at this level. In addition, although there was slavery in Cali, it was in a lesser proportion than in the Caribbean or Brazil, so there are no rituals for the ancestors or ceremonies for the orishas, no African polytheism or Santería, and no *batá* or *yuka* drums that form part of our local or regional history or that might have resonated with the clave from distant times. In Cali, contact with the percussive polyrhythm of the clave and its relatives is a phenomenon going back no further than the 1930s, when the first Cuban music groups formed in the city. And its growing incorporation into musical groups occurred late, in the 1970s (along with the height of drug trafficking), when salsa groups multiplied, musical production was intensified, live concerts and studio recordings proliferated, and show business and discographic production increased. The cowbell and cowbell player came into style, as did the congas and the conguero, the bongos and the bongo player, who began to play a part in family festivities, in salseros' get-togethers, in bars, and in *salsotecas*, spaces that also included the clave, the maracas, and the timbales. Of this group of instruments, only the timbales were used in bars and cabarets in the 1950s to accompany the music that emanated from jukeboxes in the red-light district.

This late (or recent) presence of percussion and clave-based polyrhythm is, in my opinion, the other fundamental reason for which clave is not present in the dance. But, to those who hold that salsa cannot be danced without clave, I wish to point out that salsa culture in Cali, a popular culture, generated and consolidated a particular and widely varied style, something like a dance dialect, that has its own specificity and is acknowledged among dancers the world over. Until a few years ago, it was not widely recognized in international competitions, where Puerto Ricans and North Americans are those who dictate the canon and its legitimacy.

The classic Caleño style has been consolidated over half a century as a dance complex composed of designs, steps, figures, and choreographies with their own aesthetic and has survived despite fashion changes and insurgence of other ephemeral dances. It is now time that it be recognized as its own expression, one that instead of contributing to the homogenization of dance styles has instead enriched and diversified salsa dance as a language of the body. Proof of this can be found in Caleño dancers Ricardo Murillo and Viviana Vargas winning the First Annual World Salsa Championship in Las Vegas in December 2005 in the cabaret category, in which classic Caleño style prevailed as a novel, creative expression, different from winning styles in earlier international events. In 2006 the Cali dance school Swing Latino, directed by Luis Eduardo "El Mulato" Hernández, won first prize in the group category and second prize in couples in the cabaret division in the Second Annual World Salsa Championship, also in Las Vegas. In 2007 Swing Latino again took the top awards in the Third Annual World Salsa Championship, this time in Orlando, Florida, where they had gone to defend their titles and consolidate their prestige.

A Local Dance on the Global Stage

The success and triumphs of these dancers indicate, at the very least, three changes in local Caleño salsa dancing and its internationalization. First, the qualitative transformation in ways of dancing salsa effected by these groups has enriched the style with new steps, figures, and choreographies. The development of the dance has allowed them to achieve a degree of sophistication and complexity that is difficult to imitate or reproduce without sufficient training and preparation. In turn, this more complicated new style has led to the increased professionalization of Caleño style salsa.

Second, this bodily language has now been inserted into the field of the transnational cultural industry or entertainment industry. Winning several world championships, with all the paraphernalia of big show business, transmitted exclusively by ESPN to various countries, confers a universal status to this occurrence and to the participants; it gives them a prestige analogous to that conferred by large sports tournaments in the world today. It is no longer about dancers who perform a show and then pass a hat asking for voluntary donations and a smattering of applause. Now it is about competing in the big leagues, with everything that entails—preparation, discipline, sacrifice, effort, and creativity—to develop bodily intelligence and achieve the highest level of expression and eloquence.

Finally, Caleño salsa dance (represented in Figure 8.3)—the classic style of the bailarines complemented by the spectacle of aerials and acrobatics—has vindicated this city in a way that contrasts notably with the global stigma Cali has suffered from so many years of drug trafficking and violence. The new image that is beginning to be projected at an international level will not eliminate this stigma, but it does contribute to the generation of a new perception of Cali and its inhabitants. It is significant that in the midst of the tragedy of recent decades in Colombia, dancing salsa has become a source of income for youth from the poorest sectors of this city, who have found in salsa a different alternative for their lives. Their presence in international shows and in the entertainment industry in American and European cities not only has transformed their lives, socially and economically; it also marks a new milestone in the history of salsa and popular culture in Cali, which has in this way transcended its local borders. Thanks to the dance and to them, the city now has a story that identifies it as more than the seat of drug traffic and drug exporters; it is a cradle of great dancers and an exporter of the pleasure and joy salsa dancing offers.

Figure 8.3. Salseros Miryam Collazos and Willian Valencia dancing in Cali's San Antonio neighborhood. *(Photograph by Aymer Álvarez.)*

NOTES

1. "Popular" in Spanish and as I use it here often refers to the working or lower class.

2. [The closest English translation here is *social dancers*. The term "street dancer" might also be used, as it has some currency in the salsa world; however, Ulloa is not making the spatial distinction this term implies (studio/street or inside/outside).—Trans.]

3. [For this term, the most commonly used English equivalent would likely be *studio dancers*, or professional and semiprofessional dancers.—Trans.]

4. *Viejotecas* are sites where older people dance to recorded music (see Waxer 2002).

5. Currently, the popular sectors constitute 85 percent of Cali's population, distributed among socioeconomic strata 1, 2, and 3, Colombia's designations for the lowest class, with a monthly income between approximately US$20 and $500. These are the strata in which salsa culture developed over the last fifty years in Cali.

6. It is no coincidence that current salsa world champions train from six to eight hours daily.

7. The name of the club transferred to its owner, the well-known dancer Jairo "Cañandonga" Obando, still living. Meanwhile, the dance style became so popular that La Cali Charanga recorded the hit song "El pasito cañandonga" in 1990, and Grupo Niche mentions both the place and the person in their song "Del puente para allá."

8. The description of the parties is based on the stories of Benigno Holguín, Hilda Palta, Lucho Lenis, Edgar Mallarino, Héctor "La Sombra" Martínez, and Olmedo Rosero. When they gave their testimonies in 1985–1986, all were over fifty years old and had participated as adolescents in the champú and fee dances. The latter three were professional soccer players during the time of "El Dorado" (a golden age in Colombian professional soccer between 1948 and 1960, when many first-rate Argentine players came, including Alfredo Diestefano, who was considered the best player in the world before Pele).

9. "I remember the parties in the house of Mrs. Gregoria, in the Obrero barrio, from when I was a child. . . . They danced to string bands (guitar, *tiple*, and *bandola*) and to . . . songs that played from Victrolas hooked up to an RCA Victor radio," Edgar Mallarino recounts (1988). They were popular songs like "The Broom Dance," a march by Juan Moriche and Margarita Cueto, and the tango "Ladrillo" by Juan Pulido that had come at that time to Cali. Ladies in long dresses and men in vests, ties, and hats gave a touch of elegance as they enjoyed a healthy and mild event. Of the men, only those who wore long pants (i.e., those who, having reached adulthood at age twenty-one, were allowed to wear pants) could participate in the dance. However, as a place of socialization, the party was open to everyone, producing bonding and the integration of the neighborhood.

10. According to the testimony of professional soccer player Edgar Mallarino, also a mulatto, the champú dances of the Arce family in the El Hoyo barrio were very popular and took place in an immense apartment building on Eighteenth Street between First and Second Avenues, as were the Holguín family champús in Barrio Vilachí, where Benigno Holguín was the disc jockey, and the champús in San Nicolás (Second Avenue and Twenty-Third Street) and in Obrero (Ninth Avenue and Twentieth Street) barrios. The champú dances were more than just a business to sell food and drink: they created a space for the festive and friendly meeting of neighbors and family members who lived in a particular barrio or sector. Because they were relatively large places where neighbors, family members, and friends all attended, some began to worry about having a good sound system and a comfortable discotheque, in accordance with the times, perhaps presaging the *melómanos* (music connoisseurs) and music collectors of Cali, recognized on a national level for their mania as music consumers and for the preservation of recordings. See Waxer 2002 for more on these collectors.

11. Los Cali Boys was a sextet founded in 1945 by Tito Cortés and José del Carmen Beyibo, both mulattos, to play Cuban music. The group got together in the park of Barrio Obrero, where Beyibo and Cortés lived. In Obrero, along with Sucre and San Nicolás, the most ardent listeners of Antillean music in our city were concentrated. These barrios were not only places of entertainment, prostitutes, dancers, and soccer teams but also where a large part of the native Caleño population—mostly mestizo, black, or mulatto—lived and was born.

12. Colombians often term music from the Caribbean islands "Antillean music." This category includes many popular styles, such as salsa and merengue.

13. According to Carlos F. Trujillo, in the World Salsa Congress held in Puerto Rico in 2002, two groups of dancers could be identified, a division representing the two tendencies indicated here: those who dance on-1 and those who dance on-2: "Each group prides itself on its style and manifests that pride through t-shirts, caps, bracelets emblazoned with the phrase on-1 or on-2" (2003). This binary opposition clearly defined the tensions created in the international salsa dance scene, which result from different factors, including the continual and ever-growing presence of Caleño dancers and classic Caleño salsa dance.

REFERENCES

Genner Vásquez, John. 2007. Interview by Alejandro Ulloa Sanmiguel. July 15. Cali, Colombia.

Mallarino, Edgar. 1988. Interview by Alejandro Ulloa Sanmiguel. March 15. Cali, Colombia.

Melo, Jorge Orlando. 2006. "Contra la identidad." *Revista el Malpensante* (Bogotá), December 15.

Rodríguez, Pablo. 1996. "La sociedad y las formas: Siglo XVIII." In *Historia del Gran Cauca, historia regional del suroccidente Colombiano.* 2nd ed. Cali: Instituto de Estudios del Pacífico, Universidad del Valle.

Trujillo, Carlos Fernando. 2003. Interview by Alejandro Ulloa Sanmiguel. March 13. Cali, Colombia.

Ulloa Sanmiguel, Alejandro. 1992. *La salsa en Cali.* 2nd ed. Cali: Universidad del Valle.

———. 2005. *El baile, un lenguaje del cuerpo.* Cali: Secretaría de Cultura y Turismo del Valle del Cauca.

Waxer, Lise. 2002. *The City of Musical Memory: Salsa, Record Grooves, and Popular Culture in Cali, Colombia.* Middletown, CT: Wesleyan University Press.

9

Dancing Salsa in Santo Domingo, Dominican Republic

A First Look

Rossy Díaz

(Translated by Sydney Hutchinson)

Music and dance are inherent features of Dominican culture, and the culture identifies people according to their favorite music-dance genre. This association of music with dance is such that being a *merenguero*, *sonero*, or *salsero* is a synonym for "dancer" even more than for "musician" (of merengue, *son*, or salsa, respectively).

In the Dominican Republic, the passion for dance is an enduring facet. It is not delimited by geographic or temporal styles and takes precedence over sociopolitical or cultural topics related to the music, so that Caribbean and other musics are danced without consideration for anything other than bodily enjoyment. Salsa is one of the most popular musical styles in the Dominican Republic, and that this international genre coexists with local and regional dance music styles, particularly the merengue as a "national" music, reveals the particular behaviors surrounding peoples' preferences for one genre over another.

With Dominican migration to New York City and New York's influence on the island a new and marked sense of salsero identity has gradually formed in the Dominican Republic since the style was introduced. This identity also was affected by (1) the opening of the Dominican Republic to national and international mass media after the end of the Rafael Trujillo dictatorship in 1961, (2) the son dance culture, which has been strong in older barrios of the capital, Santo Domingo, since the early twentieth century, and (3) rural migration into the capital and the resultant new social class after the fall of the dictatorship.

The mass media have transmitted cultural values and salsa itself, spreading social and cultural codes through the shared experiences of musicians and, above all, dancers, which leads to the formation of a sociocultural group with a salsero identity that parallels that of the merengue, salsa's greatest competition for a listening audience in the commercial category of tropical music in the record market. The salsa dance schools and academies are one aspect of this salsero culture, allowing interchange of social and cultural values among different social classes in Santo Domingo in addition to disseminating dance. They are also a means of economic progress, social mobility, and ascent from a marginal, or lower-class, culture for dancers.

Alongside the construction of this salsero identity within the many contemporary Dominican identities, a salsa dance cultural industry has also emerged that permeates the entertainment and tourist industries, an important part of the national economy. This salsa dance cultural industry, and the attendant salsero identity, also competes for audiences in the record market and in commercial establishments in Santo Domingo showcasing music and dance.

The Context: The Dance Music Scene in Santo Domingo

Santo Domingo has a population of 2.73 million, according to the 2002 census (Oficina Nacional de Estadística, República Dominicana 2002). A huge influx of rural migrants since the 1960s profoundly altered its social makeup. These migrants brought with them their listening preferences for rural genres, such as *merengue típico* from the Cibao region of the country or the guitar music of the Northwest, adding those musical cultures to those of son dancing, Cuban music, and other genres that already existed in the city's barrios.

In this musical setting, Caribbean dance musics like son, bolero, and salsa have come to share popularity with merengue, an autochthonous music and dance genre that has enjoyed primacy in the local scene since the late nineteenth century. Musical fusions, like merengue-son and *bolemengue*, emerged. The inherence of music and dance is evident today, especially with son and salsa: the first because it represents a cultural heritage of the old barrios of Santo Domingo, particularly those of the working and lower classes,[1] and the second because it is an expression of a more international Hispanic Caribbean and new Dominican social class, that of the return migrants, or *retornados*, of the New York diaspora.

As some Dominicans left for New York, others moved from rural areas to urban centers. Santo Domingo was the destination of 62 percent of rural-to-urban migrants in the 1960s and 1970s, and cultural friction occurred because of the conflict between traditional rural and urban lifeways (Faxas 2007: 219).[2] This demographic shift provoked a gradual mixture in the capital of the culture of the old parts of the city center (e.g., San Carlos, Villa Francisca, and Borojol) with that of the new barrios of peasant settlement, a new crucible of identities heir to the son, bolero, merengue, *guaracha*, and the incipient *bachata*. Salsa made its presence felt in this diversity of musics as a new and more modern Caribbean popular style. This new music was heard only in the capital, where there was access to mass media, and this access differentiated capital dwellers from the rest of the nation for a time. For this reason salsa was identified as a dance of the capital. In particular, it was a dance of the working-class and marginal areas of the city.

This chapter is based largely on the information, statements from informants, and participant-observation gathered during four events I coordinated as part of my work for the Institute for Caribbean Studies (INEC) in Santo Domingo during 2006 and 2007:

- Public discussion titled "The Salsa Boom on Dominican Radio" on October 5, 2006
- Meeting of salsa teachers in Santa Domingo in Santo Domingo on November 28, 2006
- Meeting titled "Passion and Style in Salsa" on December 6, 2006
- Dance workshop titled "How Is Salsa Danced?" on May 24, 2007

INEC researchers gathered basic data from participants, who usually included dancers, musicians, radio announcers, dance teachers, and fans of son and salsa. We recorded these activities in audio and video as a part of our work leading up to the Second Congress on Music, Identity, and Culture in the Caribbean (MIC2), an academic conference held in Santiago, Dominican Republic, every two years. During this project, I was an activities coordinator for INEC, which was one of the research institutions organizing the conference.

The participant-observer descriptions I present here relate to recognizing local salsa culture as a type of Dominican identity rather than to standardizing the dance itself in relation to global salsa culture. Nevertheless, on the basis of these notes and work experiences, through which I was able to observe, converse with, and dance with outstanding salsa dancers and teachers, I also outline a few of the dance's features.

As I have come to understand it, local conceptions of salsa are closely related to two cultural processes: (1) the son tradition in Santo Domingo barrios and (2) the formation of a New York–Dominican culture since the end of the dictatorship in 1961, a culture that in a few short decades would come to influence national life as a whole.

(Tras)Pasos de Baile: The Dominican Sonero-Salsero

Several social factors important for understanding son and salsa as dances of the barrios lie within this urban cultural collectivity.[3] The greatest is that salsa shares son dancing spaces in Santo Domingo. Others are that the dancer is the primary person in son and that a cultural identity is formed as an alternative to the national one. This latter aspect is especially vital to the localization of salsa dance, since Dominicans want to revive the local citizenship of son and distinguish it as existing before Cuban son. A sense of son ownership is still present among local soneros, even though the Dominican origin of son is a "myth overcome already in 1971, after establishing the absence of illustrative arguments for this old theory" (Andújar 2007: 205). This myth nevertheless creates unity among dancers of son and salsa and is why they jealously guard their dance sites, which generally are somewhat exclusive.[4] The connection between dance sites creates a cultural geography of salsa, overlapping with that of son, in certain parts of the Dominican capital.

The Dominican performer and composer Rey Reyes connects son dancing to salsa culture in the working- and lower-class barrios of Santo Domingo in his popular salsa "Patios, bateyes y callejones (de Quisqueya son los sones)" (Patios, plantations, and alleys: Son is from the Dominican Republic),[5] on the CD *Llegó la rumba* (2005). The Santo Domingo barrios mentioned in this song include Cristo Rey, El Hoyo de Chulín, Villas Agrícolas, San Antón, Villa Mella, Borojol, 27 de Febrero, Capotillo, and Luperón. Reyes is known as *el Sonero de los Barrios* because of the importance his songs give to the Dominican salsa geography.

The transfer from son to salsa culture occurred in the 1960s, when new Caribbean musical styles arrived in the Dominican Republic, as the Dominican salsa reporter and radio announcer Eugenio Pérez reveals:

> In the early 1960s, the sound of [Puerto Rican bandleader Rafael] Cortijo provoked a renewed interest in Caribbean rhythms among Dominicans, initiating a true craze. Certainly, we already had Dominicans who performed son and guaracha, but aside from Johnny Pacheco, a true luminary of *charanga* in the 1950s, it was only after Trujillo's death that locals began to excel in salsa, which had recently emerged principally in the barrios of New York. (2008: 418)

The development of communications and mass media outlets for music after the fall of the dictatorship gave Dominicans access to the outside world. But the circular relation between Dominicans inside and outside the country also mediated salsa music and dance. A large migratory flow developed after the end of the Trujillo dictatorship, and large transnational communities grew in New York and other cities, each with a local identity that participated in the "salsa movement" of the time, as Lara Ivette López de Jesús calls it (2003). But how are these two identities—the transnational and the local—related? Or more specifically, how can the local salsa sensibility[6] be defined?

Only a decade after the emergence of salsa, Dominicans in New York would become a cultural force that "affected Dominican identity on the island" (Austerlitz 2007: 97). At the same time, salsa, the most popular and most representative Caribbean diasporic music, was gradually taking over as the dance of the barrios of Santo Domingo. I found that salsa dance sites in Santo Domingo frequently had been former son establishments that were acquired by "Dominican Yorks," or return migrants, who put a salsa spin on them (Tejeda 2009).

Son and salsa fans shared an ambiguous attitude toward merengue, Dominicans' national dance. Chino Méndez, host of the radio program *Salsa Son*, noted that some bars in the 1970s and 1980s would program salsa exclusively. He reported that "in these businesses salsa was listened to, like, 'I don't listen to merengue or bachata!'"[7] Answers to questions by the INEC researchers (e.g., "What other musical genres do you listen to?") revealed that, after son, the music participants generally preferred for dancing was salsa, followed by bolero, bachata, and in a distant position, merengue, when mentioned at all. Salsa stood out as a dance that gave participants pleasure and distinguished them from others, particularly from dancers of merengue.

This preference for son and salsa brings us to what I believe is Dominicans' cultural duality as expressed by dancing to and enjoying musics that have interacted and shared space with *the* genre of merengue. But if on the one hand they see son as their own, as Dominican, and on the other they elevate salsa as the most modern, stylish Caribbean music and the most international Latino dance, that continually creates tensions of identity in the country of *the* Dominican identity and likely determines many of the characteristics of Dominican salsa culture described in this chapter.

I do not see this as a deep identity conflict because diversity has also predominated as a central cultural paradigm in the Dominican Republic. However, social analogues of the dance of son and salsa do exist beyond the poor barrios, which are basically a manifestation of the marginal sense conferred on these musics in the past. What most distinguishes soneros from salseros but also makes them resemble one another is their individuality within the local, the assumption of being both Dominican and Caribbean, with no conflict. Their decision to face the sea, not turn their back to it—just as Dominicans seem to live, even today—makes these modes of association viable.

Two important aspects of the localization of salsa are the Dominican salsa market and salsa media. Popular national and transnational Dominican *orquestas* (ensembles) combined merengue and salsa repertoires on their albums at the beginning of the salsa movement, and "although what some authors have called a 'sonic struggle' between merengue and salsa has existed, both have influenced each other mutually and their performers have practiced them together" (López de Jesús 2003: 146). A few important paradigms are apparent in the relationship between salsa productions by Dominicans on the island and those abroad. Production of salsa recordings from the 1960s to 1990s was based mainly in New York. The samples published in research by the Puerto Rican sociologist Ángel Quintero Rivera (2008: 62–64) reveal that not until the 1980s and 1990s did the number of local salsa recordings come to rival that of New York recordings.

By the 1980s Dominican artists had already recorded salsa, including well-known merengueros like Joseíto Mateo; soneros Cheché Abreu and Cuco Valoy; musicians like Johnny Ventura, who produced some recordings exclusively featuring salsa; and Wilfrido Vargas, an essential artist for understanding the fluidity of relations between Caribbean popular musics, above all during the apogee of the Fania All Stars (the signature ensemble of Fania Records). Names central to the New York salsa scene include Johnny Pacheco and Ralph Mercado, both with Dominican heritage and both of whom worked in merengue and salsa; Cuco Valoy is better known as a salsero off the island, while on it he is mainly considered a merenguero.

From the 1980s to the 2000s, musicians like Juan Luis Guerra also stood out as part of the salsa identity universe, along with merengueros like Fausto Rey, Sergio Vargas, Cherito (of New York Band), Alex Bueno, and Rubby Pérez. Dominican salseros like Raulín Rosendo and Rey Reyes were heirs to earlier Dominican salsa musicians, like José "El Canario" Alberto, Santiago Cerón, Frankie Dante, and José Bello, as well as current Dominican salseros like Sex Appeal, Asdrúbal, Manolé, and Michel. There are also Dominican composers who have written internationally popular salsas, like Palmer Hernández with his "Ven devórame otra vez," written for Lalo Rodríguez; Alicia Baroni with her "Esperándote," performed by Tito Rojas; and Fernando Arias, coauthor of "No me conoces," sung by Marc Anthony. Dominican salsa arrangers and directors include the well-known musicians Ricky González and Ángel Fernández, the latter of whom also played merengue with New York Band and Milly, Jocelyn, y los Vecinos.

This "moment"[8] well illustrates what Deborah Pacini Hernández describes as a real conflict between salsa and merengue,[9] since they have both competed in the international market as tropical music. But the point is that the output of salsa recordings is substantial in both Dominican geographies, and the quantity made abroad both confirms the importance and participation of Dominicans living abroad and affirms the influence they exert on the local market up to the present time.

The role of the salsa media in Santo Domingo is also noteworthy. The radio in particular has been important in the diffusion of salsa: as Chino Méndez described it, salsa was already on the AM band in 1969 in programs such as *La Hora Brava* with Hugo Adames on the station Onda Musical.[10] Méndez mentions many radio programs currently on FM (including *Salsa Picante, Cocinando la Salsa, Salsa Son, 95 Grados de Salsa,* and *Cimasalseando*) that have strong links with and in salsa culture and a large listenership. Their hosts are the main presenters on salsa stages as well as important figures in the promotion of salsa events and productions.

Dominican salsa radio does more than disseminate music and allow social interaction: it also promotes the culture of salsa dance in the streets and discotheques. Telephone calls to stations to request songs, report listeners, announce dance competitions, or advertise salsa businesses indicate the programs' and hosts' popularity. Teodora Lahoz Banks notes that salsa programs increased in popularity beginning in the 1990s because of dancers' desire to return to *salsa brava*, the more aggressive early salsa style also known as *salsa dura*, forsaking the softer *salsa monga* or *salsa romántica* style, which was influenced by the *balada* (pop ballad) style, that had dominated the dial (Lahoz Banks 2009). The audience was the cause for the return to playing old salsa recordings in barrios, thus constituting an unusual form of interaction between the radio and local salsa culture, something that would also be reflected in the dance and in competition.

Salsa is reemerging as a competitive dance, principally in the discotheques of Santo Domingo's outer barrios, where salsa is heard and jammed to; where scholars, promoters, radio announcers, and dance instructors come together; and where special competitive events are often organized (see, e.g., Figure 9.1). These are the area of the Manoguayabo turnoff, the western part of Santo Domingo around Isabel Aguiar, the San Vicente de Paúl area, and establishments on Venezuela Avenue in the eastern part of the city. Dance competition seasons are also televised on, for example, *9 × 9 Roberto*, *La Opción de las 12*, and seasonal programs.[11]

With and because of competition in salsa dancing, an important characteristic of the capital-city salsa dancer is defined: now the dance affords not only pleasure but also the opportunity to stand out on the dance floor. Televising dance makes people want to show off more.

Salsa dancing today is also profitable, and the dance industry has diversified; salsa schools proliferate in the outer zones of Santo Domingo (Los Mina, Alma Rosa, Ensanche Las Américas, all in the eastern part of the city) and in the western barrios (e.g., Herrera and Los Alcarrizos), as well as, more recently,

Figure 9.1. Salsa dancers at El Canario Patio Lounge, a Santo Domingo salsa club owned by the singer Jose "El Canario" Alberto. *(Photograph by Hanel Peña, 2012.)*

in the zones of the national district (Ensanche Miraflores, Paraíso, El Vergel, Zona Universitaria, Zona Colonial). Examples include Salsoteca Internacional, a school with a holistic vision of the dancer and Afro-Caribbean dance culture, located in the Colonial Zone (near the intersection of Las Mercedes and Palo Hincado) and also known as Eli Casandra School, and the Merengue, Son and Salsa Academy of Doña Chicha near the Universidad Autónoma de Santo Domingo, well known in the local salsa universe after more than three decades in business, where upper-class dancers, who traditionally did not dance salsa, have trained. Another well-known school where upper-class dancers train is Pasos Dance Academy, a successful school in business seven years in Ensanche Paraíso, an upper-class neighborhood, that has found new commercial niches in salsa dance via business exhibitions, special shows to launch products, and constant investigation into the current state of dance in Santo Domingo. Francisco "Quico" Medina, owner of Pasos Academy, attends salsa congresses, and he states that he has a book forthcoming on characteristics and technical aspects of salsa dance in the Dominican Republic.

Other schools are that of Luis Melo, which is known by its slogan "Learn to dance salsa in 21 hours" and is a dynamic business that combines classes in Caribbean and Latin rhythms, special workshops for children and for soon-to-be brides and grooms, and class sessions in discotheques and in customers' homes and also offers entertainment for events. The Dominican-French school Salsa Carib'Event, located in Las Terrenas, Samaná, offers trip packages that include salsa class programs with intensive sessions and lodging. Indeed, in recent years salsa has become a component in the Dominican tourist industry, as is the case of Pipo La Fama and Salsa Carib'Event, which is establishing itself as a model for dance academies in beach areas like Boca Chica, San Pedro de Macorís, and Puerto Plata.

Through tourism, music, and increased exposure, dancer exportation to other countries has occurred, and schools of salsa and other Caribbean rhythms are opening in countries like France, Spain, Germany, Switzerland, and Italy that project the dance industry model found in Santo Domingo.

Salsa Dance in Santo Domingo

I have emphasized in this chapter how salsa is a social action as well as a representative of a total cultural space, and for this reason particular forms of socialization exist among soneros and their salsero heirs. In particular, the use of the same spaces (bars, discotheques, *colmados*)[12] results in common musical preferences, codes of behavior on the dance floor, and the like.

Chino Méndez distinguishes the forms of salsero socialization such as recognition of the female salsa dancer. He writes of the pride many women feel in receiving invitations to dance, which he attributes to the sense of "companionship" in salsa dance.[13] Therefore, assuming that dance is an instrument of interaction between social processes and the body, behind salsa dancing's appearance of entertainment lies an expression of aspects of the cultural and social condition of the Dominican lower classes. These include an attachment to parties and alcohol as a means of evading adversity; *tigueraje*,[14] both masculine and feminine; machismo; pride in bodily form; and negritude.[15]

Salsa dancers occupy a special social position in the sector in which they live: they are known as a personality in the barrio; are admired, particularly those who compete on salsa dance programs on national television or those who appear in the videos of local salsa artists; are sought after for parties and recreational activities in the barrio; and are known by their artistic names, which are allegorical to their way of dancing, some carrying the surname Salsa (La Cometa de la Salsa, Luís Jala Rayo, El Tesoro Salsero, El Topo, Luís Estilo, Tony La Fragancia, Papito Style, Julio La Salsa, and El Catedrático de la Salsa, to cite a few). Such names connect them all as dancer personas.

In terms of the corporeal aspects of the dance, the particularities of local salsa dance are best revealed by comparison. The Puerto Rican and the New York styles, the styles most often referred to by the dancers interviewed, have "differences," asserts dance instructor Francisco "Quico" Medina (2009). "[Dominicans] use the feet more," he says, thereby confirming another element of local style, the lesser movement of the torso. Nonetheless, the basis in clave and the combination of styles like the Puerto Rican one with legwork show that there are also similarities between Puerto Rican and Dominican styles, although the local salseros habitually perform figures in a more open position.

As Sydney Hutchinson observes regarding the professional style of salsa dance in Santo Domingo, "It combines the Eddie Torres count with a foot tap on the empty count that they call '*el marque*' and use to facilitate the turns" (2008: 130). She also asserts that "many dance in reverse, with the right foot forward and the left back, in contrast to the rest of the world." This refers to the style of dance with the first step on the left foot, which I consider a special feature, closely related to the local dance tradition, and something that distinguishes us from the whole of other salsa dancers, even though "here there are very many influences," as Medina (2009) told me. This has been better identified in son dancing, from which it transferred to salsa as a stylistic value, similar to other characteristics mentioned in this chapter.

In an interview with Pipo "La Fama" Alcalá and Cathy Launay de Alcalá, founders and directors of Salsa Carib'Event, Pipo Alcalá explained:

> Dominican salsa is mostly danced starting with the left foot and is characterized by its *rumbero* [lively or festive] style—which is to say, with a lot of movement. There isn't really a "count" as we can find, for example, in the salsa called "Puerto Rican," but instead one dances along with the timbales. That is why one speaks of a *rumbero* street style. (Alcalá 2009)

External dance influences, coming especially through the proliferation of international dance schools and formulas, do not mar the particularities of some local styles, particularly from the western and eastern zones of the city. In these, dancers like Ambiorix "El Bory de la Salsa" Saldaña, who invents his own steps in the western part, and Marino "El Catedrático de la Salsa" Lizardo, a dance instructor who uses his own dance terminology in the eastern part, stand out.[16] Likewise, the dancer known as Tony La Fragancia states on his worksheet that compared with the son tradition "there are different [types of] dancers, like those who dance rumba or have more movement in their style, for the party, and the classic dancer."

Dance instructor Medina (2009) identifies the current style as a street, or *callejero*, style: "It is more acrobatic, with a marked rumba style, a busier style in which many figures that aren't characteristic of the classic dance are used." Particularly during the flourishes of instrumental improvisation in salsa, the dance is styled on the rhythm section, the clave, the *tumbadoras* (congas), and the timbales—which also shows us the styles of salsa that are preferred for dancing, such as salsa-mambo, boogaloo, and the salsa brava of the 1960s–1970s. For this reason, some disdain toward salsa romántica and the balada style persists among salseros.

In the current style the man generally combines footwork with drops and leg crosses, knee movements, and crouches, while the woman maintains the basic steps; nonetheless, dancers from eastern Santo Domingo (Herrera, Los Alcarrizos) demonstrate greater participation by the woman in terms of free turns and the leg movements, though the man still directs the turns and partial turns and decides whether to let her go or hold her in any given moment.

Within the partner dynamic, the exchange of hands occurs while changing weight from right to left and forward: they approach one another and move away while holding both hands, a step that alternates with different turns using both hands. The single-handed dynamic is similar, with partial turns to left and right, and in the faster and more complicated turns the drops, lower-leg crosses, and floor figures are often combined.

The New York influence is notable, but there is no doubt that the local salsa aesthetic has a global sense that results from the dance congresses and the boom of academies and schools of dance in Santo Domingo. During the meeting of dance teachers in November 2006, Cathy Launay described "an international salsa, with more turns and acrobatics," that is danced as a standard form in the Dominican Republic.

These ambiguities between one style and another have led to meetings between salsa schools. Angelina "Chicha" Tejeda, a well-known salsa instructor, described her impressions of on-2 and on-1 dancing:

I began teaching on-2 a decade ago, because I had contact with dancer friends in the United States who sent me dance videos, but two years ago I changed to on-1, although I am starting from the beginning again, because it is more comfortable, and it goes with the beat of the music. (2009)

Together with her spouse, Fellito, Mariel—whom Tejeda recommends as "an excellent dancer"—has a studio called On Two on Núñez de Cáceres Avenue, where only salsa is taught.

Medina pointed out:

In on-1 salsa the strong beat is not marked with the right [foot]; here this is copied. Dancing on-1 is more traditional. The man's starting foot is the right one, with the first step forward; this is the natural [style]. On-2 is American style; more eclectic, it has a bit of other dances [in it]. In the classic style the turns are not so elaborate. (2009)

On the same topic, Pipo Alcalá stated:

The 1 count allows for salsa to be learned easier and faster by those who are beginners. However, the 2 count comes from mambo, and it gets you to follow the clave, to listen better to the music, and to dance it as a consequence. The movements, steps, and turns can be more elaborate or demonstrative when following this rhythm. (Alcalá 2009)

The dance schools consulted in the INEC activities teach both counts. Tejeda told me that "they were trying to unify the on-2 dance for all the schools" to avoid the stumbles and collisions of style between salsa dancers on the dance floor (2009). When I asked this outstanding teacher how she evaluates women's contributions to salsa dance, she pointed out that in her school she notices that more women attend classes, particularly at night, and that this year she has twenty female and eight male students. She continued:

The role of the woman is to give a touch of grace to salsa. The woman uses her arms and figure; she stands out. The man has control; he sets out the guidelines; the woman works with what the man does. (Tejeda 2009)

Nevertheless, I wish to point out a few interesting cases of women in salsa dance. I noticed that, of the schools and couples consulted by INEC, the pedagogical role of the woman stood out. Many of the women danced both female and male styles. Playero La Salsa, a male dancer from the western part of the city, dances both leader and follower roles, as does his partner. La Sati de la Salsa, a young woman I met in December 2006 at a cultural activity on the premises of the Cultural and Sport Association of Gualey (Agrucudegua) is the leader of her couple and was announced as such at the event. But the convention in these circles is to announce the man by name and not identify his partner; she is just "his partner."

The founders of the school Salsa Carib'Event enthusiastically enumerated female dancers who were well known in the country, such as Miguelina, known as La Reina, who dances with José La Salsa in the Kandela review, and Yesenia Peralta, who currently lives in Spain but who excelled for many years in the Dominican Republic (Alcalá 2009; Launay de Alcalá 2009).

Also noteworthy is the ritualization of professional dance through spectacle and flashy costumes with sequins and shiny trim, which are also great differentiators from the "natural," or street, dancer or the aficionado. The prominence of professional salsa dancers, the centrality of the figure on the dance floor, usually means that such persons eclipse the nonprofessional dancers. This is further shown by the segmentation of space on the dance floor, since their different styles do not generally allow them to dance together.

This showiness has a lot to do with the mass media and with travel to dance competitions and dance congresses, which creates greater exposure to staged salsa. Likewise, the showiness has contributed to the imagining of a dancer personage, one who transcends the dance space, is recognizable in society, and thus receives greater economic benefits. A consequence, highlighted by the five or more Santo Domingo–area dance academies participating in the "Passion and Style in Salsa" meeting, is that, because these dancer personages establish dance academies, salsa is ever more frequently danced by the middle and upper classes in Santo Domingo.

Learn to Dance Salsa: A Local Cultural Industry

In closing, I return to the topic of the dance schools and academies and note that these are phenomena that transcend their function in dance culture, competition, and even the transfer and interchange of values between different social classes in Santo Domingo.

Dancing salsa in Santo Domingo is today a profession through which participants may gain space and status within the city and may transcend a life in the poor barrios. According to the participants at "Passion and Style in Salsa," this has led to the ascent of a marginal culture, the transfer of cultural values to upper classes of the capital and their acceptance of those values, and a path to higher social position for dancers, who often are the owners of the dance schools.[17] At the same time, these changes have given new energy to the original passion for salsa, and they attract new forms of association, whether in the marketplace or with local and regional musical tendencies of the times, as in the contrast between the limited circulation of salsa brava and the current popularity of bachata and *reggaetón*. This small entertainment industry of salsa dance has maintained itself and has expanded, despite market studies and current cultural policy, contributing to the two pillars of the national economy: music and tourism.

Salsa dance competition forms part of one of many Dominican identities. But even omitting its competitive aspect, salsa dance is a local cultural industry. In the absence of official cultural policy, this cultural industry has outlined its own policies based on competition among dance styles and means of promoting dance schools via the Internet, videos, radio, television, competitions, and the like, thus guaranteeing the participation of dance styles and schools in foreign commerce through their integration into the international context of dance and competition.

Many professionals already known in the local sphere for their creativity in dance are beginning to travel to congresses in Puerto Rico and New York and to participate in and promote congresses on their home island. A first successful meeting was held approximately four years before I wrote this chapter, in Santo Domingo's Palacio de los Deportes; the Dominican Republic hosted the 2002 world salsa championships; and the Punta Cana Salsa Congress has been held in the Dominican Republic since 2006. In the Punta Cana Salsa Congress professional dance groups from the United States, Latin America, and Europe come together. The second congress, held in 2008, included the maestro Eddie Torres.

However, precisely because of the lack of government backing for local cultural industries, despite the benefits of music and dance for the Dominican economy, Dominican dancers and salsa styles are not represented in the media in the way that those of our neighbors Puerto Rico and Cuba, for example, are. Dominican salsa dance receives no promotion in shows, musical videos, or other major forms of marketing.

I welcome other perspectives on salsa dance in Santo Domingo but restate the idea that salsa in Santo Domingo gives prominence to the dancer in not only the spaces in which salsa culture is articulated but also other spaces of socialization in which a dancer rises from a lower-class and generally marginal condition. Likewise, I emphasize that the cross-fertilization between the New York Dominican community and island culture that I have described has given rise to outstanding professional dancers of worldwide renown such as Tomás Guerrero, who founded the New York dance group Santo Rico over a decade ago, and Juan "Pachanga" Matos, a Dominican salsa dancer.

Finally, to put the dance into social and cultural perspective, salsa is one of the most widespread musical styles in the Dominican Republic. Yet its coexistence with local and regional dance styles, particularly merengue, is a result of its media strategy, established at the outset; of the participation of the New York Dominican community and the role of the diaspora in salsa's formation; and similarly, of the formation of a new social class in the capital after the fall of the Trujillo dictatorship, that of the lower-class barrios. The influence of the Dominican diaspora on the island and the nation's openness toward the mass media, above all in the city of Santo Domingo, brought the older barrios with a son tradition together with the new urban reality of rural migrants, who were often on their way to New York City. Despite the lack of major-label or government support, the mass media were and still are channeling these influences and mediating the new components of the passion for salsa in Santo Domingo, including multiple fan-generated elements of publicity, marketing, and local cultural industries, like the dance establishments, competitions, congresses, and dance academies.

This sociocultural group, the salseros of the Dominican capital, has maintained its identity despite commercialization and has negotiated an unfairly weighted competition with merengue. This competition coexists with a Caribbean feeling of regional identity, above and beyond the internal identity conflicts advanced by the medialized moment both musics share. The passion for salsa won out, and it is danced without consideration for anything beyond bodily enjoyment.

NOTES

Note: Work forms and guides of the Instituto de Estudios Caribeños used as part of the preparatory activities for the Second International Congress on Music, Identity, and Culture in the Caribbean (MIC2) held between October 2006 and March 2007 are available to the public in print form from the Instituto de Estudios Caribeños, Santo Domingo, Dominican Republic (http://www.inecny.org).

1. [Díaz's term is *"clase popular,"* or "popular class," which refers to the lower strata of society. Here I translate it as "working class," except where I understand the author also to refer to the unemployed. In the Dominican Republic the term *"barrio,"* or "neighborhood," is understood to refer specifically to the lower class and never applied to the middle or upper class; the term is used in this sense throughout the chapter.—Trans.]

2. Laura Faxas also refers to anthropologist Jorge Cela's work *Los imaginados* (1987), which gives a view of life in the urban lower-class barrios of the Dominican Republic and an important context: "Free-time activities in the barrios are also the basis of important social linkages, as in the role of the 'colmados,' stores in which cold drinks (beer) and rum are sold. In general, free time is dedicated to cultural and sport activities, to listening to the radio, watching television, and also to activities that are realized, according to the barrio inhabitants, in 'places of corruption'[;] . . . the poorer the barrio, the greater the tendency towards the development of 'places of corruption,' and to the love of the party and of alcohol" (quoted in Faxas 2007: 225).

3. [In this section's heading, the author plays on the common root word in dance steps, or *pasos de baile*, and *traspasos*, meaning transfers or sales.—Trans.]

4. I noticed that soneros and salseros each have days on which only their music is played at dance sites, and the merengues played are classic ones of the 1940s–1960s.

5. [Quisqueya is the indigenous Taíno name for the island that today includes Haiti and the Dominican Republic; Dominicans also use it to refer to their country.—Trans.]

6. [The word Díaz uses, *sentido*, could also be translated as "feeling" or "sense," and all these meanings play a role here.—Trans.]

7. "The Salsa Boom on Dominican Radio."

8. For more on four "moments" in immigrant musical production, see Flores 1993. [Díaz uses "momento" (moment) to refer to the current musical situation in the Dominican Republic, where both local and foreign (migrant) musics play a role.—Trans.]

9. According to Deborah Pacini Hernández, this conflict relates to the competition between Puerto Ricans and Dominicans (quoted in López de Jesús 2003: 146).

10. "The Salsa Boom on Dominican Radio."

11. Lahoz Banks also refers to the 1970s and mentions dance pairs like Los Popeyes who performed on variety shows at noon (Lahoz Banks 2009).

12. [*Colmados* are the typically Dominican corner stores, called *bodegas* in New York City, where one can not only buy groceries but also stop to have a beer and listen to music.—Trans.]

13. "The Salsa Boom on Dominican Radio."

14. "*Tigueraje*" is a local term to describe someone disposed to fun and partying, living in the most economically and socially marginal barrios of the city, and on occasion linked to illegal activities or very informal working arrangements.

15. Negritude is a form of social and racial revindication in salsa, because it is a special identity component within the Caribbean diaspora of New York and because of what it means in local culture. In terms of resistance to dominant aesthetic patterns in Dominican society, salsa represents one of the most optimal means of reassertion of this identity, which is so often denied by certain dominant sectors but which barrio culture assumes with pride from a position of marginality.

16. These two examples were pointed out by Saldaña and Lizardo themselves on the INEC work forms, and I do not have videos of performances, so their analysis is best left to another study.

17. Participants base this opinion on a selection of four schools in the eastern zone, seven in the national district, and five in the western zone. Nine salsa radio programs, five son and salsa radio programs, and two television programs were also included. The figures are based on INEC projects.

REFERENCES

Alcalá, Pipo. 2009. Interview by Rossy Díaz. May 20.

Andújar, Carlos. 2007. "La situación del son en Santiago de los Caballeros." In *El son y la salsa en la identidad del Caribe*, ed. Darío Tejeda and Rafael Emilio Yunén, 205–220. Santiago: Centro León and INEC.

Austerlitz, Paul. 2007. *Merengue: Música e identidad dominicana*, trans. María Luisa Santoni. Santo Domingo: Secretaría de Estado de Cultura.

Faxas, Laura. 2007. *El mito roto: Sistema político y movimiento popular en la República Dominicana, 1961–1990*. Mexico City: Siglo XXI Editores, Fundación Global Democracia y Desarrollo (FUNGLODE), FLACSO.

Flores, Juan. 1993. "'Qué Assimilated, Brother, Yo Soy Asimilao': The Structuring of Puerto Rican Identity in the U.S." In *Divided Borders: Essays on Puerto Rican Identity*, 182–195. Houston, TX: Arte Público Press.

Hutchinson, Sydney. 2008. "Bailando en su lugar: Cómo los salseros crean variantes locales de un baile global." In *El son y la salsa en la identidad del Caribe*, ed. Darío Tejeda and Rafael Emilio Yunén, 127–134. Santiago: Centro León and INEC.

Lahoz Banks, Teodora. 2009. Interview by Rossy Díaz. February 21.

Launay de Alcalá, Cathy. 2009. Interview by Rossy Díaz. May 20.

López de Jesús, Lara Ivette. 2003. *Encuentros sincopados: El caribe contemporáneo a través de sus prácticas musicales*. Mexico City: Siglo XXI Editores.

Medina, Francisco. 2009. Interview by Rossy Díaz. February 29.

Oficina Nacional de Estadística, República Dominicana. 2002. *VIII Censo Nacional de Población y Vivienda 2002*. Available at http://redatam.one.gob.do/cgibin/RpWebEngine .exe/PortalAction?&MODE=MAIN&BASE=CPV2002&MAIN=WebServerMain.inl.

Pérez, Eugenio. 2008. "La República Dominicana en salsa." In *El son y la salsa en la identidad del Caribe*, ed. Darío Tejeda and Rafael Emilio Yunén, 417–428. Santiago: Centro León and INEC.

Quintero Rivera, Ángel G. 2008. "Salsa, son, nación y migración." In *El son y la salsa en la identidad del Caribe*, ed. Darío Tejeda and Rafael Emilio Yunén, 53–70. Santiago: Centro León and INEC.

Tejeda, Angelina. 2009. Interviews by Rossy Díaz. March 1 and May 7.

10

Allons à la Fête—On Danse Salsa

New Routes for Salsa in France

Saúl Escalona

(Translated by Sydney Hutchinson)

Drawing from Patria Román-Velázquez's (1998) work about the development of a salsa circuit and the construction of Latino identities in London, in this chapter I analyze the salsa movement in Paris.[1] Román-Velázquez, using the notion of route, examines salsa in London by describing where it came from—and thus how it spread. She asserts that salsa, as an amalgam of rhythms and practices, is articulated differently in different cultures. If this is true in the Caribbean, which includes Cuba, Colombia, Panama, Puerto Rico, the Dominican Republic, Venezuela, and in places emigrants from these countries live and perpetuate their cultural practices, then salsa's articulation will present different characteristics in European countries, whose social and cultural characteristics are different from those of the countries of salsa's roots.

One of these characteristics is its geographic sense, meaning the transfer of the music from the Americas to Europe. Salsa transports culture, a culture that digs its roots deeply into the Latin American continent, and salsa is a reminder of one of the most painful and, at the same time, most fruitful times for the lands "discovered" and colonized by the Spanish. Integrating itself into Europe, particularly France, and establishing relations between Latin America and Europe, salsa evokes a different conception of existence, at times the nostalgia of the excluded or oppressed, alongside its collective nature and spirit of festivity, as Octavio Paz has indicated[2] in his essays.

In the early 1970s,[3] a Latin American colony in Paris was composed principally of middle-class political refugees from Brazil, Argentina, Uruguay, Bolivia, and Chile. They held *peñas*, nighttime musical parties with Andean music played on instruments like *charango* and *quena*. In 1978 the discotheque La Chapelle des Lombards[4] opened, offering tropical music, particularly salsa, to a French audience of academics, professionals, artists, students, and those who were acquainted with the Caribbean region through travel or who found the rhythm innovative.

A decade later, a new Latin American migration fit itself into this salsa route, a heterogenous migration of social classes who came to France in search of a better life. As a consequence of their different class and national origins, they propelled a musical practice in which the *charango* and *quena* were replaced by congas and bongos. Other Latin Americans in Paris and other European cities joined this tropical atmosphere, and Colombians and Venezuelans, among others, came to love salsa and learned to dance it. Although in their countries of origin salsa was regarded as a music of "delinquents" (*malandros*) or blacks or even the barrios,[5] nostalgia for home brought acceptance of and even affection for the cultural values of other social classes. In addition, salsa in distant Europe was a way to meet others as well as an expression of identity. One sometimes heard, "You are Venezuelan (or Colombian), and you don't know how to dance salsa?" This first stage culminated with a large increase in the size of the Latin American community, and salsa musicians contributed to the music's diffusion in the French musical landscape.

A New Path

My research has shown the birth of a new, commercial path in the late 1990s, in which Latin Americans are displaced from the musical world and its economic benefits, and salsa is seen as only a dance. New services flourish: food, disc jockeys, "professors" of salsa, and tourist travel to Cuba and the Dominican Republic. There also emerges a tendency to refer to Cuba for everything related to Latin music.[6] During this period establishments opened to take advantage of the phenomenon and played music while customers were eating, drinking, or talking, just as in any place in Latin America. The historic ballrooms of the French capital adapted their programming to incorporate dance classes, shows, spectacles, and the like. The turn toward this music did not occur for cultural reasons but for financial ones, and it entails the complete and definitive erasure of Latin American organizers from the scene, since the new promoters, all European, had greater economic resources and knew better the regulatory legislation for mounting events or concerts.

In this context, salsa is associated with and marketed as foreignness with a Caribbean climate, to make it a music without which one cannot live; as some followers assert, "I look for salsa because it takes me out of the routine of work—also because I want to get to know Latinos, to speak Spanish, and to travel in . . . [Latin America] in order to see if all that beauty that is so talked about is real."[7] An individual's behavior, the lifeways of a social group, and the values of a society are often influenced by publicity campaigns whose mechanisms are invisible. In this sense, although assimilation imposes a particular taste, which in most cases is linked to a desire for improved human relations, one must look at the origins and mechanisms underlying the customs of these social groups and work to establish closer ties without conventions or economic motivations. Salsa is not a part of the everyday in Europe. Salsa is another type of entertainment for European nights, nothing more or less. With these suppositions, it is logical to ask, "Isn't salsa in France more of a bodily therapy than the discovery of another culture?"

The meaning of a music derives not from its place of origin but from its function in the current location. In France a discourse tends to propose immediate enjoyment from salsa, a discourse that

> aims to erase all temporality, it must be said, history, with a notion of absolute exoticism and valorizing Cuba or Puerto Rico above the East Coast of the United States, which constitutes its true point of origin and is never mentioned. These "lands of origin" objectively constitute an environment at once more legitimate and more suggestive, seen from Europe in winter, than those "Latino barrios" with their degrading houses and the torn-up streets of the great U.S. metropolis. (Dorrier-Apprill 2001: 37)

The salsa boom has extended into various Parisian recreational settings. Román-Velázquez's (1998) description of urban space indicates that my case is different from London's: there, the majority of participants are Latin American; in Paris they are usually French, with some other Europeans and a few other nationalities. This means that salsa consumption in Paris entails only places of business like rented halls, bars, or discotheques where events are held and where the attending public is not principally Latin American. If salsa has turned into a cult because of the passion it provokes, it is also because it is a tremendously lucrative business, from record sales and dance courses, festivals, and the like. Even more, salsa has brought back social partner dancing, which had disappeared by the turn of the last century after having stayed popular through the postwar period. As a form of entertainment with social ties, social dancing thus has the feeling of being a popular French tradition (Argyriadis and Le Menestrel 2003), which salsa continues.

When inviting someone to dance salsa in Paris, the opening always begins with the famous interrogative phrase "Shall we dance?" The response is equally interrogative: "Do you dance Cuban or Puerto Rican style?" For a simple dancer things can get complicated, depending on which style he or she dances. I describe the evolution of styles, focusing on (1) the context of their and salsa's reception, (2) the types of dance styles that underlie the Parisian salsa route, and (3) the different dance steps.

The Context of Salsa's Reception

Elsewhere (Escalona 2001, 2007), I have written that the emotions of French people have become open to the "Latin spirit"[8] that many describe as a way of living full of spontaneity. The dream of the Caribbean, the openness to finding the Other—the foreigner—who is different but holds values close to ours, is a symbol of fortunate changes that enter the anthropological plane like the discovery of new sensations (Le Breton 1998). In this context of assimilation, the salsa fan develops the same gestures: how to move, how to behave in a group. These meanings contribute an image of extraterritoriality and of climate that refers to the Caribbean, as mentioned previously, and is based on interactions that designate a musical form as able to be danced and assimilated in the way of an exotic flavor or color, using expressions composed of culinary, meteorological, or erotic metaphors (Dorrier-Apprill 2001). Palpable proof is found in the posters, flyers, and messages on the Internet or disseminated by other means, announcing the weekly salsa or Latin parties or concerts, in which the recurring terms are "fiesta," "hot," "Latin sensuality," "tropics," "spicy," "encounter," "seduction," "fever," and "sexy woman." The symbolic force of 1970s Latin American music, an important vector of socialization, loses its meaning decades later, inaugurating with salsa a new period in which the audience members do not listen to music, because they only want to dance.

In this sphere, salsa is a sensual music that invokes the "Latin lover," given that these rhythms and dances come from a certain representation of sensuality or, rather, "*latinidad*" (sense of Latino identity) (Dorrier-Apprill 2001: 39). It is here that clichés are born and debated, those that posit salsa as a music that allows romantic encounters, symbolizes a consensual eroticism, and also causes imaginings, as one fan asserted in an interview: "The women who dance on the beach, each of them attractive . . . ah! What pleasure it is to imagine being in the Caribbean." Similarly, France Schott-Billmann (2001: 26), analyzing partner dances that come from South America, demonstrates that the "hot dances" provide Europeans with escape through sensuality and their effect on the audience—for example, the swaying of the body when one hears the percussion. Although this author does not refer to salsa specifically, his analysis helps us understand it as a related experience.

Characteristics of the Currents of Dance Style

In the salsa courses now given in Paris, we find three levels. The beginners start without music. The teacher contents him- or herself with simply saying *one* to indicate that students should mark the first step with the left or right foot, according to their method, and *two* to indicate the other foot. The courses last this way for one hour. At the intermediate level, the students learn with music. The movements are put together at a great speed. The teacher plays any kind of salsa piece and even completely different genres such as cha-cha, *guaguancó*, mambo, and *guaracha*, and they dance without rhythmic distinctions. The advanced students may progress more quickly, and they generally change into clothes and shoes allowing greater agility in their movements. They attentively follow the instructions of the teacher, who will say "mango," "chocolate," "hot," or any other predetermined word to indicate that students should execute a turn or let go of their partner. For salsa dance enthusiasts, the proposed styles are the only way of dancing salsa, and they do not search for other ways of dancing that might include improvisation or other means of expression. In reality, the styles most practiced today in the global diffusion of salsa dance and music—for example, "Eddie Torres," "New York," "salsa mambo," "breaking on 2," and "Los Angeles" styles—are being integrated.

The stylized movements and the attitudes of the dancers are simply codified figures of dance inspired by these styles, which many adepts will repeat similarly, dancing in successive circles without separating, executing figures in which the arms and hands play an important role, with the body very straight and without hip movement. Most of these dance styles benefit from vestiges of rock and roll, still widely danced by all generations of Europeans, a tie compensating for the difficulty of learning a new dance style. From there comes the image of the European dancer,[9] absent emotional contact and performing steps and acrobatic figures that fit into a mentality closed to the festive spirit.

Dance Steps

Parisian salsa fans emphasize steps impelling codification that have been proposed by teachers—Latin taps, ragga jam salsa, slave step, Cuban step, cha-cha—in which one sees figures like the cross-body lead, the *salto de caballo* (horse leap), and "shines," or foot- and legwork. One also notices the "sweet turns," hip movements accompanied by small jumps. Fans reach an extreme state of excitement when dancers perform shines (see Chapter 2). These movements omit those that turn partner dance into a game of seduction between a man and a woman, such as the pelvic movements or *quebrados*—that gesture in which the hands, feet, and waist follow the musical rhythm during the change to the *montuno* section in a salsa piece, as practiced in some Caribbean countries.

A Route Only for Dancing

Commercial interest in salsa translates a salsa obsession into merely an interest in a sexy music. Further, commercialization protects its interest by limiting information dissemination, whether by radio, in stores, or in the many concerts played for a public avid to learn more about composers, new recordings, music, or groups. One might say that salsa in Europe is "only dead guys," since the salsa musicians now known in most European capitals are deceased icons such as Tito Puente, Ray Barretto, and Celia Cruz (Feliciano 2006).

If the globalization of trade offers a vast field of projection for cultural products, their commercial use often divests them of all content, of any intrinsic social or cultural value. They then have no identity, only materiality. This supports my contention that salsa, a consumer product, tends to become uniform and is a "trivialization of exoticism" (Aubert 2001: 123). Its representation is manifested in dance as a type of spectacle in which each member of a couple tends to negate the corporeality of the other, if we conceive of the dance as a game of seduction.

We can see, then, that this route suggests arriving at a salsa that is a purely aesthetic representation whose codification of steps impedes improvisation and negates the joy of spontaneity, since it bestows rationality on the free expression of bodily movement and limits the ways one might move as it establishes agreed-on norms. One thus thinks of a salsa without soul. This transpires in part because salsa supporters attend courses only from a desire to learn the steps and figures proposed by a particular teacher and his or her style, thus leading to official dance practices, which all students attempt to apply to all the musical genres without distinction. Learning this step and not others, beginning to dance with the right foot and not the left or vice versa, just as is taught, some apprentices believe themselves to be salsa stars and enthusiastically demonstrate their technical knowledge, which allows them to say to other dancers, "You don't know how to do the one, two, three."

Dancers exhibit different styles of dance at salsa events to demonstrate that they are into the "salsa thing." Some dancers require a minimal space in which to move; others need a larger space to express their choreographic abilities. Other dancers, either in couples or alone, I term the "crazy dancers," because the dance floor for them is a theme park in which they are the main protagonists, or the "salsaholics," whose particularity is that they will converse about only salsa.

Salsa in France is centered on an orchestrated campaign of exoticism. Today, salsa promoters claim that it is not necessary to visit distant lands to experience exoticism: it is here, two blocks from the Metro. Other musics also generate partner dances but do not occupy much space in France, perhaps because they do not generate much economic profit. I refer particularly to the tango, which does not command a large public despite the sympathy it enjoys. Why it remains in the hearts of the French might be, in part, because the tango is a part of the French musical tradition. Since the beginning of the last century, tango has driven partner dance, and its popularity grew after World War I along with the economic boom. Also, tango is usually associated with the Sunday dances of the *guinguettes*,[10] attended by the elderly and viewed as antiquated. The participants generally come well dressed in appropriate and comfortable dresses and suits, elegant and ready to dance. The *guinguettes* do not have the same ambience of salsa concerts or parties; numerous dancers declare a sentiment similar to the following:

In practice, [*guinguettes*] show a true enthusiasm for Latin-inspired musics, which attract a large quantity of dancers to the floor to enjoy tangos like La Cumparsita, Marinella, El Caminito, forming part of a repertoire that fires the pleasures of the dancers. (Argyriadis and Le Menestrel 2003: 130)

And So We Leave

In this new path, salsa is presented to the French as an easily accessible music. As one admirer described it in an interview, "It is the only music that makes me vibrate." The public demands events, and organizers present salsa gatherings with names like "salsa meeting," "salsa dance congress," "salsa night," or "theatrical salsa group." Organizers and impresarios find a hook that will attract the public, such as the advertising for an event related to International Women's Day: "With salsa music, Latin rhythms, and the night's special feature for all [women], 'salsa kills you, man.'"[11] Salsa becomes a commercial tool, whose consumption manifests intrinsic desires rooted in an exotic and sensual imaginary in which women are told that learning or knowing how to dance salsa will help them seduce men.

Paradoxically, research has demonstrated that the movement driving salsa counteracts an individualistic life model, showing greater social openness, at least to foreigners. This is why in France salsa has contributed to a greater acceptance of Latin Americans, in particular. If French fans have assimilated the dance with all its contradictions, salsa nevertheless contributes an enthusiasm from which the French also tend to benefit, as they search for an ambience different from that of hard rock concerts, for example. Salsa, because of the environment it creates, brings together different nationalities; it widens fans' circles and opens up a different cultural panorama. Hearing, for example, that Venezuela is not in South America but in Africa is long past; today better geographic knowledge of the Caribbean and South America has come about through familiarity with the origins of well-known salsa musicians, a familiarity only deepening with time and making French salsa fans today also interested in the Spanish language.

During the summer songs appear with percussive rhythms or rhythms or melodies that resemble tropical musics. The song "Lambada," not part of the salsa genre, was heard throughout France in 1989; its popularity led to an avalanche of songs with the same type of rhythm coming out every year around the same time (see Escalona 2001). Interest in salsa has contributed to sales of musical scores with Latin American airs (for example, Cuban and mambo) and materials for learning how to play instruments like the clave, *tumbadoras* (congas), or bongos. Television and radio programs include salsa songs to seem livelier; salsa is even sometimes used in haute couture fashion shows as musical accompaniment.

Conclusion

Salsa has succeeded in Europe and in France, and in so doing has brought joy; yet there, it is a music divested of social and cultural values, exactly the opposite of what it is in its countries of origin. Nevertheless, what interests us here is to highlight the phenomenon of its assimilation—in other words, its integration into the French musical and cultural world, which conceives of it as a passionate music. For supporters, salsa creates an enthusiasm like that for an ineffable delicacy, and to some it does not matter if its message is grasped; they are interested only in feeling happy when participating in a salsa dance party or concert in Paris.

Contrasts and contradictions are evident in salsa in Paris. If salsa has an appeal, it is that it permits encounters between different communities. Salsa's effect in France is also a kind of revision of customs, a change from an individualistic comportment to a greater openness to the world, which allows establishment of new social relations between people. Following this argument, it is possible to think of the dance party as mirroring the real world and to believe that salsa, with its aesthetic essence and its contradictions, contributes its spirit of festivity.

NOTES

1. Salsa in France began in Paris. This occurrence is logical because of that city's important Latin American community. To refer to salsa in Paris thus also includes all French territory in its breadth.

2. Paz is a Mexican writer (1914–1998) of international renown for his immense literary output of poetry, essays, and more, taking on themes about Indians, Mexican identity, and contemporary Latin American culture. In 1981 he was awarded the Cervantes prize and in 1990 the Nobel Prize for Literature.

3. The French capital in the 1930s received tropical music with great enthusiasm, creating a festive atmosphere into which some Cuban musicians quickly inserted themselves— for example, Don Barreto, his brother Sergio Barreto, and the group Lecuona Boys. In the 1970s, other Latin Americans began to migrate, creating enthusiasm first for Andean music and later for tropical music.

4. La Chapelle des Lombards was opened by Jean-Luc Fraisse and his wife, Michèlle, in a medieval wine cellar on Lombards Street in Paris's first arrondisement. In 1981 it moved to 19 Rue de Lappe in the eleventh. In 2001 it was sold, and the salsa programming was radically changed.

5. [In this sense, "barrio," or neighborhood, always refers to areas inhabited by lower-class or marginal people.—Trans.]

6. In the late 1990s, I noted an emphasis on the Cuban. Taking advantage of this emphasis, French impresarios promoted all things Cuban: first, tourism, which attracted Europeans to the island and turned it into an exotic locale for sexual tourism, and, second, gastronomy. Using "Cuba" commercially is thus an important, lucrative medium. Finally, the music of Compay Segundo generated interest in Cuba in France and in greater Europe. Also see Escalona 2007.

7. Quote from an interview with a male salsa fan. The unattributed quotations in this chapter are taken from statements gathered through a survey of four hundred salsa fans in France, Germany, and Sweden, conducted by the author in 2001 and 2004.

8. From an anthropological viewpoint, this has to do with cultural differences related to a worldview and to social norms, which determine certain values and behaviors and differ greatly between the French and Latin Americans. For instance, Latin American individuals establish social relations between one another more easily than the French do. And the French, even many couples, use the formal *vous* (*usted*) more than the familiar *tu*, demonstrating social distance even in close relationships. For the French, the image of supposed sensuality relates to everything, to a lifestyle, and one often hears, "Ah! He's a Latino"—an allusion to why a person never arrives on time, for example.

9. I refer here to the dancers for whom the soul of the dance is not the communion of a partner dance but the desire to show an audience that they have mastered a style. The absence of emotional contact means that what is important is to dance to show others that one knows how to dance: "dance, dance—the important thing is that people *see how you dance.*"

10. *Guinguettes* are French establishments whose origins date to the beginning of the nineteenth century. One frequents them to drink wine; dance *musettes*, waltzes, polkas, and so on; and spend the afternoon around a dance floor remembering old times. They are located principally to the west of Paris, some twenty kilometers from the river Marne.

11. See *Paris Boum Boum*, no. 940, Paris, March 6–12, 2000, p. 24.

REFERENCES

Argyriadis, Kali, and Sara Le Menestrel. 2003. *Vivre la guinguette*. Paris: Presses Universitaires de France.

Aubert, Laurent. 2001. *La musique de l'autre*. Paris: Georg.

Dorrier-Apprill, Elisabeth. 2001. "Entre imaginaires et réalités, la géographie mouvante des danses 'latines.'" *Danses Latines, Autrement* 207:32–47.

Escalona, Saúl. 2001. *Ma salsa défigurée*. Paris: L'Harmattan.

———. 2007. *La salsa en Europa: Rompiendo el hielo*. Caracas: Instituto de Musicología/Fundación Juan Vicente Sojo.

Feliciano, Héctor. 2006. "La dernière salsa à Paris." *Courrier International*, no. 793, p. 38.

Le Breton, David. 1998. *Les passions ordinaires: Anthropologie des émotions*. París: Armand Collin.

Román-Velázquez, Patria. 1998. "El desarrollo de un circuito salsero y la construcción de identidades latinas en Londres." *Revista de Ciencias Sociales* (Puerto Rico) 4:53–79.

Schott-Billmann, France. 2001. *Le besoin de danser*. Paris: Odile Jacob.

11

Salsa in Barcelona and Spain

Isabel Llano

(Translated by Sydney Hutchinson)

The dissemination of salsa music in Spain began in the 1970s with the Fania record label's promotion of various singers; in the 1980s the popularization of musicians and groups began through radio, live concerts, and local groups that played current hits. In the 1990s discotheques playing salsa multiplied, and the teaching and learning of salsa dance began. This growth, together with the growth of the Latin American–origin population since 2000, has led to the emergence of Latin dance schools and teachers in the last decade and of radio stations dedicated exclusively to Latin music. Most of these new stations and many of the discotheques opened since 2000 have a relationship with a specific Latin American nationality. All these changes in the sociodemographic panorama coincide with the internationalization of salsa dance, particularly through dance congresses, such that, with the turn of the century, the native population's taste for salsa grows, dance companies are founded, and salsa congresses at which the majority of the audience is exclusively Spanish take place throughout the country. Currently, although there are some exceptions, the salsa worlds of Latinos and non-Latinos do not mix, and each group experiences salsa dance and other Latino musics in a different way.[1]

In this chapter I undertake a retrospective analysis of the dissemination, consumption, and production of salsa music and dance from the 1980s to the present in Barcelona. Since there is also a salsa circuit in Madrid, Valencia, Seville, Bilbao, Cádiz, Saragossa, the Canary Islands, and other Spanish cities, however, I also consider aspects that pertain to the country in general. The growth of salsa and Latin music in Barcelona is part of this movement around the world, and it is framed within a context characterized by redefinitions of identity through the ambivalent discourse about immigration and the growth of transnational circuits of cultural and commercial exchange in which music plays a crucial role. In particular, one must consider Catalan and Basque nationalist debates in Spain, as well as the debates over European identity.

At a theoretical level, my analyses revisit the perspectives of Peter Wade (2000: 210) and Jeremy Gilbert and Ewan Pearson (2003: 108) on the relationship between listening and dancing to the music and the configuration of identity, as well as those of García Canclini (2001: 14) regarding hybridization. I consider salsa dance in Barcelona to play a role in transforming cultural identities, since to a certain degree it is modifying or altering previous experiences through the body. My argument coincides with those of Wade and Gilbert and Ewan, who agree that listening to music and dancing to it are important practices for configuring subjectivity, sense of self, and in particular, bodies, and they can offer a bodily experience that either stabilizes and affirms or alters and modifies previous experiences. Dance in particular lends itself to incorporation and transformation of identity. After observing transformations in Spaniards' consumption practices regarding Latin music and Latin dances, I believe processes of cultural hybridity are occurring, since here the dance is generating new forms and new practices.

First, I note some antecedents to the establishment of Latin music in the country up to the 1970s. Second, I discuss the development of record production, radio stations, and discotheques, given their importance in relation to the listenership and enjoyment of this music and of salsa dance, which many non-Latinos see as extremely exotic and occasionally view with contempt. Third, I describe the dance teachers, schools, companies, and congresses.

I speak about not only salsa in particular but also Latin musics in general. This is because the dissemination and consumption of salsa has paralleled that of merengue and *bachata*, *timba*, and other Cuban musics, as well as other dances associated with the Caribbean with which the greater part of the Latin American immigrant population in Spain has been identified.

Precursors of Latin Music in Spain and Barcelona

Before popularization of Latin music in Barcelona began in the 1980s, a few key precursors set the stage. They include the historical ties between the city and the Caribbean and the European tours of *son* groups and singers in the early twentieth century. People and groups who paved the way for salsa include the following: The Cuban performer Antonio Machín had been a fundamental influence since the 1940s; he popularized the bolero and introduced chachachá. José Manuel Gómez (1995: 6) recalls that Pere Pubill Calaf, known as Peret, introduced songs by Cheo Feliciano, Ismael Rivera, and others, and the Argentine Javier Patricio "El Gato" Pérez rediscovered the Catalan rumba[2] in the 1970s and accentuated the genre's salsa and mestizo turns.[3] Catalan groups like Mirasol Colores and La Platería popularized well-known salsa tunes in the mid-1970s, and the orchestras of Fiestas Mayores spread dances like chachachá, son, and *cumbia*.

The record industry has, since the 1970s, promoted singers and groups by radio and through concerts. The first broadcasts of Latin music were made in the 1970s, coinciding with the promotion undertaken by New York's Fania Records. The early 1970s saw the birth of the record company Discophon, which published records from the Fania catalog and later, in 1975, from Discos Manzana, a label that maintained a line of radio promotion and specialized in re-editions of recordings from the Fania and Cuba Records catalogs. By the 1980s these musics had disappeared from radio and stores, and pop rock had completely taken over the Spanish market,[4] but not before Barcelona had seen Rubén Blades, Ray Barretto, Willie Colón, Eddie Palmieri, Luis "Perico" Ortiz, Paquito D'Rivera, and the Fania All Stars, among others, either in concert or on television.

Dissemination and Consumption of Salsa and Other Latin Musics in Barcelona

The growth of salsa discotheques and radio stations and their relationship with specific nationalities, especially since 2000, when the influence of Latin American immigration and salsa congresses starts to be evident, have been two of the most important factors in the diffusion and consumption of salsa in Barcelona since the 1980s.

Record Industry

In the late 1980s and early 1990s, record labels worked to promote Latin American singers and groups by radio. One such label was Bat Discos, which emerged in 1990 to promote the singer Lalo Rodríguez and was run by Cuban brothers Oscar and Jorge Gómez, friends of Ralph Mercado from before he created the RMM label. It became a licensee of RMM, handling Celia Cruz, Oscar D'León, Tito Puente, and others. At the same time, recordings of *salsa erótica*[5] came to Spain along with Dominican merengue and the cumbias that Colombian label Discos Fuentes promoted in addition to other Colombian rhythms through Fonomusic, a Spanish distributor that also imported Cuban music. Spain also had been an important site for distribution of Cuban music and salsa since the early 1980s.

Radio Programs and Stations

Radio has played a crucial role in disseminating salsa and Latin music. The importance of so-called Latin stations in the promotion of concerts by foreign singers and groups has been evident since 1999, when stations dedicated exclusively to programming these musics first emerged.[6]

The promotion of Latin musics by radio and the development of the record industry associated with these musics are related to the tremendous success that figures like Juan Luis Guerra of the Dominican Republic (with *Bachata rosa*) and Gloria Estefan of Miami (with *Mi tierra*) had in Spain in the early 1990s. Although Juan Luis Guerra's trademark song in this country, his idiosyncratic version of the Venezuelan song "Woman del Callao," went practically unnoticed during the summer of 1989 (broadcasting stations preferred to continue with the old recipe of Spanish- and English-language pop rock), the 1990 Spanish edition of his album *Ojalá que llueva café* was successful among dancers and deejays. This success was achieved, in part, through the spread of the lambada, which although ephemeral awakened interest in dance, as did the popularity of the *salsa erótica* song "Devórame otra vez" by Lalo Rodríguez in the 1990 carnivals. With *Ojalá que llueva café*, Juan Luís Guerra ensured that dancers became the first to perceive the difference in his subtlety of arrangements and texts (López 1993: 8).

Despite the record industry's promotion of salsa and other Latin music genres, in the 1980s opportunities to hear salsa songs on the radio were scarce. Local and national programs dedicated to Latin musics in the 1990s had weekly broadcast times of only a few hours. Up until the creation of Barcelona's Radio Gladys Palmera in 1999, no station had dedicated its entire programming to Latin music. Since 1999 the panorama of Latin radio stations has been very changeable, partly because of regulation. Thus, some appear, disappear, or change their frequencies in a relatively short time span. In late 2008, besides Radio Gladys Palmera nine other more recently formed Latin music stations broadcast in the Barcelona metropolitan area, many of which also broadcast online.[7]

Latin radio stations can be classified by the nationality of their listening publics and of their staff: some stations are associated almost exclusively with a single nationality, others with several Latin American nationalities, and still others with Spaniards with a more cosmopolitan outlook. The increase in Latin Americans living in Barcelona,[8] many of whom listen to radio music daily, even during work hours, has led to the birth of stations run by Latinos and the transformation of programming on regional public radio such as Sintonía COM 882 OM (now LatinComRàdio).

Discotheques

Currently, many discos that program salsa, timba, merengue, bachata, *reggaetón*, *cumbia villera*, or *tecnocumbia* are dispersed throughout the city and in neighboring towns according to the predominant nationality of the audience in each location or according to the discos' interest in capturing a particular audience. Likewise, audience characteristics and the musical repertoire in each disco determine the dance styles in each, so that there are clubs in which mainly *salsa en línea*, or slot-form salsa, is danced and others in which Colombian style or another style is danced.[9] In the discos frequented primarily by Spaniards, North American–style *salsa en línea* is commonly danced, while in the discos Latinos frequent, club-goers dance in their own styles.

In 1981 the only place one could hear and dance to *salsa brava* (also known as *salsa dura*) in Barcelona was the bar Tabú, on Escudellers Street in China-town. However, the Latin American community grew in the mid-1980s with the arrival of Cuban immigrants, principally 1970s exiles, and other sites began playing salsa, including the dance hall Bikini, the bar Kennedy, and Zeleste, a concert venue and important site for music from its opening in 1973 until 1987. In the early 1990s, other sites like Cibeles, Carammba, Sahoco, El Bohío, Lati-nos, Artículo 26, El Mojito, and Raíces Salsa appeared, and dance sites prolifer-ated in the early 2000s.

The *Buena Vista Social Club* phenomenon, or the son revival related to the album and movie of this name, has also been influential in the dissemination of Cuban and Latin music in Europe since the mid-1990s (see Roy 2003: 185). In the club Para Mi Gente on Lesseps Plaza, versions of the *Buena Vista Social Club*'s famous songs like "Chan chan" and "El cuarto de Tula" were played live between 2002 and 2003 by Cuban, Catalan, Colombian, and other musicians. Live musical improvisation also took place in the club, with the participation of Catalan, Spanish, and other *salsa brava* listeners and dancers.

Discotheques construct and communicate their own brands of cultural identity and can be classified according to the predominant nationality of the clientele. During my fieldwork, I could determine the nationality of the audi-ence by not only the different dance styles but also such practices as liquor con-sumption. In Spain, it is customary to sell and consume liquor by the glass, not by the bottle accompanied by water or soda, as is characteristic in Colombia, Ecuador, Peru, and the Dominican Republic, among other countries. Thus, while those who order glasses can walk throughout the club, those who con-sume liquor Latin style install themselves at a table where, although they may get up to dance, they remain the whole night to continue serving themselves from the bottle of whisky, rum, or other hard liquor. For this reason, there are usually more tables and chairs in discos with a Latino majority than in those a non-Latino or mixed public attends. In addition, the Latin discos differ from the non-Latin in their lighting: the discos with a majority Spanish audience are generally more brightly lit than the others, which are usually kept dark. The facades and advertising for the majority of locations allude to a tropical landscape—palm trees and beaches—and national insignias, particularly flags, related to the country of origin of the site's most significant audience. On the inside, the Bolivian, Dominican, and Colombian discos tend to reproduce the less cosmopolitan environment of the countries they evoke in a nostalgic way.

Among the cosmopolitan discos, Antilla BCN Latin Club (BCN refers to Barcelona), founded by a Catalan couple in 1993, is the leading dance club in Barcelona. With seventeen years in business, live weekly concerts by local and foreign salsa and other Latin groups, a dance school, "taxi boys,"[10] and its hosting of the annual Festival Tempo Latino, the Antilla has achieved wide, international recognition. Nightly activities include dance lessons interspersed throughout the evening, in which teachers encourage club-goers to dance casino, salsa, chachachá, or bachata. Since its opening, it has hosted a diverse public of Catalans, Spaniards, Colombians, Cubans, Dominicans, Venezuelans, Peruvians, and tourists and other Europeans. Principally salsa and bachata are played in Antilla, and with the diversity of the audience and staff, salsa is danced as often in Cuban or Colombian style as in the slot form. The public at the discotheque Mil Pasos, located in the Heron City commercial center, is equally varied, with both Latinos and non-Latinos in attendance. The public may be majority Venezuelan, Dominican, or Argentine according to the artists or group playing the concert, and both *salsa en línea* and other styles are danced.

Other clubs are less diverse. The sites preferred by Cubans generally present live concerts. Some, like Mojito Latin Club (also known as Buenavista), where house group La Unión Habanera plays every Sunday, have more mixed audiences but often a Spanish majority. The restaurant-club HBN-BCN (Habana-Barcelona) also offers dance classes, programs live musical performances, and presents entertainment that relies on a faithful, mainly female audience, as is common in most of the clubs. Here both Cuban style and *salsa en línea* are danced. In Dominican discos like Brisas del Caribe and Bailodromo Latino, mainly merengue and bachata are played, although salsa and reggaetón are occasionally heard, and the Dominican flag occupies a central spot in the decor. Bolivian discos tend to cater to a very young clientele and play reggaetón, tecnocumbia, and salsa. The Bolivian club Enjoy also has a dance group, presents Bolivian artists live, and as occurs in some other Latino discos, offers female and male striptease shows. Principally Spanish discos, like the now-defunct La Clave and Sugar, often also have dance schools and *salsa en línea* predominates.

Most of the discos opened since 2001 are markedly Colombian, in clientele and staff and in the styles of liquor consumption, music, and decor. In all the Colombian discos live concerts are presented, there is no dance school, and people dance Colombian-style salsa, with the exception of SalSabor, which has the most mixed audience, including a high percentage of Spaniards on Thursdays, when *salsa en línea* is danced.

Other clubs' audiences vary day to day. Agua de Luna, opened in 2000, at first had a mainly Spanish audience but now has a clientele that attends according to the program. On some days it has a primarily Spanish audience that dances *salsa en línea* and Cuban-style *rueda de casino* (see Chapter 6), while on other days it has a primarily Peruvian and Ecuadorian audience dancing bachata and salsa in their own style. Agua de Luna includes a dance school, hosts performances featuring rueda de casino on Wednesdays, and presents Orquesta Stylos, made up of Peruvian musicians, every Friday.

The characteristics of each club's audiences are related directly to the club's music, as well as the social status and reputation of the club. Nonetheless, the predominant nationality of a disco depends on not only the music played there or the audience's self-selection but also social exclusions or inclusions that occur among different Latino groups and between Latinos and Spaniards. On many occasions, the doormen or club proprietors enforce these inclusions or exclusions at the club's entrance. The causes for exclusion or inclusion include status symbols, prejudices tied to physical features, the attribution of legitimized or stigmatized behaviors, or the difference between "Latin" and "Spanish" parties, for instance, in liquor consumption. On the part of the attendees, separations are partly caused by dance styles. These and other factors cause Latinos to prefer to go to Latino discos, specifically those of their compatriots, while the non-Latinos tend to go to the more cosmopolitan or predominantly Spanish clubs.

Spaniards are ambivalent about immigration, and their attitudes and opinions toward it have changed in the past decade as the number of foreigners residing in Spain and their social visibility have grown. During the 1990s, immigration was progressively more accepted, but since 2001, as immigrants have increased, acceptance has decreased (Méndez 2007: 81). Even though most Spaniards consider immigrant workers necessary (M. Delgado 2007: 215), and the growing ethnicization of the labor force is seen as natural, the widespread perception is that there are too many immigrants and that immigration is out of control. Immigration is seen as related to delinquency and urban insecurity and as threatening dissolution of the cultural identity and is thus stigmatized (Bonet i Agustí 2006: 55). In the Catalonia region, of which Barcelona is the capital and largest city, concern for language preservation and the secession debate compound the problem. There are tensions between Spaniards and foreigners as well as among the different Latin American communities. For instance, doormen at some Colombian discos, believing Ecuadorians and Bolivians get drunk and cause problems, bar those with markedly indigenous features, which causes conflicts.

Despite the popularization of salsa and other genres, for many Spaniards Latin musics continue to be foreign. They are not able to differentiate between salsa, merengue, and bachata, since for them all these musics are salsa, or else they relate them to a so-called Caribbean mix or to the music for the *pachangueo de verano*, the summer party season. To them, to dance salsa is simply to perform steps or turns as a couple. Nonetheless, some Spaniards have taken Latin musics, and particularly dancing, very seriously.

Barcelona Dances Salsa: Teachers, Schools, Companies, and Congresses

Many discos and salsa clubs offer dance classes to a considerable number of students, so that the classes have become indispensable for the dance halls. In addition, some dance academies make agreements with dance halls so that their students can practice there. In addition to the explosion of Latin discotheques and Latin dance schools, the growth in national dance contests, concerts, and festivals in which salsa plays a central role similarly demonstrates the transformations of cultural consumption and production habits that affect musical life not only in Barcelona but on the entire European continent as well.

Teachers

Cubans were the first to begin teaching salsa in Barcelona, and perhaps in the country as a whole, in the early 1990s.[11] Most of them had professional dance training, had participated in dance companies, and had toured in Europe, principally Italy, and then remained in Europe. Yet others prefer to define themselves as *bailadores* (informal social dancers) rather than *bailarines* (professional dancers; see Chapter 8) since, other than their cultural heritage of dance, they have not had formal artistic training.

Barcelona dancers debate whether Angelito Labarrera of Havana, who arrived in the late 1980s, or Carlitín (Carlos Enrique Arditti), who arrived in 1992 from Havana, was the first teacher in Barcelona. Whatever the case, Cubans continued to arrive in Barcelona, including Víctor Méndez, teacher of rueda de casino in Barcelona, who arrived in 1996; Jorge "Camagüey" Izalguez, a teacher of timba (currently teaching in Central and Eastern Europe), who arrived in 1997; Rogelio "Macusa" Lorda Moré, an Afro-Cuban dance teacher and founder of the cultural center called Macusa, who arrived in 1998; Emilio Prieto of Santa Clara, one of the best disco entertainers (*animadores*) in Barcelona, known for mixing Cuban salsa with *salsa en línea* in Barcelona, who arrived in 2000; and Yamira Sánchez of Havana, author of articles about Cuban dance and culture that have appeared in the magazine *Salseros*, who arrived around 2001.

Next, Argentines, Uruguayans, and other South Americans began to distinguish themselves as salsa teachers in Barcelona. Some of them had prior experience; others discovered salsa after arriving in Barcelona. As was the case for some Cubans without dance training, these South American teachers found salsa dance instruction to be a way to earn a living in Barcelona. Argentine Martín Rolinski, a Barcelona salsa teacher since 1992, explains, "Salsa was an accident more than anything. I arrived here at nineteen; I was a child, because I hadn't experienced anything. One could say that I discovered [salsa] here." However, many who were his students ten years ago "now give classes in civic centers, in other schools; they put together companies" (Rolinski 2006).

Although many salsa teachers exclusively teach, some create and direct their own dance companies and academies. Around 2003, professional dancers Emiliano Sosa and Sabrina Kacheroff arrived in the city from Argentina. Emiliano had been dancing salsa since 1996 in Buenos Aires. He is now choreographer for and director of Mythical Mambo, a company whose style is based on New York mambo, which he founded in 2004, and he also teaches in the school that shares the name.[12] Kacheroff, born in Buenos Aires, founded the women's dance company Queen Style and Company and has directed Vibes, her own dance studio, since 2008.

Since 2003, many other South American teachers and professional dancers have emerged, including Adrián Rodríguez from Uruguay and Anita Do Santos from Brazil, winners of the Puerto Rico Salsa Congress competition in 2007 and 2008, and Evelyn Viana from Venezuela, also a journalist for the magazine *Salseros* in 2007–2008. Although the Southern Cone is not typically associated with salsa, the presence of so many Argentines and Uruguayans as prominent salsa teachers in Barcelona has produced a regional perception of salsa as a pan-Latin American rather than specifically Caribbean dance practice.

Finally, Spaniards like Ray Pradell, Olga Valls, Sandra Camargo, and Mario Layunta began to enter into salsa teaching in the mid-1990s. Layunta, like Ray Pradell, was a *salsa en línea* dance pioneer in Barcelona. He started dancing salsa in 1989, and by 1994 he was teaching the Cuban style he had learned. Since 2000 he has taught other styles, like Puerto Rican, Los Angeles, and New York; he is now founder, dancer, and choreographer of the company Salsa del Barrio.

Some Cuban teachers assert that *salsa en línea* is doing away with the Cuban style in Europe because performances of salsa champions since 2002 have spread and promoted it and because professional salsa in Spain has gradually incorporated other nationalities. This opinion is understandable, because from the time that *salsa en línea* has been taught and dance congresses held, Cubans have ceased to be the only ones teaching the dance.

Salsa classes were first held in civic centers, then in gyms, and only later in discos. Initially, salsa classes were scarce; salsa was intended principally to entertain. The first style taught was Cuban rueda. However, today Barcelona and surrounding towns have around forty schools that teach salsa and many other dances, including some non-Latin ones similarly classified as exotic, such as belly dance. Among these schools, 35–40 percent operate out of discotheques.

Schools and Dance Companies

Although some ballroom dance schools, like Bailongu (opened in 1989), had already begun teaching rueda de casino and other salsa-associated dances, the Buenavista became the first all-salsa school in Barcelona when it opened in the Mojito Club in the late 1990s. The early teachers, including Layunta, Pradell, Gemma Bosch, and Rosa Ginés (also the director), later would found the first dance company in Catalonia, BCN Salsa Dancers. In 2001 dance schools opened in the Antilla and Mil Pasos; since then, numerous other Barcelona discos with salsa schools have appeared, although most salsa schools in Catalonia do not operate in discos.

Dance classes are diverse, and selection depends on each school, but the most common courses include salsa, merengue, son, bachata, rueda de casino, and chachachá. One can find Cuban, Puerto Rican, Los Angeles, and New York styles of salsa (on-1, on-2, and *salsa en línea* are also advertised), as well as salsa fusion, salsa-ragga, acrobatic salsa, and even Cali-style salsa (see

Figure 11.1. The Cali-style salsa group Exhibición Baile Caleño performing in Barcelona's Sala Apolo, April 15, 2012. The show was part of the Salsa and Latin Jazz Festival organized by the famous salsa singer Herman Olivera. *(Photograph by Isabel Llano.)*

Figure 11.1). Similarly, some schools refer to certain rhythms as tropical, while others call them Latin, and it is ever more common to find modern dance, jazz, *claqué*, hip-hop, funk, samba, mambo, rumba, boogaloo, lambada, *lambazouk*, *kizomba*, capoeira, and *batuka* on the programs of schools alongside the more conventional ballroom dance, ballet, tango, *sevillanas*, and flamenco. Similarly, some schools focus on Afro-Cuban dances and more exotic offerings such as break dance, hip-hop ragga, and Bollywood. Nevertheless, some classes with an exercise, therapeutic, or body-care focus are also included, such as aerobics or dance therapy, thus creating places that are more health centers than dance schools and in which music and dance are employed therapeutically to improve physical and psychological health as well as self-esteem.

In Spain there are more than forty performing dance companies and teams; in Barcelona and surrounding areas alone there are more than ten pair teams and ten dance companies. As noted, BCN Salsa Dancers was the first company in Catalonia, and although in the beginning they danced Cuban style, they later performed L.A. and New York styles and Puerto Rican *salsa en línea*. The group first promoted *salsa en línea* through performances in Barcelona and later represented Barcelona in national and international dance congresses, creating heightened interest in participating in such events. Although it is common to find Latin American members—principally Argentines and

Uruguayans, later Colombians—in dance teams and companies, more and more new groups are made up exclusively of Spaniards.[13] Most of the current companies dance *salsa en línea*, but one can also find mambo-, Colombian-, and Cuban-style companies.

Salsa Congresses in Spain

Given the proliferation of dance clubs, schools, companies, and teams, it is no surprise that in Spain salsa congresses and competitions are held throughout the year.[14] I use the term "salsa congresses" to refer to those events of national or international character related to Latin American dances. The audience may run from 400 to 1,500 people, and the name includes "congress," "festival," "symposium," "weekend," or "meeting" depending on the event's objectives and characteristics. The growing number of those held in Spain indicates not only the importance that salsa and other Latin dances are gaining among Spaniards but also the level of appropriation occurring in the country with regard to these dances.[15]

Table 11.1 shows all dance congresses held in 2009 in Spain. Twenty-seven congresses took place, lasting between one and three days, and the congresses in Barcelona and nearby provinces (like Girona and Tarragona) usually occurred in coastal cities. Most congresses were for salsa, but other rhythms were not excluded; thus a kizomba championship was also held to choose the Spanish representative for an international event in Lisbon. The Spanish cities where dance congresses take place most frequently are those near Barcelona. The most important national congress is the Spain Salsa Open, in which Spanish champions are chosen to represent the country in the Puerto Rico Salsa Congress at the end of the World Salsa Open.[16] International events took place in Madrid, Tarragona, Lloret de Mar, Castellón, Majorca, and Cartagena.

Congresses are usually organized by clubs or associations of salseros and include workshops, dance exhibitions, and social dance. Deejays are indispensable, since live music is more an exception than a rule, as are the invited dance teams and companies, who perform their choreographies, offer dance workshops, and promote future congresses. Alongside these activities, dance merchandise is sold. Congresses are directed at Spaniards, and the Latinos who participate are usually those invited as teachers, dancers, and deejays.

Congresses have a close relationship with salsa schools and the Latin music clubs for Spanish audiences, so that the audience is composed mainly of current or former students of the salsa schools. Many of these schools' teachers participate in the congresses as invited guests, either alone or with their respective partners or dance companies. Thus, congresses are promoted in discos where dance classes are given and where parties with exhibitions by dance groups are held.

For Spaniards, congresses constitute one of the principal avenues of contact with salsa music and with other dancers. Congresses represent an opportunity

TABLE 11.1   DANCE CONGRESSES HELD IN SPAIN, 2009

Date	Name	City (Province or Region)
January 23–25	International Congress–ACM Salsa Festival	Lloret de Mar (Girona)
February 6–7	Festival de Bailes Latinos/Latin Dances Festival	Huércal-Overa (Almería)
February 6–9	Oscasalsa 2009	Huesca
March 6	Kizomba Championship	Barcelona
March 6–8	Cantabria Tropical: Tropical Gem and Friends	Camargo (Santander)
March 6–8	Murcia Fusion	Murcia
March 13–15	Barcelona Dances Salsa	Barcelona
March 13–15	Euskasalsa	Vitoria-Gasteiz
March 20–22	Latin Rhythms Congress–Murcia Dances	Murcia
March 28	Pamplosalsa	Pamplona
March 28	DH Festival–Latin Dances Festival	Seville
April 3–5	Salsa and Casino Enric and Montse Meeting	El Perelló (Tarragona)
April 9–12	International Symposium of Salsa	Madrid
April 17–18	A Coruña Salsa Congress	A Coruña (Galicia)
April 17–19	BurgoSalSon—"Spain's Most Popular Salsa Meeting"	Burgos
April 25–26	"Tarragona City" Salsa Congress	Tarragona
April 25–26	International Congress of Salsa of Tarragona	El Perelló (Tarragona)
April 30–May 3	Festival Va de Baile/Go Dancing Festival	L'atmella de Mar (Tarragona)
May 8–10	International Congress of Salsa	Palma de Majorca
May 29–31	Salsalba 2009	Albacete
June 5–7	Danzarte	Ribesalbes (Castellón)
July 3	Spain Salsa Open 2009	Valencia
July 3–4	Bizkai Salsa–Salsa Meeting in Bilbao	Bilbao
July 23–26	Benidorm Salsa Festival	Benidorm (Alicante)
October 30– November 1	Weekend Enric and Montse	El Perelló (Tarragona)
November 13–15	Carthagosalsa 2009–Third Latin Rhythms Congress	Cartagena (Murcia)

for beginning dancers to meet renowned teachers and an opportunity for dance teams and the companies they represent to show their work, enhance their résumés, and boost their reputation.

Former salsa students have turned into dance teachers with time and now direct or are members of dance companies. For many veterans, their lives revolve around salsa: besides being teachers or dancers, some are deejays, record collectors, or creators of websites dedicated to promoting the genre, and some have begun to play Latin percussion. Many current students also live for salsa; they go to discos to dance, take trips to the Caribbean, or join clubs for salseros or salsa fans. They also exchange information about music and clubs, particularly through Internet forums and e-mail.

These observations suggest that a new way of relating to dance is emerging through such events. As more than an expression of one's own culture associated with the enjoyment of music, the dance becomes a means of widening one's circle of friends, a healthful leisure-time activity, and a way to have fun while exercising. In some cases, dance also becomes a career. Nevertheless, most students from dance workshops, as well as some teachers, are interested in only dance steps and figures; they are not concerned with following the musical rhythm or with the quality of the musical repertoire. Paradoxically, the music at dance exhibitions is *salsa dura*, while the "street" dancers, who have not learned in class settings, are those who dance the so-called *salsa monga*, or limp salsa (that of Marc Anthony, Jerry Rivera, and others, also known as *salsa romántica*), which the critics have discredited. Finally, congresses constitute a dynamic national circuit with international connections through market institutions, and thus the majority of workshop teachers, dance pairs and dance companies, deejays, congress organizers, and purveyors of dance merchandise participate in several different congresses, as do many attendees.

In salsa congresses and dance practices, we see a transformation in the practices of musical consumption and, in a sense, of the cultural identity of the Spaniards who tie themselves closely to Latin musics, since "salsa has never been far from us in Spain, [although today] the general public and the non-specialized mass media hardly distinguish one rhythm from another" (Gómez 1995: 6). Those who approach these musics to learn about them have begun to make them their own, and for many, the musics begin to take on a fundamental importance, similar to the importance of popular music and singers in Latin American intimacy and identity. As for dance, despite the close cultural relation between Spain and Latin America, in general non-Latinos have had to attend classes to learn the steps of salsa and other Latin rhythms. Among these students, few are interested in feeling the rhythm of the music, and more are concerned with how they look on the dance floor or with counting how many steps to take before a turn. Nevertheless, given the growth in salsa dancing, it is possible that right now children are beginning to dance at a very early age, imitating their elders in their own homes, as it has been in Latin America. Salsa dance is thus playing a role in transforming cultural identities, since to a certain degree it is modifying or altering previous experiences through the body.

As I mention at the beginning of this chapter, Spaniards' changing musical consumption practices show that cultural hybridity (García Canclini 2001: 14, 22, 29) is occurring.[17] Since Latin dances, particularly salsa, are turning into a global language, I further argue that "the hybrid seems to be dethroning the exotic" (Gruzinski 2000: 40).

Conclusion

The development of salsa dance, as well as of other Latin musics and dances, has been tied to the growth of the Latin American immigrant population on the one hand and to the internationalization of salsa congresses on the other, with the music business having a hand in all these developments.

The importance of music and dance to Latinos has been a determining factor in the appearance of radio stations, clubs, dance teachers, musical groups, and discotheques. Dance and music can help alleviate uprootedness and marginalization, the precise topics that many salsa songs discuss. In this sense, discotheques have permitted Latinos to express their cultural identity beyond the geographic borders of Latin American countries.

By analyzing salsa discotheques and Latin music in Barcelona, it is possible to analyze Latinos' and non-Latinos' differing practices of reception and consumption of these musics and their dance. These practices, depending on the specific case, can be a motive for inclusion or exclusion among Latino groups and by non-Latinos of Latinos. In general, Latinos bring to Barcelona practices of musical consumption that are customary in their countries of origin, and they influence the music and dance scenes in various ways: Latinos consume liquor in Latino style; many discos present striptease shows or concerts featuring singers popular in Latino countries of origin; Latinos do not dance *salsa en línea*; and although in general discos play salsa, merengue, bachata, and reggaetón, they play this music alongside rhythms particular to the predominant nationalities of their clientele.

In terms of non-Latinos, although they consume liquor, it is not unusual for many to drink only water or soft drinks; they have generally appropriated *salsa en línea*, although they also like Cuban casino; their method of practicing dance is different from that of Latinos (it is more associated with what they have learned in class); and they have special dance footwear (some even change shoes in the disco). These differences in the ways of experiencing the event, the music, and its dance mean that discos are classed according to their clientele's nationality and that few have an audience of diverse nationalities. This analysis also reveals disparities and social conflicts, since the inclusions or exclusions correspond to the existence of social prejudices and conflicting attitudes regarding immigration, and some discos have trouble maintaining order. One might also say that *salsa en línea* has become dominant in Barcelona because of non-Latinos' attendance at salsa classes and congresses where it is the most frequently offered style.

Salsa and Latin music radio stations constitute one of the most important means of promoting discos and concerts and creating a communal feeling among the different Latin American populations. As with the discos, the radio stations can be classified according to the predominant nationality of the listening public and the staff. The radio stations and discos that have an audience in common establish relationships and promote each other, demonstrating the interdependence of listening, dancing, and consumption practices.

The discos associated with particular Latino communities do not offer dance classes, but they often present live concerts by singers and groups. The discos with a non-Latino clientele do offer dance classes and, instead of concerts, present exhibitions by dance companies, often as publicity for dance congresses.

In Barcelona as well as nearby cities, some dance schools are associated with discos, and others are not. School offerings include all types of dances taught by Latinos and non-Latinos. In the 1990s the teaching of dance was fundamentally the charge of Cuban teachers who taught rueda de casino in cultural centers; since 2000, Argentines, Uruguayans, and Spaniards have begun to teach salsa, particularly the línea styles, thanks to the salsa congresses and the consequent relationship between local, national, and foreign teachers and dance companies.

By promoting instruction in other styles of salsa dance and formation of companies, teams, and new schools, salsa congresses have contributed to growth in the non-Latino population's attachment to the dance. Congresses show even more clearly that non-Latinos practice the dance differently from Latinos. Although some attend congresses to specialize their training as dancers, in general, non-Latinos attend these classes as they would aerobics classes at a gym. Many do not improvise while dancing; on the contrary, they dance the steps they have learned and are concerned with only exhibiting their skills. More concretely, Latinos do not separate music from dance, but many non-Latinos privilege dance and do not feel the music to the same degree. Nevertheless, this is changing: more non-Latinos dance salsa all the time, feeling and enjoying the music, and they identify with salsa in such a way that salsa and other Latin musics and dances are transforming their cultural identity to some extent.

Finally, this retrospective makes evident the power of Latin music and dance—particularly salsa—and the importance they have in the lives of *rumberos* (dancers or partiers), both in Spain and in Latin America. However, this music and dance do not always succeed in bringing together different groups of Latinos or uniting Latinos with non-Latinos, since enjoying them does not mean that all fans enjoy them *together*. Nevertheless, salsa continues to be internationalized, to be globalized, like jazz, tango, samba, and many other musics. In particular, it is evidence of and part of a social phenomenon: the migrations of Latinos, first those of the 1960s to the United States and, later, in this past decade, to Europe.

NOTES

Acknowledgment: I thank Mamá Inés for providing information on Alberto Bonne, Silvio González, and the 2009 Puerto Rico Salsa Congress.

1. I use the category "Latino" to refer to the Latin American population living in Barcelona, but this category includes people from different countries, regions, and cities, with diverse ethnic, social, and economic characteristics. "Non-Latinos" include the native local population and diverse non-Latin American nationalities; this, of course, also entails a heterogenous group.

2. Catalan rumba is a musical genre born in Barcelona, created by gypsies, and derived from gypsy rumba mixed with Cuban dance music and rock and roll.

3. See Pérez's website at http://vespito.net/gato.

4. During the early years of the post-Franco transition in Spain, a countercultural movement, La Móvida Madrileña, emerged. It spread throughout the country until the late 1980s and was characterized by interest in alternative or underground culture, including pop rock groups and singers different from those sponsored by multinational record companies. Many are still around today.

5. *Salsa erótica* is also known as *salsa romántica* (see Washburne 2002).

6. Some discos and stations have the same owner, thus the stations promote certain discos, and in most cases, the predominant nationalities in the discos coincide with the stations' nationalities. Some advertisements on stations are addressed to the community that frequents the respective club, and radio personalities are linked to particular discos as the people in charge of maintaining dancers' enthusiasm in the disco.

7. See Llano Camacho 2008: 26–27, 231–233 and Llano Camacho 2009: 7–32 regarding Latin radio stations in Barcelona.

8. Foreigners in Barcelona grew from 53,428 in 2000 to 282,178 in 2012, so that 17.4 percent of residents are immigrants. Of these, 40 percent are Latin American, principally from Ecuador, Bolivia, Peru, Colombia, Argentina, Brazil, and the Dominican Republic. Spain as a whole is home to almost six million immigrants, or 12 percent of the country. See Barcelona Government 2012; National Statistic Institute 2010. See also Delgado and Lozano 2007.

9. *Salsa en línea,* or salsa danced in a slot format, can be performed on the beat (on-1) or in a syncopated way (on-2) (see Chapters 2, 4, and 7).

10. Some discos hire two or three taxi boys, young men to dance with women who have no partner, each night.

11. For instance, Cuban teacher Saúl "Papa Rumba" Barbosa Ventosa now lives in Castile–La Mancha and has resided in Spain since the 1980s, when salsa had only just begun to spread in the country.

12. In Argentina, the taste for salsa music and dance is principally a result of promotion by Cuban Alberto Bonne (1966–2001). He taught Cuban dance first in La Plata and later in Buenos Aires and all of Argentina, where he also worked in radio, organized dance congresses, and created the group AmeriSalsa. See Maani 2001 and "Alberto Bonne" 2001. Argentines now also play important roles in congresses and as performers. The Argentine Silvio González of 2X4 Mambo is responsible for the International Salsa Open; for competitions in Spain, Argentina, and Puerto Rico; and together with his partner, Sandra

Ferreira, for part of the organization of the Puerto Rico Salsa Congress. See "Argentina en la cima" 2009.

13. The presence of Argentines and Uruguayans in Spain stems from (a) the interest many Latin Americans have for Spain and Europe as places to develop as music and dance professionals, (b) the economic recession that began in 1998 in Argentina, provoking the *corralito* (bank freeze) in December 2001 and the bank crisis in Uruguay, and (c) the fact that many Argentines and Uruguayans have European citizenship through their parents, allowing them to reside and work in European Union countries.

14. Likewise, congresses held at local, national, and international levels have been an incentive to form dance companies and teams throughout Europe.

15. Dance teacher Saúl "Papa Rumba" Barbosa Ventosa, organizer of the congress DanceArt (Danzarte), states that dance congresses began to take place in Spain in 1999 (*Salseros*, no. 15, January 2009, p. 45). The Congreso Mundial de la Salsa (World Salsa Congress) indeed first took place in Spain in 1999.

16. Salsa congresses emerged initially in the United States and because of their commercial success have since been exported to other countries. The Spain Salsa Open functions as a branch of the Puerto Rico Salsa Congress, organized by Albert Torres, who also created the Los Angeles Salsa Congress.

17. The processes of hybridization are "sociocultural processes in which structures or discrete practices, which existed in separated form, get together to generate new structures, objects, and practices" (García Canclini 2001: 14).

REFERENCES

"Alberto Bonne: A dos años de su fallecimiento, sigue estando con nosotros." 2001. *AmericaSalsa.com*. Available at http://www.arteshow.com/abonne/index.htm.

"Argentina en la cima del 'Salsa Congress.'" 2009. Fundación Nacional para la Cultura Popular, August 7. Available at http://www.prpop.org/noticias/ago09/salsa_congress _ago07.shtml.

Barcelona Government. 2012. "Població estrangera a Barcelona." Available at http://www .bcn.cat/novaciutadania/pdf/ca/estudis/pob_estrangera_2012.pdf.

Bonet i Agustí, Lluís. 2006. *Diversitat cultural i polítiques interculturals a Barcelona. Dinámicas Interculturales*, no. 6. Barcelona: CIDOB.

Delgado, Lola, and Daniel Lozano. 2007. *Latinos en España: Cómo son y cómo viven colombianos, argentinos, ecuatorianos, venezolanos*. Madrid: La Esfera de los Libros.

Delgado, Manuel. 2007. *Sociedades movedizas*. Barcelona: Anagrama.

García Canclini, Néstor. 2001. *Culturas híbridas: Estrategias para entrar salir de la modernidad*. 2nd ed. Barcelona: Paidós.

Gilbert, Jeremy, and Ewan Pearson. 2003. *Cultura y políticas de la música dance: Disco, hip-hop, house, techno, drum'n' bass y garage*. Barcelona: Paidós.

Gómez, José Manuel. 1995. *Guía esencial de la salsa*. Valencia, Spain: La Máscara.

Gruzinski, Serge. 2000. *El pensamiento mestizo*. Barcelona: Paidós.

Llano Camacho, Isabel. 2008. "Músicas latinas en Barcelona: Espacios de reafirmación y negociación de identidades." In *La política de lo diverso: ¿Producción, reconocimiento o apropiación de lo intercultural?*, ed. Fundación CIDOB, 227–235. Barcelona: CIDOB. Available at http://www.cidob.org/es/publicaciones/libros/monografias/la_politica _de_lo_diverso_produccion_reconocimiento_o_apropiacion_de_lo_cultural.

———. 2009. "Inmigración y música latina en Barcelona: El papel de la música y el baile en procesos de reafirmación e hibridación cultural." *Revista Sociedad y Economía* 15:7–32. Available at http://www.redalyc.org/articulo.oa?id=99612494001.

López, Carlos, ed. 1993. *Juan Luis Guerra*. Madrid: Luca Editorial y SGAE.

Maani, Refah. 2001. "Alberto Bonne: Para recordar siempre." *AmericaSalsa.com*, October 11. Available at http://www.americasalsa.com/notas/alberto_refah.html.

Méndez Lago, Mónica. 2007. "Actitudes de los españoles ante la inmigración: Una mirada desde las encuestas." In *La inmigración en España en 2006: Anuario de inmigración y políticas de inmigración*, ed. Eliseo Aja and Joaquín Arango, 68–81. Barcelona: CIDOB.

National Statistic Institute. 2010. "Notas de prensa." April 29. Available at http://www.ine.es/prensa/np595.pdf.

Rolinski, Martín. 2006. Interview by Isabel Llano. June 14. Barcelona.

Roy, Maya. 2003. *Músicas cubanas*. Madrid: Akal.

Wade, Peter. 2000. *Music, Race and Nation: Música Tropical in Colombia*. Chicago: University of Chicago Press.

Washburne, Chris. 2002. "Salsa Romántica: An Analysis of Style." In *Situating Salsa: Global Markets and Local Meaning in Latin Popular Music*, ed. Lise Waxer, 101–132. New York: Routledge.

12

Diffusion and Change
in Salsa Dance Styles in Japan

Kengo Iwanaga

Salsa dancing is now performed in daily life around the world, whenever salsa music is heard. This form of everyday salsa dance, often called "street salsa," is distinguished from the stylized type of dance discussed later. Sheenagh Pietrobruno argues, "Since many people who grew up dancing to salsa music started as children, they have acquired their dance tradition through numerous years of experience and practice" (2006: 117). Thus, it follows that it is impossible for people living in a cultural context in which street salsa dancing is not practiced to dance in the same way. It is also difficult to teach the style because "salsa learned in a lived context does not distinguish between the steps and turns of the dance and how the total body moves in dance" (Pietrobruno 2006: 125). In contrast to street salsa, "studio salsa," which originated in the 1980s in the United States and in other countries, is a more elaborate form based on social dance styles that is gaining popularity around the world (see also Chapter 2).

Salsa music was brought to Japan concurrently with its birth in the 1970s. However, salsa dancing did not gain popularity there until the 1990s. Earlier studies on the migration of salsa have examined salsa dancing in European cities such as London and Paris and in the Canadian city of Montreal. All these studies focus on cities where immigrants from Latin America lived and on how they brought salsa into the local communities. In contrast, in Japan the acceptance of immigrants has been limited to a small number of Latin Americans of

This chapter is a substantially altered version of Kengo Iwanaga, "Changing Salsa: How Salsa Dancing Was Assimilated into Japan," *Journal of Latin American Studies* 37 (2009): 13–21, a publication of the Institute for Latin American Studies at Rikkyo University.

Japanese descent who arrived in Japan following changes made in the Japanese immigration laws in 1990. It is clear that the impact of immigrants on Japanese society, culturally and economically, proceeded in a substantially different way from what was experienced by the countries investigated in other studies.

Salsa dancing's diffusion in Japan would also have been different from that in other countries owing to the rarity of physical contact in Japanese culture. Couple dancing involving a man and a woman is commonly found in Western cultures. In other words, pair dancing is part of the Western cultural habitus, or shared bodily practices and customs. In contrast, in Japanese culture there is little physical contact in public in daily life. The Japanese have few opportunities to witness social dances involving couples.[1] In this chapter I analyze the diffusion of salsa dance outide its original cultural context, examining the popularization of salsa dance in Japan through the application of Pierre Bourdieu's methodology and concepts of field and habitus.

Definitions of Terms

According to Bourdieu's concept, *habitus* is "necessity internalized and converted into a disposition that generates meaningful practices and meaning-giving perceptions" (Bourdieu 1984: 170). The *field* is "a network of objective relations (of domination or subordination, of complementarity or antagonism)" (Bourdieu 1996: 231). Bourdieu conceptualizes the "literary field," which is a structure that includes authors, editors, publishers, and literary works. In the field of cultural production, those who participate in a particular field compete regarding how to differentiate themselves from others and how to relocate themselves into a higher position of that field to obtain legitimacy. However, according to Yojiro Ishi, the measurement of legitimacy is neither constant nor absolute and may change with the social space.[2] In *Distinction* (1984), Bourdieu argues that Bach's music is seen as aesthetically legitimate among listeners of a high social class, but if his music is popularized, it would then be outside their index of legitimacy. In this study, I apply these concepts to salsa dance in Japan. We can assume that the "salsa field" includes those who conduct or take lessons, salsa events and studios, informative magazines, and relevant Internet information. Those who dance in the salsa field also fight for legitimacy in the field.

Salsa Dancing and Habitus

Studio salsa dancing was invented by incorporating the movements of social dance into a more formal framework. Since then, various salsa dance styles have been created and performed worldwide. They are named after the place of their birth, such as New York style, L.A. style, Cuban style, and Colombian style, and each style is distinguished by its rhythmic or movement characteristics (see Chapters 2, 4, 6, and 8 herein). Salsa dancing styles born in the

Americas have been imitated and developed in Japan; no local dance styles, such as Tokyo style, have been distributed.

Although the basic movements are similar among the styles, the actual technique is relatively different. Therefore, mastering one style does not mean mastery of the other styles. Despite the variations between salsa styles, salsa enthusiasts can easily distinguish one style from another.

In my opinion, the habitus is different for each style because the attitude, wording, and atmosphere of the field are unique. Salsa students judge whether the habitus of the style they are learning fits their own habitus. Let us examine the difference between the habitus of followers of the Cuban and the L.A. styles in Japan.

The habitus of Cuban-style dancers in Japan in the era of emergence (discussed below) is authenticity oriented. A key criterion of the style is to demonstrate a close connection to the features of the culture in which the style originated, such as its music and language. Cuban-style dancers in this era place less importance on the accoutrements of appearance, such as shoes, attire, and accessories. Cuban-style dancers are often seen sporting T-shirts and jeans. The teaching method of Cuban-style instructors is to focus on the basic flexibility of the body, the flow of the dance, and improvisation. Adherents of the Cuban style are interested in aspects of Cuban culture, such as Cuban music and the Spanish language, and some of them even visit Cuba. Cuban-style instructors are well acquainted with Cuba and its locals. Most teachers were either born in Cuba or have resided there.

In L.A.-style salsa in Japan, however, the habitus is exhibition oriented. The purpose of the style is to be noticed by the audience. Dance movements are precisely taught, even up to the degree to point the toes. Followers of the L.A. style also place high importance on the selection of attire and shoes. They spend time learning to dance to particular songs, and they are enthusiastic about performing on stage. However, unlike Cuban-style enthusiasts, they are less interested in the elements of Latin American or Latino culture, such as local life and music. Japanese instructors of the L.A. style are typically experienced in other styles of dance, such as ballroom dance.[3]

The Expansion of the Salsa Field

In Tokyo today, the majority of salsa enthusiasts dance the L.A. style, but when salsa dance first emerged in Tokyo, the majority danced the Cuban style. This change occurred simultaneously with an influx of people who had a different habitus. The following factors outline the process of change while focusing on the expansion of the salsa field in the Tokyo metropolitan area.

The Era of Emergence

Even the greatest musical artists in Latin America are little known in Japan. One example of this is the singer and composer Juan Luis Guerra, who is very popular in the Dominican Republic and throughout Latin America but who is a big unknown for most Japanese. However, some internationally popular Latin songs, like "Bésame mucho" and "Lambada," have become famous in Japan and can even be heard in Japanese karaoke bars. Thus, when salsa arrived in Japan in the 1970s, a period I term the era of emergence, its audience had little prior knowledge of the style on which to build.

My own experience in salsa is illustrative. I first came across salsa music on a CD by Japanese salsa group Orquesta de la Luz, which a friend of mine had lent me in the summer of 1993. I did not realize that salsa was both a form of music and a type of dance until I attended a salsa concert and saw a few audience members dancing. I began learning to dance salsa in a salsa club, and it fascinated me so much that I eventually decided to quit my job to travel to Latin America. This travel experience expanded my interest in the culture of Latin America. I thought that the reason people were interested in salsa was because it was viewed as something novel and easy to take up, compared to other types of dance, such as ballroom dancing and Argentine tango,[4] which require special dance attire or shoes and long physical training. When I returned to Japan, I studied anthropology and sociology as a graduate student, and I then conducted field research on the popular music of the Dominican Republic. Meanwhile, I also taught salsa in a course open to the public at Seisen University and contributed to a serialization of salsa dance in the monthly magazine of a Spanish language course.

The first club exclusively dedicated to salsa dance was inaugurated in 1992 in Roppongi, one of the largest nightlife districts in Tokyo. Additional salsa clubs soon opened, mainly in Roppongi, but they were seen in other areas also, such as Shinjuku, Shibuya, and Yokohama. At the same time, salsa instructors began to appear. In 1994 Japan had three salsa instructors; the number had risen to thirteen by 1997 (Salsa Hotline Japan 1999: 112).

The number of salsa clubs in the era of emergence was small, and the majority of customers were Latinos of Japanese descent and people who worked for American military bases in Japan. For example, at a salsa club in Motomachi, Yokohama, Latinos made up the majority of customers who danced till dawn on Sunday mornings, with only a scattering of Japanese people. Salsa dance events, such as the Cuban Salsa Festival, hosted by the Cuban Embassy in Japan since 1996, and the dance event Folkcuba Japan, held since 1994, also occurred. Beginning in 1995, the Tokyo Caribbean Connection held monthly salsa events attracting several hundred people. The promoters of salsa dancing in this era were embassies or salsa enthusiasts who organized salsa events.

Also during this period, some Japanese salsa musicians enjoyed international prominence. The best-known Japanese salsa group on an international level is Orquesta de la Luz (see Hosokawa 2002), which formed and began its musical activity in 1984. In 1989 it went on a self-funded tour across the United States and in 1990 released its first album, *De la Luz*. In 1993 the group appeared on the NHK television program *Kohaku Utagassen*, one of the most widely watched New Year's Eve shows in Japan. Up until its breakup in 1997, the band gave concerts in Japan and overseas, but its fame in Japan was much less than abroad. Nonetheless, several groups still occasionally play salsa in Japan, one of which formed in 1978, before Orquesta de la Luz, and is called Orquesta del Sol.

The Turning Point

The turning point of the salsa field occurred between 1998 and 1999. In 1999 salsa's popularity intensified because of several factors, such as the success of the French film *Salsa!*, a NHK television program dedicated to salsa, and an article published in a magazine belonging to a credit card company. Gen Ohgimi, a founding member of Orquesta de la Luz, criticized the salsa dance boom, questioning the trend of teaching the movements. Asked, "What do you think about the recent attention to salsa as a gorgeous pair dance?" Ohgimi said, "Salsa is not a subject to take lessons. Dance schools popping up are okay, but you can dance without mastering dance steps" (Salsa Hotline Japan 1999: 123; my translation). Nonetheless, interest in learning and performing salsa only grew.

An important factor contributing to the increase in the number of people who were practicing salsa at this time was the improved availability of information on salsa events and clubs. Sources providing information on salsa dance had consisted mainly of flyers or word-of-mouth publicity. A change occurred in 1998 when a magazine called *Salsa Hotline Press*, published by Salsa Hotline Japan, was widely distributed in Japan. *Salsa Hotline Press* provided information about salsa music, salsa dance events, artists coming to Japan, and salsa clubs in New York City. In addition, Internet sites also provided information on salsa.[5]

Another factor that contributed globally to the expansion of the field was salsa dance congresses. In Japan, the Japan Salsa Congress has played a significant role in uniting Japanese salsa lovers with the global salsa industry (see Figures 12.1 and 12.2).

George Watabe, a Tokyo-born Japanese and the publisher of *Salsa Hotline Press*, started organizing salsa dance events as a business proposition. He says, "I wanted to establish salsa more widely and deeply in Japan on the basis of my experience in the music business. I take risks in my business, and I did not want to do volunteer work" (Salsa Hotline Japan, n.d.; my translation). In 1999 Watabe organized the Japan Salsa Festival, later renaming it Japan Salsa Congress. In 2002 forty groups and four hundred people participated in the event. In 2004 the organizer moved to a larger venue, and in 2007 the numbers rose to four hundred and four thousand, respectively. According to Watabe, the Japan Salsa Congress became "the biggest salsa festival in Asia."[6]

The Japan Salsa Congress is the largest annual salsa event in Japan, and it is internationally oriented. During the event, international guest dancers conduct workshops for dancers. At the 2008 Japan Salsa Congress, Eddie Torres and eight other invited dancers gave lessons for two days. No workshops were

Figure 12.1. Japan Salsa Congress, 2011. *(Photograph courtesy of Salsa Hotline Japan.)*

Figure 12.2. Salsa lesson at the Japan Salsa Congress, 2011. *(Photograph courtesy of Salsa Hotline Japan.)*

offered by Japanese dancers, however. At the shows held during the congress, dancers perform and are ranked according to criteria such as technical competence, creative expression, and audience appeal. However, only one person judges the performances. He is Albert Torres, organizer of salsa congresses worldwide and one of the presenters of the event.[7] Winners at the congress are eligible to compete in the world salsa congresses held in Los Angeles and Miami. For instance, winners of the 2008 Japan Salsa Congress qualified for the Fourth World Salsa Championships held in Miami.

The number of people who have entered the salsa field in Japan since the late 1990s has increased, and these new dancers possess a habitus different from those who began dancing in the era of emergence. The recent entrants generally do not have direct experience of Latin culture but have gained an understanding of it through television and the print media. These people are interested in salsa dancing itself and its physical movements rather than the cultural elements such as music and language. According to one DJ, there is a pronounced lack of interest in salsa music itself. He says, "I have been a DJ for various genres of music, but the toughest one is salsa. I feel playing as a DJ for salsa music is worthless . . . because the audience is only counting the tempo and not feeling the groove" (Salsa Hotline Japan 1999: 136; my translation). In addition, there are few opportunities to dance salsa with live music in Japan. For example, during the dance time after the shows at the Japan Salsa Congress, music is played by a DJ, and no live music is performed.

Dance locations have become multipolar. Latinos of Japanese descent mainly dance in the nightclubs in the suburbs of Tokyo and are less often seen in salsa clubs in Roppongi. The polarization of people into street salsa dancers and studio salsa dancers can also be observed. The people who started salsa dance from the turning-point era mainly claim distinction based on differences of body movement. This change provokes the selection of dance styles that are visually representative, such as the L.A. style, rather than the culture-oriented Cuban style.

Salsa Today and the Systematization of Dance Movement

I have examined the diffusion of salsa dancing in Japan with regard to two phases: the era of its emergence in the early 1990s and the turning point in its popularity in 1998–1999. In each period, the habitus of participants in the salsa field differs, and the differences relate to various dance styles. I now turn to the current salsa scene in Tokyo and undertake a brief analysis of the systematization of the dance.

Salsa Schools: Three Types

To achieve a deeper understanding of salsa's spread, we cannot overlook the salsa-dancing schools that brought together teachers and students. On the basis of announcements for salsa classes published in a free monthly magazine called *120% SALSA*, in August 1998 there were ten salsa instructors in the Tokyo metro area, and the total number of classes was fifty per week. By March 2007 these figures had grown to sixty-three instructors and two hundred classes per week. The majority of those interested in salsa discovered it through the salsa schools.

Salsa is taught in three types of settings:

1. Salsa clubs, where during the first hour of the evening people can participate without making a reservation
2. Dance academies that have a fixed schedule and offer classes at various levels
3. Cultural centers or fitness clubs

In the first setting, that of the salsa clubs, a context that has existed since the emergence of salsa teaching in Japan, the majority of classes begin at 7:00 or 7:30 p.m. on weeknights and last for an hour and a half. Dance teachers change every day, and people who participate in multiple classes can learn a variety of types and levels of dancing at a single club. Classes cost 2,500 yen ($25),[8] and the price includes a drink. Students do not need to make a reservation to attend class, thus the number of participants changes for each class and each day.

In the second case, that of the dance academies, the majority of classes are at night, but on Saturdays and Sundays there are also classes during the daytime. The schools generally charge tuition and a monthly fee. The monthly fee is between 8,000 and 10,000 yen ($80 to $100). There are different classes depending on the level of the participants.

In the third case, at cultural centers or in fitness clubs the salsa class is one activity among a variety of courses offered. Course duration varies between one and three months. As with dance academies, the school collects tuition and a monthly or semester fee. A typical cost for a semester lasting three months is 23,000 yen ($230) for ten classes.

Salsa Instructors (Teachers) and Students

Most instructors are Japanese, but some are foreigners, including Cubans and Japanese-Peruvians. Instructors usually have another steady job, but those who earn their living from dance teach classes every day in several clubs and dance schools.

The types of people who attend salsa classes vary according to the types of classes discussed above. In the case of the first type, the salsa clubs, and the second type, the dance academies, participants tend to be workers between twenty and thirty years old. They work downtown, and the clubs are located in the downtown nightlife districts, near their offices. In the case of the third type, cultural centers or fitness clubs, participants vary widely, ranging from college students to retirees.

Overall there are more female students than male. According to a survey conducted by Salsa Hotline Japan in 2004, 19 percent of respondents had been dancing for one year, and 31 percent had been participating for one to three years. The most common reason respondents started dancing salsa was because of "an invitation from friends" (40 percent). The frequency they went out dancing was "once or twice a week" (57 percent) or "three or four times a week" (15 percent) (Salsa Hotline Japan 2004: 39).

Systematization of Dance Movement

For students who want to learn salsa, having standardized salsa dance styles, such as L.A. style, removes the shame from dancing salsa. Japanese generally have few opportunities for physical contact in daily life and almost never have the chance to dance in pairs or to synchronize their body movements with a partner. Given these cultural circumstances, dancing as a couple is out of the ordinary and creates a feeling of shame. Following a particular, codified salsa dance style serves to alleviate this feeling. To count and follow the steps of the style serves as a rule that removes the shame.

Systematization—that is, making or creating a rational format—is also helpful for salsa instructors. First, one can situate oneself within a particular salsa-teaching trend, emphasizing style X, which clarifies one's position. Second, systematization can create some degrees or stages of learning and clarify the criteria that establish the level of dance. This system can stimulate students' desire to improve, which helps retain students over the long term. Instructors regularly give students the opportunity to demonstrate the results of their learning by dancing for an audience. Instructors also recommend that students attend salsa congresses and that they purchase learning DVDs. One salsa dance instructor requires students to learn the steps shown on the DVD; they cannot move up to the next level until they can perform the moves perfectly. Instructors use these activities and techniques to encourage students to continue learning to dance salsa.

Recently, there has been a movement to establish organizations for salsa dance in Japan to pursue systematization. An incorporated nonprofit organization called Japan Salsa Association was established in September 2009. The head of the organization, Mika Takenaga, explained that she established the association because there was no organization in Japan for salsa dance like there were for other acknowledged dance forms, such as tango and flamenco, and she wanted to introduce salsa dance to the public and unite people belonging to different dance styles and factions. According to her, salsa dance can be enjoyable without being associated with any organization; however, she felt that introducing salsa into public events or schools would be easier if it was promoted by a private studio or institution.

The organization performs two main activities: (1) hosting the Japan Salsa Festival and (2) granting qualifications. The Japan Salsa Festival, also known as the Japan Cup, consists of three dance categories: pair, team, and trial. The first festival was held in November 2009. To progress through the levels of salsa dance, one must pass a test with the organization in which qualifications are granted on the basis of ten grades. For example, grade 10 is for beginners and mainly consists of a variation of cross-body lead and under-arm turns, and grade 9 is a variation of inside and half turns. Takenaga suggests that "the qualification is a good method to keep motivation for dancing salsa." It "provides a definite target for dancers to achieve, and is not just about enjoying dancing in a salsa club" (Takenaga 2009; my translation). Apart from the Japan Salsa Association, the Japan Salsa Professional Federation was established in April 2010 and plans to hold events such as an annual dance event.

As I have explained, every year salsa attracts more and more Japanese participants. But the spread of salsa in Japan seems to follow the traditional Japanese way of learning—systematization—such as observing strict rules, creating currents or factions, and placing emphasis on the distinction of styles.

To dance salsa, Japanese need to learn a number of rules, such as dance steps and partner positions; men need to learn how to lead, and women must learn how to follow. By mastering these movements, and by following dance styles, the Japanese seem to enjoy salsa. Other types of learning situations can further illustrate the idea of systematizing dance or, rather, creating or observing a current or a form in a dance that was essentially free originally. For instance, there are various currents (or schools) in the case of the tea ceremony; there is also an association for examining and evaluating the students of this art. The students must practice the appropriate form over a long period until they are able to make the movements naturally.

Because there is so great a distance, not just physically but also culturally, between Japan and the place where the music was born and nurtured, it is difficult for Japanese dancers to imagine salsa's cultural background—how the general public enjoys the music and dancing—without having experience of the Latin American world. Outside the dance's original cultural context, dancing often follows standardized styles of physical movement, regardless of the culture in which it was born. The case of salsa learning in Japan is thus an interesting example of the encounter between Latin American and Japanese culture.

Conclusion

In this chapter, I have described how the habitus of participants in the Japanese salsa field has changed from the era of emergence in the early 1990s, through the turning point of 1998–1999, and up to the current time, with its trends toward organized salsa, a qualification system, and emphasis on the salsa dance style—with "systemization" as a key word. I have also indicated how these changes relate to concepts of salsa dance styles held by Japanese dancers.

This case study highlights the following points, which require further research and analysis. First, to clarify the structure of the salsa field, we need to understand the changes in dance styles discussed in this chapter. Second, we need to analyze the activities of participants in the field, such as salsa instructors and DJs. Finally, we must conduct studies of fields, such as the salsa congresses and salsa clubs.

By taking this study further, we may come to understand how Japan has been embracing foreign cultures. As mentioned previously, in the 1990s salsa dance began to spread rapidly in Japan, and the foreign salsa dance was adapted to the traditional Japanese way of learning practices. More specifically, in Japan the method of adaptation is to create definite formats of learning, such as systematization of movement of dance styles, or the habitus people prefer. This way of learning has been commonly observed for quite a while in the tea ceremony and art of flower arrangement in Japan. This chapter has focused on the localization of culture in the field of salsa dance—a global cultural phenomenon.

NOTES

1. For instance, the hero of the movie *Shall We Dansu [Dance]?* (1996) is very reluctant to reveal that he is learning social dance.

2. See Ishi 1993 for details on the possible change of legitimacy.

3. In the case of one salsa instructor, she started to learn social dance at the age of eight and became a champion of ballroom-style Latin dance.

4. See Savigliano 1995 for more on the diffusion of tango dance in Japan.

5. "Salsa Japan!" (http://www.salsa.org), one of the pioneers, has provided salsa music and dance information since 1996.

6. Numbers are taken from the back cover of the DVD of the 2007 Japan Salsa Congress.

7. The organizer of the Japan Salsa Congress, Watabe, has been appointed a judge of the Los Angeles Salsa Congress and the World Salsa Championships.

8. In this chapter, $1 is calculated as 100 Japanese yen.

REFERENCES

Bourdieu, Pierre. 1984. *Distinction: A Social Critique of the Judgement of Taste*, trans. Richard Nice. Cambridge, MA: Harvard University Press.

———. 1996. *The Rules of Art*, trans. Susan Emanuel. Palo Alto, CA: Stanford University Press.

Hosokawa, Shuhei. 2002. "Salsa No Tiene Fronteras: Orquesta de la Luz and the Globalization of Popular Music." In *Situating Salsa: Global Markets and Local Meanings in Latin Popular Music*, ed. Lise Waxer, 289–311. New York: Routledge.

Ishi, Yojiro. 1993. *Sai to Yokubo*. Tokyo: Fujiwara Shoten.

Pietrobruno, Sheenagh. 2006. *Salsa and Its Transnational Moves*. Lanham, MD: Lexington Books.

Salsa Hotline Japan. 1999. *Salsa! Koisuru salsa book*. Tokyo: Ongakuno Tomo Sha.

———. 2004. *Latin Dance*. Vol. 1. Tokyo: Byakuya Shobo.

———. n.d. Home page. Previously available at http://www.salsa.co.jp/zzz/outline/contact.html (accessed November 11, 2008).

Savigliano, Marta. 1995. *Tango and the Political Economy of Passion.* Boulder, CO: West-
    view.
Shall We Dansu *[Dance]?* 1996. Directed by Masayuki Suo. Tokyo: Daiei.
Takenaga, Mika. 2009. "Salsa Interview." *All about My Salsa*, November 14. Available at
    http://aams.blog72.fc2.com/blog-entry-312.html.

Contributors

Bárbara Balbuena Gutiérrez is a full professor in and dean of the Department of Dance Arts at the Instituto Superior de Arte in Havana, Cuba, where she also coordinates the master's program in dance theory studies and serves as secretary of the Commission on Academic Ranks. She received Cuba's National Research Prize for her monograph *El íreme abakuá*, an honorable mention at Cuba's annual research awards for her work *El casino y la salsa en Cuba*, and Cuba's Annual Prize for Cultural Research for her book *Las celebraciones rituales festivas en la Regla de Ocha*.

Katherine Borland is an associate professor of comparative studies in the humanities at the Ohio State University. She is the author of *Unmasking Class, Gender, and Sexuality in Nicaraguan Festival* and *Creating Community: Hispanic Migration to Rural Delaware* and coeditor (with Sydney Hutchinson) of *Latin American Dance in Transnational Contexts*, a special issue of the *Journal of American Folklore*. Currently, she is researching the history of humanitarianism and human rights activism in Central America and India.

Joanna Bosse is an assistant professor of ethnomusicology at Michigan State University whose research involves the ethnomusicological study of couple dances in the United States. She has presented papers at numerous meetings, including conferences held by the Society for Ethnomusicology, the Society for American Music, and the Society of Dance History Scholars, and her work has appeared in the *Journal of American Folklore*, *Dance Research Journal*, and *American Music*. In 2001 she was awarded a Nahumck Fellowship for dance research from the Society for Ethnomusicology.

Rossy Díaz is a graduate student in art history and criticism at the Universidad Autónoma de Santo Domingo in the Dominican Republic. She has conducted research for the Institute of Caribbean Studies in Santo Domingo and was a member of the 2005 and 2007 Organizing Committee of the International Congress on Music, Identity, and Culture in the Caribbean. She currently coordinates the Bahoruco Community Culture Program and serves as consultant to the Dominican Network of Local Cultures. In 2011 she published her first book, *Rumbas barriales: Aproximaciones al análisis del merengue de calle.*

Saúl Escalona, a sociologist living in France, is a researcher at the Center for Intercultural Research in Latin American Cultural Fields. He writes for the journal *Fermentum* at the University of the Andes in Venezuela and is the author of *La salsa: "Pa' bailar mi gente." Un phénomène socioculturel; Ma salsa défigurée; La salsa en Europa: Rompiendo el hielo . . .;* and *Si La Peña m'était contée . . . ! Une histoire de la salsa à Paris* and coauthor of *Parole et musique dans le monde hispanique; La fête en Amérique Latine; Musiques et sociétés en Amérique Latine;* and *Músicas, sociedades y relaciones de poder en América Latina.*

Sydney Hutchinson is an assistant professor of ethnomusicology in the Department of Art and Music Histories at Syracuse University. Her articles have appeared in publications including *Ethnomusicology, Popular Music, Yearbook for Traditional Music, Journal of American Folklore, Folklore Forum, Revista Dominicana de Antropología,* and *Centro: Journal of the Center for Puerto Rican Studies.* In 2008 she received a De La Torre Bueno Prize Special Citation from the Society for Dance History Scholars for her 2007 book *From Quebradita to Duranguense: Dance in Mexican American Youth Culture* and a Nahumck Fellowship for dance research from the Society for Ethnomusicology.

Kengo Iwanaga studied at the Institute for Latin American Studies at Rikkyo University in Tokyo. He is a member of the Japanese Association for the Study of Popular Music and has delivered presentations at its annual conferences. His research involves a sociological and anthropological analysis of Japanese society's adaptation and transformation of music and dance derived from Latin America.

Isabel Llano is a doctoral candidate in the Department of Journalism and Communication Sciences at the Universidad Autónoma de Barcelona. Included among her research projects are *Situación social del músico en Cali* and Historia Social de la Música en Cali en el Siglo XX (both funded by the Ministry of Culture in Colombia). She has taught at the Universidad Javeriana and the Universidad Autónoma de Occidente in Cali, Colombia.

Jonathan S. Marion is an assistant professor of anthropology at the University of Arkansas in Fayetteville. His ongoing research—geared toward understanding the construction of personal and collective meaning and identity—explores relationships between performance, embodiment, image, aesthetics, gender, translocality, and activity-based communities. He is a board member of the Society for Humanistic Anthropology and president-elect of the Society for Visual Anthropology. He is the author of *Ballroom: Culture and Costume in Competitive Dance* and the coauthor of *Visual Research: A Concise Introduction to Thinking Visually.*

Priscilla Renta is a doctoral candidate in performance studies at Northwestern University whose research focuses on Afro-Latino dance and music performance in the United States and the Caribbean. Her essays have been published in the anthologies *El son y la salsa en la identidad del Caribe* and *Technofuturos: Critical Interventions in Latina/o Studies* and in the journals *Centro: Journal of the Center for Puerto Rican Studies* and *AHA! Hispanic Arts News.* Renta, who has performed with various Afro–Puerto Rican music and dance groups, was a founding member of Puerto Rico's first all-female music ensemble.

Alejandro Ulloa Sanmiguel is a linguist, anthropologist, music researcher, and professor of social communication at the Universidad del Valle in Cali, Colombia. His publications include *La salsa en Cali*, *Pagode a festa do samba no Rio de Janeiro e nas Américas*, *El baile: Un lenguaje del cuerpo*, and *La salsa en discusión: Música popular e historia cultural*. Since 2010, he has been developing Cali Cultura Salsera—El Mulataje Musical entre el Barrio y la Ciudad Global (http://caliculturasalsera.univalle.edu.co), an interactive online virtual museum that narrates and represents the memory of a musical culture linking Cali with New York, Cuba, and Puerto Rico.

Index